About the Author

After finishing two years in the sixth form and, failing to obtain the grades for a university place, Mike Winser joined the BBC at the age of eighteen, which was the only job offer he'd received.

Following three months of training to be a television engineer, he failed the exam and, was due to be dismissed but was given a second chance to train as a cameraman.

Twenty years later, he was nominated for a television craft award three years in a row.

He now describes camerawork as something he did in the last century and, in Spring 2011, he became the full-time carer for his wife following her disabling stroke.

He now lives on his own among newfound friends in a retirement village, enjoys listening to music, loves cooking and the red wines of Tuscany.

Hurry Up and Wait

Mike Winser

Hurry Up and Wait

Vanguard Press

VANGUARD PAPERBACK

© Copyright 2024
Mike Winser

The right of Mike Winser to be identified as author of
this work has been asserted by him in accordance with the
Copyright, Designs and Patents Act 1988.

All Rights Reserved

No reproduction, copy or transmission of this publication
may be made without written permission.
No paragraph of this publication may be reproduced,
copied or transmitted save with the written permission of the
publisher, or in accordance with the provisions
of the Copyright Act 1956 (as amended).

Any person who commits any unauthorised act in relation to
this publication may be liable to criminal
prosecution and civil claims for damages.

A CIP catalogue record for this title is
available from the British Library.

ISBN 978 1 80016 662 2

This is a work of creative nonfiction. The events are portrayed to the best
of the author's memory. While all the stories in this book are true, some names
and identifying details have been changed to protect the privacy of the people
involved.

Vanguard Press is an imprint of
Pegasus Elliot Mackenzie Publishers Ltd.
www.pegasuspublishers.com

First Published in 2024

Vanguard Press
Sheraton House Castle Park
Cambridge England

Printed & Bound in Great Britain

Dedication

For my darling Wendy, who gave me the confidence to be myself.

Acknowledgements

My early reading group who gave me the encouragement to keep writing.

Carol and David Noyce, Cathy and Chris Matthews, June and David Cureton, Diane Winser, Val Ponya, John Chapman (for suggesting 'Astronomy and Gastronomy'), Noel and Jeannie Brown, Brian Robinson, Barbara Hodge and the team at Pegasus. Andrea Roux for proof reading. I must have driven her mad with all the extra spaces between words that she had to remove—

Front cover photograph by Wendy Winser
Back cover photograph by Doug Whittaker

Chapter One
To begin in the middle...

It was at the end of 1990 that I realized that I could not recall having made a positive career decision in my life. I'd made several other decisions over the years, to which two marriages, one divorce and no children were testimony. Having reached the second half of my forties, I found myself reflecting, with increasing frequency, the path along which chance had taken me.

As the late autumn dusk fell, I could see through the rain-splattered window of my room, the games teams dispersing from the playing fields that surrounded the school opposite. Most of the boys, aged between eleven and fifteen and still in their blue and red vertically striped kit, were boarding single decker coaches. A select few were being collected by their parents whose car headlights glistened on the damp road. The few leaves that remained on the trees were orange and rust, crumpled and tired.

My room was number five on the first floor of the pub across the road from the school. It was barely twelve feet square, just adequate for a night or two. I was reminded of a colleague's description of a hotel room, "I wouldn't say it was tiny, but a marked increase in volume could have been achieved by removing the wallpaper". It did, though, contain all the necessary amenities, each of them lined up along the wall opposite the bed head. At the right hand end, a cubicle toilet with combined light and extractor fan, to its left a shower with a Redring electric shower unit that produced a very fine spray containing more air than water, closed in by a plastic curtain that convection currents sucked against the body. One undersized bath towel was provided. Next to the shower a sink, above which was a shaving mirror with a combined electric shaver point and light, and finally a small wardrobe, on top of which was the smallest available colour TV, for which there was no remote control so that it was necessary to get out of bed to switch off. To the left of the four feet wide double bed there was a small chest of drawers, sufficient for a few jumpers, socks and underwear but only enough room to put an alarm clock on the top, as the rest of the space was occupied by a small tray with tea-making facilities, apart from the kettle that is, which had to be on the floor, the other side of the bed where the one available power socket was. The only other piece of furniture in the room was a straight-backed chair more suitable for the dining room than the bedroom, and the only place to put a suitcase.

I, however, was coming to the end of my second week here and had brought four assorted cases. Two of them, the larger ones, were full of clothes to provide for every climatic eventuality over a period of three November weeks. I had tee-shirts, long sleeve shirts, thermal underwear, pullovers, dress shirts, one suit, working trousers, down filled anoraks – one short sleeved, one long, – and an assortment of footwear that ranged from trainers, through fell boots to my one pair of smart black Bally dress shoes. The other two smaller holdalls contained reading material, mostly computer magazines, and a small relatively cheap laptop computer, a Sinclair ZX90, with which I tinkered at writing, and the shooting schedule, cast list, and scripts for the six-episode Children's Television Drama I had been working on for the last nine weeks.

The drama's story revolved around a fourteen-year-old boy, whose father had accidentally killed his wife, the boy's mother. After the tragic death of his mother, the boy took increasing amounts of time off from school to look after his father, who had, not unnaturally, sunk into a depression. The Social Services department tried to get the boy to appreciate that he must keep up his attendance at school, but he continued to abscond and was eventually put into care. The boy meets up with the niece of a showman and they hatch a plan to get his father out of an institution and escape to a fun fair in the country. The story was being shot entirely on location, the first seven weeks in and around Hampton in Middlesex, where the school, the boy's home and the Social Services foster home were located. Apart from one day in Richmond, to shoot the court room scenes, the remainder of the series was being shot in the country, at the winter quarters of a travelling fun fair, hence the title, "Dodgem".

This Saturday, late in November, was a rest day before the final week of shooting. The various members of the television production team, the actors, the director, the design team with its painters and chippies, the electricians, the prop boys and the make-up ladies were all variously accommodated in hotels, pubs, and bed and breakfast establishments, mostly within a fifteen-mile radius centred on the Wiltshire town of Devizes. What the different members of the team did with their free days varied tremendously, but they were all trying to achieve the same end. Some went shopping or browsing through book shops, others would team up and share a car trip to a nearby tourist attraction or beauty spot, visit local museums, art galleries or a National Trust property. Often a small specialist team would take it upon themselves to do an intensive, day long, survey of the local hostelries. All, in their different ways, were trying to escape from their hotels to experience something different, inhale a change of air, alter the scenery, the company—anything to charge their batteries after the long days of continuous concentration.

The previous weekend's day off, I had gone to Stonehenge in the morning, lunched at a wine bar in Devizes, wandered the book shops and newsagents in the afternoon and joined Geoff, the Lighting Director, and Dave, the Vision Recording Engineer, for a Chinese meal in the evening. This Saturday I very much wanted to be on my own. I was tired of communicating, tired of standing, tired even of the proximity of other humans and I chose to stay in my room. I spent the day, not unhappily, drifting between reading my magazines, writing up my timesheets and expense forms, making cups of tea and coffee, smoking the occasional cigar while staring out of the window, and thinking. But mostly, I was thinking.

Was now the time for a change of direction? I'd been in my present job, as an Outside Broadcast Television Camera Supervisor, for ten years, and in the same department since 1964. There hadn't been many programmes that had been regularly serviced by my department that I hadn't worked on at some time or other in my career. My job had taken me all over the country, exposed me to people and places that as a member of the public I would never have had the chance to meet or see. It had taken me abroad, to Barcelona, Hamburg, Geneva, the Swiss Alps, a monastery in Central France; most memorably it had taken me to Africa, to an Ethiopian refugee camp in the south east of Sudan and to the Game Reserves of south west Kenya, and with Patrick Moore to Astronomical Observatories throughout the USA, Hawaii, Chile, Australia, the Soviet Union and South Africa. I'd worked on the flight deck of an Aircraft Carrier, flown in helicopters, slept in mud huts, spent days in Land Rovers eyeball-to-eyeball with a pride of lions. To anybody who didn't work in the business it would seem a truly glamorous and enviable job. But the challenges were becoming less frequent, the programme commitments that generated excitement were getting fewer and that essential adrenaline buzz was not pumping through the nervous system as often as it used to.

Did I want to apply for the management post I knew would be vacant within eighteen months to two years? My boss, the Head of Cameras, Television Outside Broadcasts, was retiring in the August after next and the consensus among my colleagues was that it was imperative that someone from within the department took over. If it was a challenge I was after, then here, surely, would be something to get my teeth into. With the Government-imposed deregulation of the industry and the ever-increasing financial restrictions, there would be staff cuts, increased pressures on those that remained to provide the same standards in less time and with fewer resources and, almost inevitably, a lowering of morale. If someone from outside was appointed to the post then it was very likely that my colleagues would become depressed and demoralised, and I was certain that, if I did not at least apply for the job myself, then I would have no right to complain. Low down the list of reasons why I should apply, but no less important, was the fact that my pension would be enhanced considerably if I got the job.

Did I want to go freelance? I'd been tempted for some years to make that leap into the unknown. I was quietly confident that I had a more than reasonable reputation as a good exponent of my craft. What I feared was that freelancing would run away with my life. All the feedback from colleagues who had taken the step had indicated that you were a fool to turn anything down, because you might never be asked again. Under the Corporation's present conditions of service about the only time off you could be guaranteed was that which you took leave for. Booking theatre tickets or agreeing to a dinner party was always a gamble, and if you did have to work, it was highly unlikely that there would be any compensation. But at least you could book annual leave and know that you would get a holiday. Freelancing would even mean giving up all thoughts of holidays booked months ahead, and breaks would have to be taken where and when they happened.

Could I cope as a freelance if I had to? I couldn't answer that question for myself, let alone ask anyone else to solve it for me. There was more to freelancing than just the ability to operate a camera. I would have to think of myself as a small business. Should I just make my skills available, or should I invest in equipment and sell the complete package? Either way, I would still have to get to grips with cash flow, VAT, marketing and self-promotion, and maybe bank loans, rate cards, agents and, possibly, even hiring other staff. I was fairly convinced that I didn't have the instinct, the smell, that innate business acumen, needed to survive in a whole new world that I knew very little about.

Could my wife cope and, what's more, should she even be asked to? I was convinced that she would hate it. Her first husband had been a staff director in the BBC's drama department for many years and had taken the plunge into the murky freelance pool. From the day he took that step he was worried about where the next job was coming from. He had to generate work. He formed an independent production company of one. He had to understand inputs and outputs for VAT, deal with corporation tax, accountants, solicitors. He spent less and less time doing what he was good at, and died, aged sixty-two, a bitter, stressed, and, ultimately, disillusioned man.

Or should I stay in my present job with the Corporation until I reached fifty, when I could take my pension and quit the business for good? The thought of leaving that early was very appealing. My wife was ten years older than I and I knew that if I stayed the distance until I was sixty, she would more than likely be too frail to enjoy my retirement with me. But if one thing stressed me more than anything else, it was the feeling that I had lost control of my life, that my employer and my responsibilities, over which I seemed to have very little control, were writing my agenda, day after day, week after week.

Time and again though, I have felt that I have lost sight of who I am, where I was going, whether I'd achieved anything of substance and that my life was slipping through my fingers at an exponentially increasing rate. As far back as I can remember, I'd tried my hand at various ways of self-expression in a search for something the world would think I was good at. I'd tried the guitar and got as far as being able to pluck the tune of "Yesterday", but I was never able to form my fingers into chord formations fast enough to be called rhythm. I moved onto painting, daubed oils about in thick Van Goch like swirls, which I very quickly found too embarrassing to show to anyone. I'd been interested in still photography since I was ten years of age and had saved my earnings from a Saturday job on a market stall to buy my first camera. Since those days I'd accrued a fine collection of cameras, lenses, studio flash equipment, an enlarger and processing equipment, and, in great bursts of enthusiasm lasting anything up to a year at a time, I'd throw myself at the pursuit of photographic excellence. I still retain a desire to take more photographs, to produce pictures that others would like to hang on a wall, but it's not all-consuming and it drifts down the list of priorities.

Over the years I have also suffered waves of the desire to write, but I never seemed to produce anything that I would be prepared to let anybody else read. It's more than likely an excuse, but I reasoned that it would not be fair to lock myself away in a room on my own for eight to ten hours a week, the minimum sort of period I considered necessary to give myself the chance of really getting something down on paper. Chasing after time, trying to make efficient use of each day, was eating away at my heart, my humour and my sense of balance and was stopping me enjoying what I had. For reasons beyond the comprehension of outsiders, I would become extremely and irrationally irritable as I felt the days slipping away from me. The track "Time" from the Pink Floyd album "The Dark Side of the Moon" sums up, in that way that only pop music can, the feelings of madness associated with the lack of control over the relentless disappearance of valuable, limited time.

It was not as if the job I had with the Corporation didn't require some creative input from me. There were times when the demands were all-consuming and very satisfying and would leave me with little energy to attend to anything else, but television programme making always was, and will continue to be, a team game. But the business was rapidly changing and, to me, not for the better. The Government was seeking to impose free market forces on a creative industry. They were trying to enforce the laws of the production line on an industry that succeeds through flair, talent and in an atmosphere in which people should be allowed to dare to fail.

For nearly thirty years, my entire time in the industry, I had believed that the BBC was the finest example of Public Service Broadcasting in the world and that its reputation for the quality and range of programmes that it made was enviable. I was not alone in thinking, that now, following a meeting between Rupert Murdoch and Margaret Thatcher, it was being pressured into effectively committing suicide to appear financially efficient, lean and competitive to a philistine government bent on free market dogma that apparently saw the Corporation as a £1.6 billion a year industry from which profits must be made. They had imposed for a second term, a Chairman of the Board of Governors who'd appointed as Director General of an industry whose raison d'être was to make programmes, an accountant who had never controlled a television channel, overseen a production department, let alone made a programme, and, to cap it all, placed as DG elect a man whose only apparent claim to fame was that he brought the nation 'Blind Date'. Under the guise of a restructuring plan, attractively and simplistically called 'Producer Choice', they were introducing internal business units whose imposed financial plans would not pass muster with the village post mistress let alone any one of the expensively hired management consultants brought in from the city. While the top levels of the Corporation's management took over entire hotels for long and expensive weekend seminars, plans were being hatched to dump the very programme making staff on which the

Corporation's worldwide reputation was founded. No wonder then, that given the obvious uncertainties of the next few years, I had absolutely no idea what I should do next.

Chapter Two
Safawa So Good

Heathrow, Tuesday December 17th, 1985.

As I boarded the British Airways Tri-Star, my overriding concern was where on Earth I was going to put the Sony 330 Camera I was carrying as additional hand luggage. My request of the cabin staff for a sensible suggestion had been met with a casual "In front of your seat, Sir". That left me thinking that the eight-hour flight was going to be more than usually cramped. It wasn't until I was shown to my seat that it sank in. We were to travel First Class. It had seemed to me that we were getting preferential treatment, because we had been told to rendezvous outside the Concorde lounge at Heathrow, away from the usual hoard of business travellers and pre-Christmas holidaymakers, but the space and comfort of the aircraft's First Class cabin was much more than I had ever expected.

Eighteen months earlier, Michael Burke had brought to the nation's attention the plight of the Ethiopian and Tigrean refugees who had streamed into Sudan in their tens of thousands, suffering from starvation, disease and the ravages of a civil war. Now, we were to go to a refugee camp in Southeast Sudan to see how well the aid agencies had done and to link the Save the Children Fund workers with their relatives, live on BBC1, Christmas morning.

The idea for this programme insert into the Noel Edmonds Christmas morning show had hatched in the minds of two young women about the beginning of November. Helen Fielding, an Assistant Producer on the Noel Edmonds Late Late Breakfast Show, and Jane Tewson, a charity fund raiser for the newly formed Comic Relief, had been discussing the waning media interest in the plight of the refugees and the lack of any reports on exactly what the relief organisations had achieved with the monies that the public had given in recent months. A previous Late Late Breakfast Show Christmas day special that had included live links with British Forces in the Falklands had been considered a success, so Helen suggested to Producer Michael Hurll that this year's show should include a live link-up with Aid Agency staff from a refugee camp in the Sudan. I am led to believe that Michael did not think that this was achievable but told Helen that if she could do it very cheaply and on her own as Producer, Director and Presenter, then she could try and set it up.

To find out if it was it technically achievable, she got in touch with John Scott, Head of Television Outside Broadcast Telecommunications. Sudan had no telephone contact with the rest of the world, let alone a telecommunications network, so sending back the sound and pictures over a landline was not an option. The remaining alternatives were overland radio link hops into Khartoum to the Satellite ground station there or take our own mobile Satellite Earth Station to the chosen refugee camp and fire the signals up to an Indian Ocean Satellite. Both options would require cajoling Intelstat, the operators of a cluster of telecommunications satellites over the Indian ocean, into turning one of them so that it's spot beam, normally directed at western Europe, would aim at eastern Africa. A rational decision could not be taken without a recce, (TV shorthand for a reconnaissance trip).

On 20th November, John Scott and Helen flew to Khartoum, and then travelled by road, mostly metalled, to Gadaref where Save the Children Fund had a safe house with accommodation and storage facilities, and then on out across the desert to two refugee camps, Safawa and Wadcowlie, to see how to get the department's mobile satellite dish there. Twelve feet in diameter with a box of electronics the size of a one-person Portaloo, it was mounted on a trailer some twenty feet long. Towed behind a Radio Link vehicle, it could be taken by normal roads to anywhere in Europe and beam signals back to London via geostationary telecommunications satellites. But East Africa? Roads aren't their strong point, and the valves that generate the power to fire communication signals up to the satellite are quite fragile.

For the project to happen at all, the good offices of several organisations were going to be needed. In short, would British Airways donate the flights for the staff that were going to go? Would a company called Heavy Lift, who were flying their Belfast aircraft to Khartoum with aid and equipment on a regular basis, have room on a flight for the satellite dish and the Radio Link vehicle? And, as the Christmas morning programme was going to show televised footage of how we got to the camp, which would include pictures of a British Airway's Tri-Star and the dish being loaded and unloaded from the Belfast, would this help?

Fortunately, Khartoum wasn't an overbooked Christmas holiday destination and there was space on the BA flights. Heavy Lift had room on a Belfast going out on Thursday 19th of December. Helen and John met up with the Save the Children Fund fixer, Derek Probert. If anything needed constructing or installing, getting water to or from, connecting to a generator, starting, stopping or maintaining, then Derek was your man. Once a decision had been taken on which camp to do the broadcast from, he would be happy to clear a two and a half kilometre long runway in the desert if Heavy Lift wanted it. They were sure they could land the plane in the desert, but they were not prepared to gamble on getting it out again. They would happily fly our equipment to the airport in Khartoum. That left us with the overland option. The Radio Link lorry could tow the dish to Gadaref, but for the bumpy desert track to the camp, the dish and its trailer would have to be put onto something with better suspension and a method of cushioning it from shock would have to be devised.

When projects like this are meant to be, everything falls into place and Iveco, the truck company, happened to be planning to move some of the lorries they had donated to the aid effort down to the camps in southeast Sudan. Apart from the fuel and food they were already moving, they were prepared to make another lorry available to put the dish and trailer on. As well as the Radio Link lorry and the satellite dish, we needed to take two Sony 330's cameras, one as a spare, one I would take as hand luggage, two 1 inch video tape machines so that we could edit material before sending it back to London on Christmas Eve, a Time Base corrector to put the signal through before sending it over the link, (don't ask me but John said we needed it), two sets of the fragile power valves for the Satellite Up Station, two towable generators for our power requirements and assorted cables, television monitors, microphones and speakers, 12volt car battery and charger. It was going to be quite a convoy, and that convoy was going to Safawa. The decision had been taken. I'm not quite sure of the rationale of choosing Safawa over Wadcowlie, but it might have been something to do with the fact that Princess Anne, the then Save the Children Fund's President, was to visit Safawa in early December, and that would give the camp a rehearsal, for our visit.

So, nine of us, except Dave Purdy and Eddie our Rigger Drivers who were coming out on the Belfast, settled in to our comfortable, reclining seats, and sipped our Champagne cocktails awaiting take-off. John Scott and his two radio link engineers Chris Cobb and Steve Clifford, Vic Godrich the Sound Supervisor, George Wagland our Vision Supervisor, a British Telecom Engineer whose name I have forgotten, Helen Fielding and Jane Tewson from Comic Relief. Nobody could say for certain that we were going to be able to make the programme, as there were yet many problems to be solved.

Travel Permits had to be obtained, permits to photograph were needed and we still didn't know how we were going to get the dish and it's trailer on to the Iveco lorry. And that wasn't all. The satellite dish, designed for use in Europe, could only tilt up to 45°; the Indian Ocean Satellite we were to fire signals at was at an elevation of 55°. But as the plane climbed away from Heathrow, all thoughts moved on to the meal that was about to be served and the accompanying wines, port and brandy, probably our last alcohol for ten days, which was hopefully going to ease us into a few hours of sleep.

The Tri-Star touched down at Khartoum International Airport at four thirty a.m. Sudanese Time. We were met by Peter Benchley or Beazley, (I can't now remember which), but he was the Transport and Shipping Manager for Save the Children Fund. Sudanese officialdom demanded to go through every piece of luggage and attempted to take the camera off me, but I managed to hang on to it. Immigration was no trouble for most of the party. We all had visas that lasted for three months. John and Helen, who had been out on the recce in November, thought their visas were fine and would last through to the New Year, way after the time we planned to return. Nobody, however, had picked up on the fact that they were not 'multiple entry' visas. They were once only. We had to leave them at the Airport. Peter stayed with them, obtained the services of a very good Arabic-speaking interpreter and, eventually, it turned out to be seven hours, got the authorities to let them into the country.

Dawn was upon us by the time the rest of us got out of the Airport to our Toyota Land Cruisers supplied by a local Safari Company called "Nile Safaris". These were going to carry some of the kit, pull the generators once they had come off the Belfast, and be general crew transport. We were driven to our hotel, via the Save the Children Fund Headquarters where we offloaded the bags of food and presents that we had brought out with us. We finally got to the Khartoum Hilton Hotel about six thirty a.m. Once inside the foyer we could have been anywhere in the world, but the view from the window of my room on the eighth floor was not. It was of the confluence of the Blue and White Niles. Black Kites were swirling past at eyeball height, and down on that triangle of dusty soil, bordered on one side by the White Nile, on another by the Blue, were plots of fenced off land containing goats and chickens and a white swathed, hunched and knobbly man tilling the soil with an ox drawn plough, wind-blown dust backlit by the rising sun. The scene appeared not to have changed from one's imaginings of what life was like two-thousand years ago.

After about an hour's sleep and a coffee, we gathered and returned to the Save the Children Fund Headquarters to sort out the bags of presents that we had left there earlier. Helen and Jane had persuaded Woolworth and Marks and Spencer, amongst others, to come up with a few presents for the aid agency workers. Tee shirts, little tubes of Christmas wrapped multi-coloured knickers, shampoo and toiletries, and Ghetto Blasters that Woolworth had given were representative of the presents that were to be distributed to staff at Wadcowlie, the other camp down in the southeast not that far from Safawa, and a further camp out west. We ourselves had bought some Christmas gift-wrapped items for the staff at Safawa. After all they were going to give up their individual Toukals, the wattle and mud daub huts they called home, and pair up so that we had somewhere to sleep.

Outside the Hilton Hotel the wind had got up and there was a dust storm blowing. Visibility was down to about two-hundred and fifty yards. As we drove through one part of the city, lines of women and children, swathed in off-white, sat on the edge of the pavement, hunched up, hugging their knees, their feet in the gutter. It was a queue for the hospital. The Save the Children Fund Headquarters was a tatty, run-down, ex-consular building constructed from brick or stone, in stark contrast to most homes we had passed on the way which were constructed from cubes of mud. Once inside SCF HQ, we realised that a lot of the presents had gone missing. There were in all thirty-two items of personal luggage that went on and off the plane, but about fifteen of them were large nylon sports bags with zip tops that had not been locked. I guess Sudanese officialdom had got its baksheesh after all.

While we had a cup of coffee, Chris Eldridge, SCF Field Director for Sudan, gave us a brief overview of the situation. Sudan was economically destitute, flat broke. It owed money internationally. At a million square miles, it was bigger than Europe, but it couldn't even afford to buy its own grain and move it to areas where it was needed. Growing conditions had been bad; this had been the first reasonable year for fifteen. Not that long ago the drive between Gadaref and Safawa used to be through forest now that forest had gone. The nomadic tribes cut it down to make fires to cook with. Deforestation took place followed by desertification, leaving the soil in a state where nothing will grow. Those tribes that stay in one place long enough to plant crops, eat the flour or cereal and use the stalks as wattle to make their huts, which they cover with mud in the wet season. Everything was used, so nothing was returned to the soil, the result was more infertile dust bowls.

As the hub through which information from London and the camps is channelled, Chris's immediate concern was the rumours of another influx of Ethiopian refugees about to come over the border. The estimates were that it would be another two-hundred thousand, which would mean that every single SCF worker would have to be totally involved in dealing with the problem.

"If it happens, they won't have time to play at television," he said, "The camp at Safawa is already dealing with forty-thousand refugees."

That afternoon, Helen and Jane went off to get the Travel Pass, the required official permission to drive the vehicles to Safawa, and a Photo Permit, to allow us to shoot material on the way down. Not just the cameraman needed this, everyone in the party had to fill out the form, in triplicate. The travel permit took two days to get, and we only just got it in time for our departure on the Friday morning. It was a stunning example of Sudanese officialdom. It was a page ripped from a lined exercise book, with Arabic characters scrawled on it and half a dozen Sudanese £5 stamps stuck to the bottom of the page. It turned out to be one way only, and we had to get another one to come back! Having got the Photo Permits, there was still quite several restrictions on what we could or could not "film". We were not allowed to photograph Government Buildings in Khartoum, we were not allowed to photograph bridges anywhere in the Sudan, and we were strongly advised not to photograph in the Souks.

After completing our hellos and pleasantries at SCF HQ, we returned to the Hilton in a local Taxi, my first experience of the "life is cheap school of motoring". The law of the land is that you drive on the right, but this is taken to mean that you only needed to miss on-coming traffic left side to left side. Normal driving is down the middle of the road and moving to one side was left until the last possible moment. The taxis were all yellow, all old, all tatty, and mostly Toyotas. Internally they were wall-to-wall carpet. The floor, the seats, the roof lining, the doors, but the dashboard had an altar cloth with tassels on it, which may account for the drivers' blind faith in his avoidance skills. Back at the Hilton, lunch was Pigeon Broth with Spinach Noodles, and Spiced Lamb kebabs. Having not eaten since the plane, we were hungry. With nothing on the agenda until dinner I went to my room to rest and to watch the Black Kites as they soared outside the bedroom window.

The BBC entertained Chris Eldridge and an assistant by the name of Nick to dinner in the Hotel's "Ivory Club" Dining Room. Wednesday Night in the Ivory Club was

"*Gastronomique* Buffet" Night, and at S£40.00, or just over £10, maybe £12, a fairly good meal as I recall. A relatively cheap and sober affair as the meal was washed down with Evian water.

Thursday morning two of the three Toyota Land Cruisers went away to have the tow hitches fitted so that they could pull our generators, while Vic, George, Chris, Steve, the BT engineer and I went in the third Land Cruiser to the airport to await the arrival of the Belfast and its cargo of our equipment. To this day I don't know why. We were shown where to park, out on the perimeter tarmac in full sun, where we sat for six-and-a-half hours unable to do or see anything. Fortunately, I had my Sony "Walkman", a few audio cassettes, and a book with me to help pass the time. Finally, we were told that everything was off the Belfast and we could follow the equipment back to SCF HQ.

Once the vehicles were parked up, Dave, our Rigger Driver, went off to get insurance. Although the kit and vehicles were covered by the BBC's own insurance, Sudanese Insurance, like the Travel Permits and the Photo passes, was just another piece of official paperwork that had to be obtained before we could move out of Khartoum. He went to the address given him by BBC Transport Department. This turned out to be useless, so he came back to SCF HQ, obtained the services of an English speaking Arab and, with his help, found a 'company' prepared to provide the necessary insurance cover. Having filled out the forms Dave offered to pay in US$. The "insurance" man would have none of it. He wanted paying in Sudanese

£s. In the Hotel reception, the exchange rate was S£2.45 to US$1.00, and we had all been given our subsistence allowance in US dollars because that was what the Hilton wished to be paid in. The English-speaking Arab interpreter told Dave it was a long way back to the hotel and said he knew of a place where he could exchange money that was a lot closer. He took Dave into a Souk where they found an open-backed, covered lorry, with a man sitting on the tailboard clutching a wicker basket, prepared to hand out S£4.90 for every US$1.00. The bill for the Insurance came to S£13.50, or about US$2.75; thankfully, we never had to claim on it.

Friday morning and it was time to move on. Firstly, we had to get one of the Land Cruisers into a state so that we could use it to "film" out of. We had to get George set up in the back with the 1" tape machine, a monitor and a box for controlling the exposure, black level and colour balance of the Sony 330 camera. (These were the last few months before the television cameraman was released from the historical grip of engineering department and allowed control over the exposure). All this was to be powered by a 12volt car battery. We also had camera batteries and a video cable for emergencies, but George preferred the engineered set up, where he retained control of the technical quality of the camera's output. We were to lead out the team of lorries and Land Cruisers and move on ahead to photographically interesting spots so that we could "film" the convoy moving through the landscape. Visually, I was preconditioned by the back row of the two and nines, and David Lean's "Lawrence of Arabia". I was expecting horizon to horizon of sweeping sand dunes the moment we left the city gates. How wrong could I have been?

Getting out of Khartoum took an age. First, we had to pass through one of the many Souks, multi-coloured, bustling with hustling, stalls constructed of upturned wooden vegetable crates selling earthenware pots, aluminium kettles and saucepans, reams of vibrantly coloured cloth, transistor radios and, out of soft wicker baskets various vegetables. We managed to "film" some shots of the bustle and colour of the street market, albeit covertly from within the Land Cruiser. At the outskirts of town, where contrary to my imaginings, there was no fortified gate marking the boundary, the vehicles picked their way along rutted tracks, past haphazard collections of mud cubes with holes in that let the wind blow through, the light in and the smoke from a fire, out. Children scuttled about, some on donkeys, others in little makeshift carts, contrived from a few planks of wood and a couple of old bicycle wheels. We recorded shots as the vehicles moved through, close ups of wheels picking their way gingerly through the rutted tracks and the faces of bemused locals. Then we went way ahead to the top of the first rise and looked back to see the convoy snaking across the barren landscape between us and Khartoum, stirring up the dust and making it almost impossible to see the camel trains with their white-clad, masked riders. Souk trucks, piled high with more kettles, pots and vegetables and with humanity clinging on to every available grab-handle, roared past us towards the city.

Once away from Khartoum the road improved somewhat and became mostly metalled and we started to put some miles in at reasonable speeds. Often though, we would come across a section of road, maybe three to four hundred yards long, where the intense heat had melted the tarmac. This was now rutted and, in some places, quite soft and had to be carefully negotiated. We had already passed several souk trucks on their side, enthusiasm having exceeded skill, and we didn't want that to happen to us. The desert wasn't sand. It was arid soil. Occasionally we would pass an area of sorghum growing on one side of the road and a small collection of four or five wattle and daub huts. Then nothing. Ten miles would go by and then, in the distance, through the heat haze, a cloud of dust. Not Omar Sharif on a camel but another souk truck thundering towards us.

Twice between Khartoum and Gadaref, we pulled up at the equivalent of county boundaries. We were told we had to, or we would be fired on by the armed guard. These "border posts" consisted of a small stone building with two doors, an 'in' and an 'out', and large enough for a desk and a chair, and outside, a ramshackle collection of stalls, assembled from rough-hewn wood, selling strong sweet tea or goat curry and mountains of crates of Pepsi Cola! Was nowhere safe from the mighty corporate tentacles? We had to all get out of the vehicles and file in through the office for the official to look at everyone's papers. The process took up to half-an-hour and, knowing we had time to kill, those of us who had been first in the queue, went off and bought some of the local tea or a bottle of Pepsi.

After recording more pictures of the convoy moving through the landscape, it was time for a break and a stretch of the legs, especially for the drivers. Lunch was a picnic in a lay-by beside the Nile. Tomatoes and hard-boiled eggs that Helen had organised. We were close to a small settlement and quickly attracted a crowd of inquisitive locals, animatedly chattering away in Arabic, when out of the crowd stepped a young Sudanese man, speaking perfect English. He asked,

"Did we sing on the Live Aid record, 'Do they know it's Christmas'?" and "Can he say how much they all appreciate what we are doing".

We moved on. Mid-afternoon, just five days before Christmas and the heat was intense. Heaven knows how many miles we were from Khartoum, and there hadn't been a sign of habitation for an hour or so when we encountered, fifty or so yards off to the side of the road, striding purposefully, a lone figure with a bundle of sticks and twigs on his back. We presumed that he had been foraging for firewood for some time and that he must probably be days walking away from his home. He waved cheerfully as we went by.

It was dark by the time we finally got to the Save the Children Fund safe house at Gadaref. We'd had an hour of waiting on the outskirts of town until Derek the fixer, and Jim Atkinson, the Safawa camp administrator, had found us and could lead the convoy to a secure, guarded compound for overnight parking of the bigger vehicles. Then we all piled into two Land Cruisers with our personal effects and were driven into the walled compound of the safe house. The property served as a self-catering guest house for those in transit between the camps and Khartoum, and as a staging post for a lot of the medicines, which was the main reason the gates were guarded. Wrapped in white, holding large sticks and squatting on their haunches, the locally employed guards leant against the gateposts, with their eyes closed. We were there for two nights. We were shown to a long, glass roofed conservatory on the side of the building containing nine or ten iron-framed beds, each with a mattress. Picking a bed each we rolled out the cotton sheet sleeping bags and hung up the mosquito nets that we had brought with us. Washing and teeth cleaning was achievable at the sink outside, next to the front door of the building, but the water supply was extremely intermittent, and we were urged to make best use of it when it was on or clean our teeth in Pepsi.

Supper was to be heated up tinned Marks and Spencer Steak and Kidney meals that we had brought with us. While we were heating that up, Jim Atkinson & Helen went off to the souk for eggs, bread and tomatoes for Saturday and Sunday lunch. George was not feeling at all well. He was running a temperature, sweating and feeling sick. He went to bed before supper and if he had not improved by the morning, then we were going to have to get him some medical help. It was nearly two hours before Jim and Helen returned. Not only had they found the supplies for lunch, but they had also managed to purchase some illicit alcohol. In glass, litre bottles with screwed up polythene stoppers was some amber liquid, which the label described as "*Grand Fine Champagne*" Cognac. Made in Addis Ababa.

The main task for Saturday was to get the satellite dish and its trailer onto the back of the Iveco lorry and sort out the method of shock-proofing, and to "film" it as it happens. Derek, the fixer, had the solution to both problems. Back at the overnight lorry park there was a huge crane and a pile of lorry tyre inner tubes. The plan was to connect chains to the four corners of the dish's trailer and lift it up, over and down onto the back of the lorry. Insert the inner tubes between the floors of the trailer and the lorry, fill them with air until they just started to support the trailer and then strap it down. Brilliant! That it took three hours to accomplish had a lot to do with the communication between Derek and the Sudanese crane operator. He obviously thought it was cold, it was Winter after all, as he was wearing a long duffel coat over layers of woolly jumpers, and I doubt that his hearing was improved by the woollen balaclava.

Sunday, we set out on the final leg of the journey to Safawa. Now, there were no longer any roads, just tracks across the desert where someone had been before. Helen, George (who was feeling a lot better), Vic and I were again in the lead vehicle, this time Jim's Land Rover 110. Derek was driving the Iveco truck with the dish on, Dave the links van, with Chris and Steve beside him. The others followed line astern. Again, we would pull away and find a spot to get out the camera to "film" the convoy going past. On one occasion we pushed on quite a way ahead and pulled off into the middle of a massive field of six-foot high sorghum. To get any shot at all I had to put the camera and tripod on to the roof of the Land Rover. There was nothing but blue sky and horizon-to-horizon sorghum to be seen. We recorded the obvious shot of the dish travelling across the horizon but knew we could not transmit it. Christmas Day was not the time to go into why, when there were masses of acres of cereal here, the country had a food crisis. We made one final stop for tea at a small village just under an hour out of Safawa. Helen also wanted me to shoot some pictures of a traditional water pump they had in the village. We soon attracted a crowd, and I was dismayed at the high proportion of people, especially the younger ones, that had eye diseases, and how tolerant they were of the flies that crawled across their faces.

As we got nearer to Safawa, we often had to slow down, sometimes stop, to let the herdsmen on camels move their goats across the track ahead of us, and on the outskirts of the town drive carefully to avoid the young boys leading donkeys carrying rubber sacks bulging with water. We stopped the convoy just short of the camp so that we could get the camera in place to "film" the arrival. Once that was achieved, we could greet our hosts properly and take stock of where we were.

The SCF camp was the first of three or four aid agency compounds out on the outskirts of Safawa, all perched on the edge of a hill overlooking a wide flat valley. Down in that valley, row upon row of off-white "tents" stretching into the distance, the haze of camp-fire smoke putting a gentle blue wash over the scene. Assembled from rough-hewn wooden poles and covered in large sheets of cloth, plastic, linen or sacking, these temporary structures were home to complete families. They were organised into villages but constantly in a state of flux. As families felt better, they picked up their little bits and pieces of bed roll and cooking utensils and set off back to where they had come from in the hope that it might just be better than when they left.

The SCF aid agency workers compound, where we were scheduled to spend five nights, consisted of ten Toukals, one for each of the staff based there. There were two shower units and two loos. They were corrugated iron cubicles – the showers were the ones with the oil drum on top and the loos the ones with the deep hole in the floor. Then there was the dining hut, a wood and canvas structure, containing tables and about twenty chairs, and the kitchen, a few cupboards and a protected area for an open fire. The SCF staff had agreed to double up to release five Toukals for us to sleep in. With Jim's advice ringing in our ears, that we shouldn't put anything on the floor and to always check our shoes for scorpions, George and I went off to spread out our sheet sleeping bags and erect our mosquito nets.

There was a lot to do before we could relax though. First, we had to find a position within the compound where we could park the lorry with the dish on, not only so that it was pointing east out over the Indian Ocean but preferably on a slope so that we could achieve some of the ten degrees of extra elevation that we needed. Then by putting blocks under the front stabilising jacks of the dish's own trailer we should be able to gain the rest of that ten degrees. Failure to find the satellite would mean that everything we'd done so far would be wasted. We also needed to find a protected area for our generators so that the sound from them would be muffled by surrounding Toukals when we came to do the live broadcast from the compound. Having done that, we needed to run power cables from them to the radio links van and the Satellite Up Station. We put television monitors and a sound feed into the dining area so that the staff could see what we were doing and wouldn't feel excluded. To start with, this rather un-African industry made initial relations with the SCF staff rather tentative, but we were all desperate to make sure all the kit we had brought was going to function and to give ourselves the maximum time to fix anything that didn't. George was in the deepest trouble as the second VT machine was not happy and the Time Base corrector didn't work. Editing the material we had shot might prove to be impossible.

Finally, we stopped to eat. The tinned food we'd brought out with us was put into store for the bad times, and we ate local produce. I haven't the faintest recollection of what it was, apart from the fact that it was washed down with orange juice made up from a crystalline powder. Helen desperately needed to see what we had shot over the last few days and to start working out how it was all going to cut together. Someone in the team, I can't remember who, suggested that if George was going to run the material for Helen to review, then maybe the camp staff might like to see it and we should put it through to the monitors in the dining hut. This seemed to meet with general approval and, from then on, tensions eased and the SCF and BBC staff started to relax and interact. Happy in the knowledge that we had achieved a great deal in getting staff and kit to the location, most of us retired to our Toukals for our first night in the desert and went to sleep listening to the sound of mice in the straw roof over our heads. Chris and Steve decided to sleep on the floor of the radio links van.

We were up and out quite early the next morning, Monday, to get as much "filming" done before the day heated up. Start early, take a long lunch break, and go back when the heat starts to abate was the order of the day. The SCF, and the other aid agencies too, had adopted this pattern of working for their doctors and nurses. There was absolutely no sense in putting the health of the trained doctors and nurses at risk from heat exhaustion. For the same reason, they ate well and employed locals to cook and do their laundry. Our morning was spent recording material of the hospitals, education centres, weighing rooms and play areas that had been erected. The hospitals, like the tented villages in the valley, were built from rough-hewn wood capable of supporting a canvas, or in some cases straw, roof and accommodating four rows of ten to a dozen beds. At one end a makeshift counter served as a dispensary for the medicines. On the beds were mostly children in a variety of states of health. Some still obviously malnourished, lay there motionless, their lazy, hazy eyes apparently not registering the outside world, others, quite clearly stronger, were sitting on the edge of their beds making coloured drawings in exercise books. A nurse from Sussex, who had been at Safawa for almost a year, took us to a bed where a young Ethiopian woman had just given birth. She took up Safawa's newest refugee in her arms and with moist eyes said,

"She weighs 1lb 12oz".

Jim explained that one of the most pressing problems that had to be dealt with at a camp like this was boredom. Not for the SCF staff, but for the refugees. At home, their days would have been spent working at getting the food, water and firewood needed to be able to prepare meals. If the agencies made it all too easy, then boredom would set in as they would have nothing to do. So, supplies of fresh, clean water are set up some way away from the camp, so that the refugees must go and get it. It can't be too far away, otherwise they will go to the nearest river and probably get infected with cholera in the process. Likewise, the distribution of grain and flour is organised to be at set times, and for small amounts at a time, so that the process takes up some good part of a morning and becomes a daily routine. Classes were arranged in general health care, attendance at which was rewarded with biscuits. Children were being encouraged to wash their hands after going to the toilet, again with some small reward of food.

On the way back up the hill, away from the refugee camp, I noticed that Helen was looking pale and a little shaky. Given that she had spent seven to eight weeks hectically setting up the project, and as a production team of one, was having to do the interviewing, and carry on the functions of Producer and Director, it probably wasn't surprising. And in forty-eight hours' time, she was going to have to present our segment of the programme live on BBC1. I made a mental note to try and take some of the strain, the last thing we needed was for her to fall ill. Back at the compound, there was some great news. Chris and Steve had found the satellite. They had managed to centre our dish onto a satellite out over the Indian Ocean and had picked up its identifying signal.

It was probably just before four p.m., when we went back to record some more of the work that was being done by the SCF staff, but first we were invited to witness a presentation ceremony. We were told that a Sudanese family from the village were coming to see one of the SCF nurses, who had helped their young child back to health, and they wanted to give her a present. It was a lovely scene with lots of hand shaking and hugging, but heaven knows what the nurse was going to do with her present of a goat!

In one tented "classroom" a Sudanese lady doctor was telling stories with a hygiene message to forty or fifty children aged five and over, while in another, babies and toddlers were being weighed and having their height recorded. Music was being made, some older children were banging makeshift drums, an adult was bowing a stringed instrument that looked a bit like a half-size cello, and the toddlers danced. Dotted about on the dirt floor sat smiling Mums with their babies, clapping along to the rhythm. I knelt beside a young mother and her child of about eighteen months, it could have been a bit older, to get a close up of his smiling face. Spotting me behind the camera, he held out a hand to me as I filmed – what could I do but put my hand into shot and take his.

Helen and I discussed the material we had and decided that we had enough for the pre-recorded inserts that London was to show. There were to be two inserts, the first about three and half to four minutes on how the team and equipment got to Safawa, which they planned to show before they came live to us, and about five minutes on what the SCF do here at Safawa and what they have achieved, which Jim was to "voice over" during the live transmission. So, we called a halt to anymore "filming" and returned to the compound. Obviously. another bunch of English-speaking westerners was a novelty around these parts as we had many visits from the staff of the other aid agencies, in particular Help the Aged and GOAL, the Irish charity. While generally chatting and drinking tea, I was taken to one side by John Scott.

"Helen is in her Toukal in a complete state," he said, "she's lost her notes and has no idea where on the tape the different shots are. Do you think you could help?"

The original plan was for Helen to edit the two pieces in time to send them as transmittable packages over the satellite to London VT during the two-hour window we'd been allocated on Christmas Eve. It was, at this stage, unlikely that George was going to be able to fix our second tape machine so, in a way, that eased the pressure. When we had established communication with Television Centre, we were going to have to tell them that they would have to find the time and the machines to do the edit, but that we would tell them the shots and the editing order. The SCF staff would be very happy to see what we had shot today as most of it was about themselves, so while they were watching in the mess tent, Helen and I could sit quietly in the radio links van with George and remake the shot list. All we then had to do was persuade George to re-run 'the journey' just for us and we should be back on top of the problem. Happier now that we had a plan of campaign, Helen and I went to see George.

"The bloody time base corrector is never going to work, and I don't know whether VT in London can take raw video," he said.

Steeped in the formaldehyde of traditional television outside broadcast engineering, George was never comfortable in the company of young producers, especially if they were female, but we eventually convinced him that we all had no other option. The process of logging all the usable shots with 'in' and 'out' time code, durations and descriptions took the three of us until about one o'clock in the morning.

Christmas Eve morning and I struggled to the communal washstand to drown my face in the cold water that the camp got the same way as everybody else around here - on the back of a donkey. We'd all discovered that the only time to have a shower was at five or six in the evening when the sun had heated up the water in the oil drum on the shower roof. That night before retiring, Helen and I agreed that we would spend the morning working out an edited order of shots and the video tape time codes so that, when our two hours of satellite time direct to VT at Television Centre became available, we could play the tapes in the order that we shot the pictures but tell London the edited shot number. There was insufficient time in our two-hour window to spool backwards and forwards through our tapes to send them our pictures in edit order.

When we met, I could see that Helen was still stressed and very concerned about fronting the programme on Christmas Day and was finding it difficult to concentrate on what needed to be achieved first. I reassured her that she would be fine. She knew that she found it easy to talk to Noel back at the office, and I suggested that if she just thought about the programme as sitting down and having a chat with him and introducing some friends to him, rather than thinking of herself as having to be a formal TV presenter, then it would work very well and he, as the professional would lead her through it. We then sat down to work out an edited order of shots for the two sequences. For the first sequence— the story of how we and the equipment got to Safawa—I suggested that we shouldn't send London the pictures of our arrival at the camp and that the last shot should be of the convoy still travelling through the dust. That way the viewers could be left guessing as to whether we made it, until Noel came to us live. Helen agreed. While we were talking, one of the aid agency workers from Help the Aged walked into the Save the Children Fund compound with a live turkey under his arm.

"Hello," he said, "I thought when you've finished tomorrow, we could all have lunch together."

While Helen and I had been sorting out the programme content, John, Chris and Steve had been working on getting the technology in place. Intelstat had turned the satellite's transponder and the vision and sound circuits had been established. The minimum requirement for the programme to work was pictures and sound from us to London, sound from London, that is Noel, and a phone line so that we could communicate with the production gallery in the London studio. Anything else would be a bonus, and bonuses we got. The communications system worked perfectly; we had vision and sound both ways which meant that we could see and hear BBC 1's output as well as them seeing and hearing us. We also had two-way talk-back to the gallery and a phone, in fact we were an internal number on BBC Television Centre's PABX. Everything we would have had if we had been in the studio next door. While the rest of the team went to lunch, Helen and I continued with the paper edit.

With George operating our one working video tape machine, Helen and I were just ready with the shot list by four p.m., Sudanese time, when we could start sending over our material. Helen explained our intentions to the VT editors in the basement at Television Centre. As George ran the tape with the first shot, Helen told them which sequence it was for, gave them an edited order number, and 'in' and 'out' points.

"This is for the travelling sequence, it's to be our shot nine, 'in' as the dish appears – 'out' as the close-up wheel leaves frame."

George then spooled forward to the next usable shot on the tape, and we repeated the process. Working to the time coded list we had assembled, we sent over all the shots for the two sequences. As the material had been recorded over four tapes, George's tape changes, as efficient as they were, seemed to take ages but we got all our shots over the link with just five minutes to spare. Although Helen knew the editors would refine the edits, at least it was her cut and the pieces would look pretty much how she intended them to look. Also, she knew she could brief Jim on the piece about the camp, it's activities and staff that he was going to talk over during the live transmission. There was no more we could do until the rehearsals with London the following morning.

Having achieved all that we needed to do with the satellite communication system, John said to BT that the link could be shut down. As the BBC had to pay for it by the hour, this seemed a sensible suggestion. BT replied that they were quite happy to leave the link up at no charge and continue to feed us the sound and vision signals, so that people could watch BBC1. We fed it through to the mess tent, but not only did it kill all conversation, it seemed somehow inappropriate, even trite, and after less than half an hour, we said,

"Thank you, finished with the pictures but could you leave the phone up, it might just be useful."

Might be useful! I'd never seen a little green box give so much pleasure. We offered the aid agencies' staff the opportunity to phone home,

"Just dial '9' and then the number you want."

It remains one of my most enduring memories, the images of those young men and women queuing up in the fading light for their three minutes on our field telephone, so that for the first time in almost a year they could talk to their parents or partners.

"Hello Mum, it's me, Pauli, calling from Sudan."

Then a moment of silence.

"Hello Dad, what happened to Mum?"

Later, when the queue had gone, I phoned home and got the answerphone.

As we were two hours ahead of UK time, we had a relaxed start to Christmas Day, compared to our compatriots at Television Centre and at the top of the BT Tower, as that was where Noel was presenting from. The scheduled transmission time for the Noel Edmond's Late

Late Breakfast Show Christmas Day Special was eleven a.m. to one p.m. That to us, of course, was one-to three p.m., the hottest part of the day and, with a two-hour transmission to do, with, for the most part, the camera on my shoulder, I'd reckoned on getting rather warm and moist. Looking like a superannuated John McEnroe with sweat bands on both wrists and one around my forehead to stop the sweat from running down into my viewfinder eye, we rehearsed the sequences we were to do for the live programme, first, on our own and then, with the studio in London. About twelve noon, our time, we had a break for coffee and, on the way to the mess tent, I noticed an old oil drum on its side, the ends missing, a wood fire on either side and, inside sitting on four or five metal rods pushed through the sides of the drum, the gently roasting turkey.

By twelve-forty-five p.m., we were set up ready for the live programme. In the middle of the compound sitting on chairs brought out from the mess tent were all Safawa Camp's Save the Children Fund nurses and doctors together with Derek, Jim and Chris Eldridge, who had come down from Khartoum. Helen sat in the middle holding the microphone, and at the back of the group, adding a bit of local colour, a donkey and a camel. Shortly after "The Late Late Breakfast Show" went on air, with some of the relatives of the nurses and doctors there in the BT Tower with him, Noel Edmunds announced that a crew had set off a few days earlier with a satellite transmitter, heading for the Save the Children Fund camp. The edited pictures of our journey were shown ending, as we had planned, with the shot of the convoy motoring through the dusty terrain between Gadaref and Safawa, and Noel concluded his voice-over of our pictures by saying something like,

"And if they have managed to get there, we should be able to go live to Safawa in about half-an-hour".

It must have been a wonderful feeling for those parents in the audience at BT Tower when London finally cut live to our picture and they could see their son or daughter for the first time in twelve months. Helen, who once Noel had started chatting to her very quickly relaxed into her role, introduced the assembled group and the surroundings, including a walk over to the nearest Toukal to show the people back in England the living quarters of the staff. We had, of course, planned and rehearsed this, and Dave was on hand with a battery light inside the Toukal.

The schedule was for the last half hour of the programme to be devoted to allowing the nurses and doctors to talk to their relatives and to exchange stories and Christmas greetings, but before that London came live to us twice more. The first time was to allow Chris Eldridge to talk about the refugee situation in Sudan as a whole, and what progress has been made by the Aid Agencies in general, and the second slot was to allow Jim Atkinson, Safawa's Camp Administrator to talk over the edited pictures that we had shot in and around the camp. It was during this piece that the Mums and Dads could get some insight into the jobs their children were doing, the general public could see what had been achieved with the donations they had given and, sitting in front of her television set, my partner saw a hand come into the picture and take the hand of a small, smiling Ethiopian child, and realised that the adult hand could only have been mine.

When Michael Hurll finally said over talkback from the studio gallery in London,
"Thank you everybody, we are off the air",
I almost dropped the camera as I sank on to my haunches. What with the heat, the length of time with the camera on my shoulder and the emotions of not only the SCF staff and their families but of our achievement in getting the programme inserts on the air, I was completely drained. I made absolutely no contribution to the derig. I was vaguely aware of Dave, Eddie, Chris, Steve and Vic rushing backwards and forwards to the van with monitors, microphones and cables, and it all seemed packed away very quickly. We all then went to the mess tent for a full Christmas lunch. Turkey, sausages, stuffing, roast potatoes and vegetables. I don't know where it all came from, but it was a magnificent feast, the enjoyment tainted by the fact that outside, down in the valley, forty-thousand refugees were on survival rations.

The original plan was for us to spend Boxing Day clearing up and to move out on Friday, but as everything had been packed away very quickly, John suggested that we should let the SCF staff have their Toukals back and that we should leave in the morning.

Having sneaked away from the mess tent and put myself to bed well before nine-thirty p.m. the previous evening, I awoke before dawn on Boxing Day. I crept into my clothes, trying not to wake George, and wandered out to the edge of the escarpment overlooking the camp in the valley. I watched the sun come up over the camp, the colours of its first rays muted by wood fire smoke, and I watched as the males wandered out from their tents and, some two-hundred yards away from the camp, squatted in loose circles chatting to each other as they crapped. I felt that I could quite happily have spent a few more days there, the simplicity of it all, the single purposed nature of the work, which gave me for a short while a great sense of peace and, when the time came to leave, I along with the others, did so reluctantly.

Even though we had decided to leave a day earlier than scheduled, Helen still handed over half our subsistence rate for the five nights, in US$, to Jim who said that the funds would be sufficient to have a new hospital built which they would call the "Satellite" hospital in our honour. The journey back seemed so much quicker and less memorable. Getting the dish and its low loader off the Iveco truck onto a metalled road just outside Gadaref took minutes. Derek found a dry lugga that was the perfect height. He drove the truck down into the dry valley and backed it up to the bridge and we rolled the low loader off onto the road. That night we ate and slept in the safe house at Gadaref and on the Friday morning set out for Khartoum. This time at the "border stops" we went straight to the makeshift tea bars and bought something to eat or drink. Feeling a bit hungry, I had a bowl of curried goat, more bones than meat but very tasty all the same. Having spent some money, the border guards were not interested in our papers and just waved us on our way. Once in Khartoum, Dave and Eddie took the vehicles straight to the airport, ready to be put aboard Heavy Lift's Belfast. We went back to the Hilton, and, as requested, phoned the flight crew to tell them we were back as they wanted out as soon as possible. Then a long soak under a shower, I'll never take running hot and cold water for granted again, a meal and a short sleep. At two a.m. we left for the airport for the return flight, this time in steerage, back to Heathrow.

The programme was very well received by the 'powers that be' back in London, including the controllers on the sixth floor at Television Centre, and much appreciated by Save the Children Fund Headquarters. We had the following letter, addressed to John Scott, from Nicholas Hinton, their Director General.

"Thank you very much indeed for all that you and the crew did to make the transmission from Sudan on Christmas Day a reality. The whole show was very entertaining and the link-up with Sudan, when it eventually arrived, was very moving. I know how hard you and others worked to overcome the considerable obstacles – we are most grateful."

John himself passed on the reactions he'd received, via this letter, to the rest of the crew.

"Since we have returned from Sudan, I have received nothing but praise and commendation from all quarters for the contribution you all made to the L.L.B.S. on Christmas Day.

The arrangements would have been difficult enough in this country, let alone Sudan. The conditions, with such high temperatures and dust, were almost impossible and the welfare facilities were at a minimum. Despite all these difficulties, the end result was of the highest standard and only possible because of the enormous determination and enthusiasm shown by all of you."

I also had a most generous and gracious hand-written letter of thanks from Helen, and a suggestion that we should meet for lunch.

"Watching a tape of the broadcast back, although there are a dozen things I deeply wish I'd done differently, I still felt really proud of it and know how much of that was down to you...The shots of the journey were sensational and those two magical sequences in the feeding centre just made me really sorry you didn't have three weeks to make the programme you could have done...I want to say thank you for all the things you should not have had to do, but did so wonderfully, the directing, the editing and supporting. And sorry, really sorry that I wobbled.... I can't tell you how much it meant having you there."

About a fortnight later we met at a bistro in Holland Park, and over lunch we re-visited the key moments of a ten-day experience that will forever remain burnt into both our memories. Around two-thirty p.m. we walked out into a crisp January afternoon and our paths have never crossed again.

Helen Fielding went on to write the "Bridget Jones" novels.

Chapter Three
Two Bs and a C or B.B.C.

I was born at the Royal Navy Maternity Nursing Home, in Gillingham, Kent, on Midsummer's Day 1945. My father, George David, was at that time a Chief Petty Officer in the Royal Navy and had served on HMS Norfolk at the time of the sinking of the German Battle Cruiser, "Bismarck". My mother was Algar Blanche Stanley, before she married, and Algar was a Christian name I could not recollect having heard anybody else being called, then or since. It was sometime later in my childhood that it was explained to me that my mother was born on 21st October, the anniversary of the battle of Trafalgar, hence the unusual name.

My maternal grandmother lived in Gillingham, in the same rented two-up-two-down with an outside toilet, from well before my mother was born, in 1919, until a few years before she died, well into her nineties. It was only the storm that swept through the South-East of England in the late Autumn of 1987, causing damage to the roof of the house, that finally convinced her that she should leave and move into a retirement home. By then, my parents were living in Rhos-on-Sea, North Wales, and it was there that Grandma Stanley finally passed away.

That house in Livingstone Road held the most memories of my earliest childhood. The afternoon teas of thin, hand-cut, slices of white bread and butter with dark brown sugar on, (sourdough, whole meal, stoneground, mixed grain, were never heard of then—bread was white, milk had cream on the top and coffee contained caffeine). I can still recall the stone-coloured, earthenware hot water bottles and the hot milk and bread cubes with sugar, "slops" it was called, with which I was cosseted when I was ill in bed with measles.

Grandfather Stanley had worked at Chatham Naval Dockyard for his entire life. My recollections of him were few, other than the only hobby I recall him having was bowls, and that he had tremendous patience, allowing first myself, and a few years later, my younger sisters, June and Diane, to play hairdressers with his thin, shiny black hair, for hours at a time.

18, Livingstone Road was not the only home I had in Gillingham, but my memories are blurred by the ravages of time. Cameo pictures drift through the colander of my brain, but I cannot recall them at will or place them chronologically with any certainty. I can remember that two or three doors down the road was Billy Bragg's Cycle Shop, where there always seemed to be an Alsatian dog, (which we are now supposed to call a German Shepherd Dog, and probably because Alsace is now French), and there must have been more than one, because the memory "snapshots" cover a period of at least twenty-five years, firstly, when I lived in Gillingham and, afterwards, when I visited my Grandmother during holidays. Billy always had a kindly word for me, whether he was behind the sales counter or more often, in the workshop, hands covered in grease, repairing bicycles. When Billy retired, his son, Barry, took over, but that was the end of the family tradition because the grandson, Bobby, went into showbusiness as a stand-up comedian and the cycle shop is now, probably, an Estate Agents, or more likely a Chinese Take-Away. I can recall running errands for Gran, mostly to the Co-op. where I had to remember to quote her membership number to make sure she got her dividends, or her Christmas bonus. Quite often Grandma Stanley would take me with her on the bus into Chatham to shop, and I can remember being shown the statue of General Gordon of Khartoum, which dominated the entrance to Brompton Barracks, the home of the Royal School of Military Engineering somewhere between Gillingham and Chatham. Little did I realise then, that one day I would see Khartoum for myself.

Grandma Stanley's sister, Ethel, lived forty yards further up Livingstone Road at number 21. She was married to Walter Rogers, a small, dapper, and to me, mild-mannered man, who, when I was about fifteen, took me to my first football match at Gillingham Football Club, then languishing near the bottom of one of the lowlier divisions of the Football League. We stood on the open terraces behind the goal and I was taken totally by surprise by a new side to my Uncle Walter's character. He spent the entire first half loudly barracking the goalkeeper, swearing and doubting his masculinity and his parentage. At about the same time, but it may not have been the same visit, Walter said to me, although I cannot recall what might have provoked such a statement,

"Get yourself a cage first, you can always get a bird to put in it later."

It's not advice I've heeded but Walter would seem to have done so. Unlike Granddad and Grandma, Walter and Ethel had bought or were buying their house. They seemed to be reasonably well-off as they used to holiday quite often in Cape Town and Durban, travelling there by Union Castle Line ship. There was several pieces of very dark South African wooden furniture in the house, which they presumably had shipped back, and a Black Boy ashtray holder which stood in the lounge.

***

For the first few years of my life, father was based at Devonport naval dockyard, Plymouth, so my parents took a flat there. My paternal Grandparents had lived in Plymouth all their lives and my aunts had also made their homes there. Grandpa Winser had been a shipwright in the Navy, so it was deemed quite natural for my father to do the same and join up, although he was given the option, when leaving school at fourteen of going into the dockyard. My only memory of that flat was of an evening around the fire, when a mouse shot out of a corner of the room and into the hollow brass fender, and while my mother kept well away from the fender, father rushed from one end to the other attempting to trap the mouse.

It is probable, from conversations that I had with my parents later in life, that mother wasn't too happy in Plymouth, because they were not in the flat for very long before father's base was moved to Portsmouth and the family moved back to Gillingham. There my parents rented a two-up-two-down of their own, number 27 Franklin Road, which was a few minutes' walk away from Grandma's, down Livingstone Road, past the junction between Barnsole Road and Napier Road, across the Gillingham Road and on up towards the cinema, where, on a later visit to Grandma's I was taken to see Fred Astaire and Leslie Caron in "Daddy Long Legs". The only memory of the house was the seemingly long entrance hall, dark coloured with a dado rail. Often when father came back from a tour of duty, he would put his navy cap on my blonde, curly haired head and allow me to tricycle up and down the hall imagining I was a bus driver.

My education started in Gillingham at Barnsole Road Primary School, but I was only there for one term because, at about that time, my father was demobbed from the Navy. If there was a period of unemployment between the navy and father starting at S.G. Browns, the gyro compass manufacturer, then I was completely unaware of it. I have no doubt in my mind that since then my father had remained fully employed right up to his retirement at sixty-five. My admiration for my father grows every time I consider his achievements. He had left school at fourteen with the minimum of qualifications and, once he had left the navy, applied himself to five years of night school to obtain a HND in electrical engineering, the closest thing to a University Degree a Technical College could award, while at the same time, helping to bring up three small children and hold down a full-time job.

S.G. Browns was based in Watford at that time, so it was necessary for the family to move away from Gillingham. My parents made an offer on a Victorian house in Enfield, but the deal fell through, so due to the need to move quickly, they bought a caravan on a site at the top of Tom's Lane on the outskirts of Kings Langley, in Hertfordshire. It was the depths of the country to me. The caravan site of maybe forty vans, with its mud and shingle oval perimeter road, was surrounded by hot, hazy hay fields, gently grazing cattle, hedgerows and scrub land, filled with eye-high cowslips, field mice and kor-korking pheasants. On more than one occasion I stumbled across a nest in the long grass and, knowing no better, brought the pheasant eggs back for Mother to cook.

The four-berth caravan itself was about twenty-two feet long, with a pair of large wheels at its centre and four adjustable jacks at the corners. It had the usual towing "A" frame, where the "Calor" gas bottle sat providing the fuel for cooking and lighting. There was an Anthracite burner in the front room, which served as entrance hall, dining room, lounge and my parents' bedroom. Every night before they could get to sleep, they would have to collapse the dining table, put it between the two bench seats and, using the cushion backs as mattresses, make up their bed.

That dining room table was the centre of family life. Not only for eating off, but it served as the office, the study, the workshop, for sewing and dress making, for changing the nappies of youngest sister, Diane, and as a modelling table when father and I built our balsa and tissue paper glider.

From that multi-purposed room, a narrow six-foot long passage passed between the galley kitchen on the one side, and the toilet and bathroom on the other, to the small twin-bedded room that my elder sister and I shared. Clothes were stored in short wardrobes on the bulkhead wall over my feet, in drawers under the bed and in aircraft-type overhead lockers above the window at the back of the caravan. I would often stare into the unpolluted blackness and marvel at the countless points of twinkling lights and can recall vividly the cold Winter night shortly after being told about the existence of other planets when, unable to sleep, I sat chipping the ferns of frost off the inside of my bedroom window with my thumb nail and saw for the first time what must have been a shooting star. I was scared rigid, thinking that an invasion from another planet had started. For what seemed like an eternity, I never moved, every sinew straining to concentrate on listening, waiting for some ominous, approaching sound.

The shops, school and nearest public telephone were all over a mile away, down in the valley through which meandered the Grand Union canal, in the village that had grown up around the Ovaltine factory, that during the second world war had turned its hand to making balsa wood tailplanes for the Mosquito bomber. Even back in the early fifties, the Kings Langley Village Primary School was overcrowded. My first classroom was a wooden hut, across the road from the main school and more suitable for a group of Cub Scouts, but it was there that I was taught joined-up writing with a dip pen that had a wide nib so that the results were almost like copperplate. It was my second year there before I moved into the Victorian main building. The classrooms were typically Dickensian, with very high ceilings and all the windows near the top of the walls so that neither could anyone climb or see out of them. I can remember being fascinated by one particular schoolgirl who had one brown and one green eye, but can only picture her in the playground, backed up against the boundary fence, surrounded by four or five other boys. There were girls in my class, but I presume that they did not like me very much, as my only memory of them is of being stabbed in the back with a pencil, the lead from which remains beneath my skin.

The only holidays I can recall were visits to relatives, which meant either back to Gillingham to Grandma Stanley's, or to Devon to stay with my father's parents, or his sister, my Auntie Betty. Once or twice, it could have been more, my sisters and I would be put on the train to Plymouth by ourselves, and Auntie Betty would put us up for a fortnight. Betty and her husband Girvan, a bus driver for the Plymouth Corporation, had one daughter Margaret, and an almost permanent lodger called Wilf. He was treated, and behaved, like one of the family, and to this day, no one is quite sure of how he came to be there. Still, I called him Uncle Wilf, and it was he that took me shrimping in the rock pools around Bigbury Bay. For a time, my paternal Grandparents had a bungalow, with an acre of garden, at Gunnislake in Cornwall. It was shortly after Grandfather had retired from the navy and they were attempting to grow all their own vegetables, with enough left over to sell to supplement their pension. Grandma Winser was a wholesome cook; steak and kidney puddings, lashings of potatoes and gravy, steamed sponges, spotted dick and plenty of cakes and scones. She made her own clotted Devonshire Cream, and my real all-time favourite was "thunder and lightning", thin slices of white bread with Golden Syrup and the homemade clotted cream. Every morning grandfather used to walk to the nearby farm to collect the day's milk, which came in quart bottles, the top three inches of which was thick yellow cream. One morning I was up early enough to go to the farm with grandfather and was given one of the large bottles to carry back to the bungalow. When I got to the front door, the bottle slipped out of my hand and smashed on the stone doorstep. I burst into tears but was amazed to find myself laughing almost immediately as I heard Grandfather say that,

"There was no point in crying over spilt milk".

Our family stayed in that caravan at Kings Langley for close on six years, and we must have been friendly with the people in the neighbouring caravans, because the first time that I ever saw a television was in the next-door caravan where we all sat waiving small Union Jacks on sticks at the flickering black and white pictures of the Coronation of Queen Elizabeth II in 1953.

On Sundays we would go regularly to the Baptist Church in the Village. Our family became friends with two families who lived in houses further up Tom's Lane. They had cars and would pick us up on the way to the church on all but the finest days. The Wymans, Rene and Alf, the pillars of the church, were in their late fifties with one son, John, who was a Bank Manager. The name of the other family is totally lost to me, but I can remember the daughter's name. It was Rosemary. It was she who suggested that I walk her home one Summer's day after Sunday School. It was she who suggested, as we reached the railway bridge at the bottom of Tom's Lane, that we climb up through the long grass to the top of the embankment. It was Rosemary who first pressed her lips to mine, who slipped her tongue into my mouth and made my pulse pound in my temples so loudly that it drowned out the train from Kings Cross steaming northwards over the bridge. Looking back, it was probably no bad thing that father changed his job and our family moved to Hatfield. I stayed on at the Wyman's for a week after they had moved to sit my eleven plus exams.

***

The fifties produced a rash of developments around the periphery of London, some known as Garden Cities, of which Welwyn and Letchworth were the obvious examples in Hertfordshire and the New Town

Development Corporation had planned a similar, but down market and cheaper version, to the south of the historic town of Hatfield. The old town had grown up to the west of Hatfield House, in the grounds of which the young Elizabeth I had been told that she was to become Queen in the C16th. The rows of new houses were mostly terraced, small but three-up-three-down with gardens back and front. The architects had struggled manfully to inject some variety into the layout of the streets. They had introduced crescents, where the terrace of houses matched the gentle curve of the road, producing individual units that were wedge shaped, the houses being two foot narrower at the back than the front, causing problems for anyone trying to lay floor covering. Another stroke of design genius was the mono-pitched, corrugated aluminium roofs, presumably chosen because they were quick to erect and cheap to make. With high winds in the right direction, the roofs acted like a giant aerofoil, creating a vacuum over the back of the houses, rolling up the strips of aluminium and leaving the crescent looking like an empty, discarded sardine can.

78 Cherry Way, the house my parents rented, was more conventionally designed, and the end unit of a block of six. Cherry Way sloped gently down-hill to the south towards Potters Bar, halfway between the Hatfield bypass, now the A1, that passed the De Havilland aircraft factory where father had got a job working on the guidance systems for the Blue Streak missile, and the old A1, now the A1000. The slope of the road meant that the front garden of our house was two feet higher than the damp

course of number 80, the first house in the next block of six houses and I can remember all too painfully the days spent helping Father landscaping the garden by carrying earth from the front of the house through to the back in an old, galvanised tin bath.

***

Senior School was something that I endured rather than enjoyed. My memories are few and of survival, of scraping through, rather than of success or happiness. I was not very sporting. I made the school soccer team on only one occasion, when the entire team turned up at our school changing rooms and sat around waiting for the opposing team from Welwyn Grammar to appear, only to be confronted by an irate, and out of breath sports master who wanted to know why the team was not at Welwyn for the away match. (Obviously, it wasn't his fault that we all turned up at the same place). Frantically, we all cycled the four miles to the other school to arrive, shattered, an hour late, and not surprisingly, were soundly beaten 11-0.

Hatfield Technical School, in Roe Green Lane near the A1, and a mile-and-a-half's cycle ride from Cherry Way, was half of a symmetrical building, twinned with the Technical College – the whole building is now the University of Hertfordshire. The school was structured towards technical subjects. The first foreign language that pupils were taught was German, followed by Russian, and you had to be a girl before they would consider letting you take French. Now, I regret very much not being able to understand that language, or Spanish and Italian for that matter, not that I was any good at German. In fact, I was not very good at English, History, Art or Geography. Encouraged by my father, I had concentrated on Mathematics, Pure and Applied, on Physics, on Chemistry and Technical Drawing.

Out of school I took a job as a paper-boy. The round took me almost twice as long as it should because I would spend so much time with my head buried in the magazines I was supposed to be delivering. "Motor Sport", the "Angling Times", "Model Maker", and the "Eagle" were my literary diet for years. Those journals were responsible for the hobbies that remained with me right through to well into my mid-thirties, and I still maintain an interest in Grand Prix motor-racing, although the scrapbooks containing photographs of Sterling Moss, Jim Clark, Graham Hill, Phil Hill (the American who drove for Ferrari), John Surtees, Lorenzo Bandini and Jochen Rindt, the Championship tables I drew up for myself, the race reports and lap times culled from the magazines, are long since consigned to dustbins, all part of the detritus dumped as I moved from bedsit to flat to house through my late teens and early twenties. Gone too are the racing cars whittled from balsa wood, the pre Scalextric electric car racing circuit, a home-made figure of eight constructed from hardboard, with aluminium sticky tape conductors, along with the 12th scale plastic construction kits of Formula One Racing Cars, lovingly painted to represent my heroes, the World War II fighter aircraft, the Fokkers, the Fireflies and the Phantoms.

The rear garden of the house in Hatfield backed straight onto fields and farmland, and many a school holiday Summer was spent fishing a deep dark pool which lay, most unusually and to this day incomprehensibly, on the top of a hill in the middle of the farmland and twenty minutes' walk from the house. I started fishing, like most boys of that age, with a bamboo cane, black cotton, a matchstick and a bent pin. Bait was a firm flour and water dough, rolled into a ball the size of a small pea, and on a good day, in excess of twenty, two to three-inch-long roach, would impale themselves on the end of the line. Inspired by the weekly articles, illicitly read in the "Angling Times" on my paper round, I graduated to a proper rod and reel. The rod was in three sections, the first bamboo with a cork handle and aluminium reel clamps, the second split cane and the third, solid fibreglass with an agate tip ring. The sections slipped together perfectly, the brass ferules setting the whole thing off beautifully. Having picked out the rod in the shop, the three weeks it took me to pay for it went by agonisingly slowly as I imagined the other anglers getting to the fish before I could. Ten shillings was the deposit. The following Saturday I handed over another ten, and at last, with the final payment of nine shillings and eleven pence, it was mine. By the standards of the day, let alone the improvements in rod design that would be brought about by the introduction of hollow section fibreglass, and later carbon fibre, that rod was pathetically inadequate with little power or flexibility in the middle and butt sections, but I felt that I had the tools to take on the largest of fish that the pond was rumoured to hold. Bankside stories of 20lb Carp, and huge Pike abounded, and the great splashes amongst the reeds and overhanging bushes that shattered the drowsy peace of those summer afternoons would add further excitement to the myths.

My technique improved, finding the feeding depth, ground baiting and the use of worms instead of paste, produced Roach and Perch of a 1lb. each and I even managed to land a 3lb. Jack Pike, which, unlike all the other fish, I did not return and took home for my mother to cook.

In addition to the seven day a week paper round, I took a Saturday job in Hatfield market, helping on a flower stall for a £1 a day, which coincided most usefully with my father giving me a six-foot by eight-foot plot of the back garden to look after by myself. I cannot remember what I put in it or for how long I remained interested.

***

It was while I was in Hatfield that I learnt the rudimentary basics of photography. My interest was aroused on one of our holiday visits to Devon, where I was lent a box Brownie to take pictures to show to my parents on our return. The paper round and the Saturday job enabled me to save up for and buy my first camera, an Ilford Sportsman, that cost £11.19s.11d. It was a proper camera, with control over aperture, shutter speed and focus, and it took 35mm film. A local youth club leader taught me how to process and print black and white film, and in 1961, when I went on a school youth hostel trip to Italy, I took colour transparencies using Ferraniacolor, which father had processed by one of his colleagues who worked in de Havilland's photographic laboratories.

That Easter holiday trip to Italy, my first ever trip abroad, remains in my mind as a glorious two weeks of new and exciting sensations. The overnight train to Venice, with everyone clutching a newspaper with Gagarin's picture on the front, stopping at Basle on the border of France, Germany and Switzerland, the gun-carrying police moving through the train and checking for I didn't know what and me leaning out of the carriage window at dawn as the early morning sun came shafting through the snow-covered Swiss Alps, the air, cold, clean and sharp to the nose. I was amazed at how far it was possible to walk in Venice, imagining that all travel would be by canal, and I found the buildings and the paintings awesome.

It was in Venice that I had my first taste of wine. Returning early to the youth hostel from a free morning to wander the city I tried to explain to the cook that I was thirsty and needed a drink of water. With a despairing look and a shake of the head she disappeared into the darkness of the kitchen to return with a huge flagon of Chianti under her arm, a ten times larger version of the raffia wrapped bottles that, buried under years of yellowed candle wax, adorned the gingham tables of Italian restaurants in England, and proceeded to pour me a huge tumbler of the wine. Unable to communicate, and not wishing to offend I was forced to consume all the sharp, acidic, warm liquid, tasting as it did like a combination of the worst medicines I'd had to endure when ill. Afterwards, not only was I thirstier than before, but to make matters worse, I had a headache. It was probably nigh on a decade before I drank any form of red wine again, preferring the sweeter wines from Germany, like Blue Nun and Black Tower.

From Venice, the school trip went to Florence, the enduring impressions being the heat, the light and the earthy redness of the buildings. My knowledge of spaghetti was until Florence, entirely of the Heinz tinned variety, so fresh pasta and the way in which the locals ate it was fascinating to me, twisting it round their forks and biting off the hanks of excess strands so that they fell back to the plate. The youth hostel was outside the city in the foothills and was rumoured to have been Mussolini's Summer palace. A long, low two-storey building, set in a large ornate garden in need of some attention, being mostly overgrown by uncontrolled Wisteria, it overlooked the city. The group of sixteen-year-olds, after spending the day walking the art galleries, churches and markets, took their pasta, salad and bread suppers on the veranda in the evening light, with the smell of the flowers and the lights of the city twinkling in the Arno valley as the sun sank. I regret not being able to share those moments with someone close to me, being acutely aware that while others were pairing up to walk amongst the gardens in the heady exotic night, I was left alone.

The Italian tour continued to Pisa, where only the weird sensation of walking to the top of the leaning tower remains in the memory from that part of the trip, and then back to England via Milan. A valuable learning experience which my parents were to repeat for my two younger sisters when they got to their fifth years in their respective schools, although the girl's trips were more expensive than the £25 it cost for me to go to Italy.

***

Nearer home, the school laid on other excursions outside of the normal curriculum, which looking back, I was glad that I had been part of. At the end of the Christmas term in the fifth and lower sixth form years, the pupils were marched into Hatfield town to the cinema for a special afternoon performance of Olivier's film versions of Richard III and Henry V. In my last year, the sixth form was transported by coach into London, to the Old Vic, to see a stage performance of a Shakespeare play, from the upper balcony. Who was in it or what it was called have long since been erased from my randomly accessible memory. I also took up the option for several seasons to attend the Saturday Morning Children's Music Concerts at the Royal Festival Hall, on London's South bank, getting the train direct from Hatfield Station to King's Cross and the tube across to Waterloo. Whether I did this before I got the Saturday job on the market stall, or after, will remain a mystery to me. But then perhaps the order of events is insignificant anyway, and it is not necessary to remember when, only that they happened and that they had an impact.

Academically I continued to scrape by. I had absolutely no idea what kind of a job I wanted or any inclination of a career direction. My father had always regretted not having the opportunity to go to University, and desperately hoped that I would go there for him and preferably to study electronics. He was sure that electronics was the coming science and that there would be an increasing need for qualified electronics engineers. Having only passed five 'O' levels, I was allowed to stay on in the sixth form but only on the understanding that I successfully resat one of my failures. So, by adding Geography to Maths, Physics, Chemistry, English and Technical Drawing I managed to avoid making any decisions about life after school for another year. My time in the upper sixth was probably no more traumatic than any other seventeen-year-old, but I found studying for my three 'A' levels and applying for jobs, when I didn't know what kind of a career I wanted, put me into a bit of a spin. On top of that, father had successfully applied for a new job with Ferranti in Edinburgh, and the plan was for the family to move to Scotland the first week after school broke up for the summer. Having applied to both Standard Telephone & Cable and the Ministry of Defence for sandwich course training that would lead ultimately to a degree, and, failing in both cases at the interview stage to be offered a place, I only had two options left to me as I sat my 'A' levels, one of which was a place at Leicester University to do a general science degree.

If it hadn't been for John Green, probably the only boy in the sixth form at school with whom I had anything approaching a rapport, who drew my attention to an advert in the Radio Times for Trainee Technical Assistants and

Trainee Technical Operators I would have been reliant on getting two 'Bs' and a 'C' in my exam results so that I could take up that university place.

The Radio Times advert, with text printed over a picture of a cameraman riding the front end of a studio crane, explained that Technical Operators could progress to be Sound Operators or Cameramen, and that Technical Assistants were trained in the electrical and electronic engineering aspects of the television system. I was more attracted to the Technical Operator course, but given my father's advice over recent months, I applied for and was offered a position as a Trainee Technical Assistant, and the offer was not conditional on my exam grades.

Whether I achieved high enough grades to enable me to take up the Leicester University place or not, I was going to start a new life a long way south of Edinburgh sometime in September. I couldn't see the point of leaving Hatfield, where I had lived for the last seven years, to move to Edinburgh for six or seven weeks. So, it was arranged for me to stay, as a paying guest, with a family from the church my parents attended. Father also arranged for me to have a summer job at de Havilland's Aircraft factory down on the A1. As an assistant in the works canteen.

"How long do I cook these potatoes for?"

"Till they're done, sonny".

I probably cleaned or scrubbed about a ton and a half of potatoes in the six weeks I was there, and I'm quite amazed that I was not put off cooking for life. One of the jobs I had twice a week was to make the mixture for the hamburgers that were to be offered at lunch. Minced meat was but a small proportion of the mix, the bulk of it being the remnants from breakfast; congealed eggs, bacon bits off the plates, cold toast - whatever was left - it all went into the mincer.

***

One 'B' and two 'Cs', so the decision was made for me.

My first contact with the BBC was the dark green coach with the grey stripe down the side that met the train from Paddington at Evesham station and bussed the nervous newcomers to the Corporation's residential training school at Wood Norton, three miles out along the Pershore road. All the information I had been sent indicated that all new entrants into the BBC would have a four-week induction course, where they would be shown around the various departments in order to start their careers with a broad understanding of the corporation's activities. For some reason that was never satisfactorily explained, September 1963's intake of trainee Technical Assistants were told to report directly to the training school.

The three-month course was a mixture of struggling by day with the mysteries of the valve, the amplifier, the transistor and the transmission system and surviving the nights of pranks and partying. Lectures and practical work were structured in a way that was not unlike school but at five 'o'clock the similarity ended. Now we were away from home with money in our pockets. Occasional sorties were made to local hostelries, but the evening's entertainment usually centred around the BBC Club, which then, was in a large Victorian house in its own grounds on the outskirts of Evesham. Apart from one or two female Sound Operators from another planet called the BBC World Service at Bush House, Wood Norton's courses were populated by males, mostly in their late teens or early twenties. Over time, the BBC club members had built up an ongoing symbiotic relationship with a Nurses Training College in Worcester, and this provided a constant supply of female company, rumours and gossip. A few of the course members had their own cars and I can remember many a midnight dash back to Wood Norton via the nurses' lodgings in Worcester, six or seven of us shoehorned into a car. A lot thinner then, I used to sit in the middle of the front bench seat of an imported 'Maigret' Citroen with its dashboard gear lever and, under instruction from the driver to my left, change gear.

I cannot remember what I did with most weekends during the three months of the course. Most of the others went back home. For anyone who lived in the Midlands or the Home Counties, the cost, in time and money, was reasonable. For me to get to visit my parents in Edinburgh would have meant travelling all day Saturday to get there and all-day Sunday to get back. On two or three weekends, I was invited back to the Guildford home of Peter Belcher, a fellow trainee with whom I got along quite well. He and I bought tickets, in an Evesham record shop, to a couple of music concerts at the Cheltenham Odeon. There were regular buses to and from Cheltenham. The first concert, on 8th October, was part of the Rolling Stones 1963 UK tour, and on the bill with them were the Everly Brothers, Bo Diddley and Little Richard. Quite a noisy affair but nothing compared to the concert a few weeks later, on 1st November. We went to hear The Beatles. We heard hardly a thing apart from the screaming and yelling of thousands of teenage girls. National newspapers next morning declared that Beatlemania was everywhere.

On the morning of the final Friday of the course, the entire intake of trainee Technical Assistants assembled in one of the larger lecture rooms, to be told which BBC department or station they were to be allocated to. The possibilities were many. Trainee engineers were required in all the English regions, Television Outside Broadcasts based in the "Palace of Arts" in Wembley, the studios at Television Centre in White City and many of the transmitter stations around the country. Wherever we were to go, we were all to report at nine-thirty a.m. on Monday January 6th, 1964. The assistant head of the training school read out, in alphabetical order the list of postings.

"Belcher, Monitor Test Room, Television Outside Broadcasts Wembley".

Peter looked happy, quite clearly, he could commute from Guildford. As more of the names were read out, I realised that all the five or six people I had warmed to on the course were all going to Wembley, and as the penultimate name on the list, I was hoping that I would be posted there too.

"Winser, Monitor Test Room,...Television Centre".
"Woolmer, …"

I didn't hear where the last chap was going, it didn't matter. I hadn't got the posting I was hoping for.

"Right. Any questions"

My hand shot up.

"Excuse me, sir, but is the allocation set in stone, I mean, can it be changed as I would have liked to have gone to Outside Broadcasts?"

"Er, I suppose not."

A moment's silence.

"OK Winser you report to Wembley and, er, let me see…"

With two simple strokes of a pen my wish was granted. I often wonder what happened to the poor chap who went to monitor test room at Television Centre instead of me.

My first job at Wembley was attempting to fix non-functioning monitors in the test room. A job that I was not at all good at, and, when the end of course examination results were announced in early February, I had failed. I was to report to Mr. B. Head, personnel officer, at Threshold House in Shepherds Bush to be formally dismissed. I had been at Television Outside Broadcasts for about five weeks, long enough to have realised that the guys having all the fun were the cameramen. At the dismissal interview I explained to the personnel officer that, against my instincts, I had applied for the Technical Assistant course because my father thought I should, and that what I would have preferred to do was the Technical Operators course. He thought for a minute and then told me that, in this case, it might just be possible for me to re-muster as a trainee Technical Operator. I should go back to Wembley and within two weeks I would be written to and told whether I could start training as a cameraman.

Chapter Four
Musiara Memories

September 1989

The sound of hoovering on the carpet outside my bedroom slowly permeated my brain. Minutes later a knock on the door revealed a dusky hotel maid, asking if it was all-right to make up the room. Peering through leaden eyelids at my watch I saw that it was seven-thirty a.m. and realised that I had been asleep for just two hours. I mumbled something approximating to "not yet" and shut the door. I guess the maid understood, which was fortunate, as this was the Jacaranda Hotel, Nairobi, and my Swahili was non-existent. It was at two p.m. the day before, that I had set out from my home in suburban Southwest London to meet with five colleagues from BBC Bristol at Heathrow Airport for the flight to Nairobi. The Natural History Unit was embarking on its most ambitious live 'Nature Watch,' and as a cameraman based at London Television Outside Broadcasts, I was extremely fortunate to be part of it.

London Television Outside Broadcast resources had only been required on three previous occasions in the past decade to assist the Natural History Unit with the live 'Watches', twice at the RSPB's bird reserve at Minsmere in Suffolk and once at the Naadermeer in Holland. I had the luck to be in the right place at the right time when, in May 1981, London had the first single camera Outside Broadcast Unit (SCU4 – I have no idea about 1, 2 and 3) and the programme's producer wanted to use it to prerecord material at Minsmere for insertion into the live transmissions. Live 'Watches' are by nature a risky business. Wildlife behaviour cannot be guaranteed to happen during pre-planned transmission times and it is essential to prerecord some material to be able to tell the whole story. Accompanied, informed and inspired by Assistant Producer Robin Prytherch, an ornithologist whose knowledge of birds, their behaviour and song, continues to leave me astounded, several sequences were satisfactorily gathered and edited.

"Better the devil you know" is a maxim I am sure all programme departments apply at times and so it was that SCU4 and I went to Holland for 1987's live 'Watch' from a colony of thirty-thousand Cormorants. It was there that Robin Hellier, the Director of the live transmissions, and following John Dobson's retirement, the Producer, was discussing further expansion of the live 'Watch' programmes. The following year, I think, "Reef Watch" from Israel took place, but preliminary research and recces were well in hand for a 'Nature Watch' from what is arguably the ultimate wildlife watching destination, The Masai Mara National Reserve in Southwest Kenya.

The BBC's Natural History Unit is world famous for its Wildlife documentaries, considered and crafted programmes filmed over many months, often years. The production philosophy behind the live 'Watches' was different in that they attempted to convey the impression of what it is like to be at one or other of the renowned Wildlife reserves for a day, to communicate the excitement of being there and to show some of the animal behaviour potential visitors might see if they were to come themselves. At most of the British Bird reserves, visitors are in hides, so camera placement is relatively simple, but with 'Africa Watch,' the problems were different. Visitors who come to the Masai Mara watch the Wildlife from free ranging Safari Trucks. The animals are constantly on the move and, consequentially, so must be the watchers.

The Masai Mara National Reserve is six-hundred square miles in area; therefore, it was necessary to find a smaller defined location within the reserve that would have a consistent throughput of animals, a hill on which to site radio link equipment, and mobile cameras in vehicles able to transmit pictures back to that base and be data controlled from that base. Using an extension of 'Golf Buggy' technology, developed to allow cameras to follow golf games unhindered by cables, London Tel OBs were to provide four Sony 330 cameras and cameramen, engineering support, radio links and one Video Tape editor. Bristol was to provide the Engineering Manager, three more Cameramen and cameras, (two Ikegami HL79's, one Sony DXC3000), the Sound and Vision staff, the flyaway studio gallery, editing facilities and another Video Tape editor. An extremely costly exercise, only possible if co-production money was available.

Fortunately, Robin Hellier had managed to persuade, convince, or cajole the Discovery Channel of America, TVE of Spain and NHK of Japan to co-operate on the project.

A suitable location was found in the Northwest of the reserve that provided the appropriate combination of wildlife activity and technical feasibility. This was the Musiara Marsh, a spring-fed area of the Mara's undulating grassy plains that remains wet the whole year round, to which the animals would gravitate for water, bordered down its western side by the Mara River and at its Northeast corner, by an approximately one-hundred-foot-high hillock. An ideal site for the control tent and radio communications base.

With the major problems of finance and technical feasibility surmounted, there remained the question of when and who. If anywhere in the BBC had the expertise to decide on the time of the year that the programme should be scheduled for, it was the Natural History Unit, and middle to late September was chosen, to give the best opportunity to see as much of the abundance of East African wildlife as possible. It was decided that two weeks pre-shooting was required, with two Land Rover based crews recording material not just around the Marsh itself but from within a much larger area of the reserve to ensure enough behavioural material to flesh out about twelve hours of live transmission to four countries. Two Natural History Producers, with past experience of the Mara and the behaviour of its animals, were to lead the crews and drive the Land Rover 110's. They were John Downer, notable for his series "Supersense" and Keith Scholey, producer of the Rift Valley programmes. One cameraman from Bristol and one from London OBs were to operate so that they could learn about the area and the animals and then lead pairs of camera vehicles for the live transmissions during the fourth week of the trip. Alan Hayward, then in charge of the Macro Studio at Bristol, and who worked mostly with film on natural history projects, was until the late seventies, a London Tel. O.B. cameraman. He was to work with John Downer and I with Keith Scholey. So, it was on the afternoon of Friday 1st September 1989 that Alan and I renewed our acquaintance on the BA flight to Nairobi.

Robin Hellier, Keith Scholey and Robin Prytherch, who was to spend most of the next fortnight in a darkened room, (accompanied by two BVW75's video tape recorders and the editor Dave Channing), had flown out a couple of days earlier to meet the pre-shoot equipment, organise the Land Rovers and collect the car mounts. They were then going to drive the hundred or so tortuous miles from Nairobi to the Mara River Camp just outside the northern boundary of the reserve, which was to be our base for the next two weeks. We six, the aforementioned Dave Channing, the two Bristol based Sound Recordists, Bob Lassiter and Tony Briscombe, John Downer, Alan and I had just to get ourselves and our personal luggage to Jomo Kenyatta International Airport where we would be met and bussed to the Hotel. Just personal luggage in my case included my two Nikon 35mm cameras, thirty rolls of fujichrome and an assortment of lenses including a hired 300mm f2.8 plus two times converter and a Nikon to Ikegami converter kindly loaned by Nikon UK, a combination that produced a fixed 0.8-degree f5,6 lens when attached to the front of the television camera. Useful for the occasional Very Big Close Up.

After the dusky maid and her hoover had retreated further down the corridor, I did not return to bed but stared out of the window at the antics of the Black Kites, one of the worlds commonest birds of prey, but an absolute rarity in Great Britain, and the Pied Crows as they searched for edible titbits in and around the grounds of the Jacaranda Hotel. I breakfasted alone assuming the others to still be asleep, only to discover subsequently that they had rushed off into the city centre to a well-known discount bookshop. A missed opportunity that I was to regret later. I spent the morning in the hotel lobby reading the Guidebook to the Masai Mara Reserve provided by the production team and scanning the pictures in the Field Guide to the National Parks of East Africa, which I'd managed to purchase from a bookshop in Kingston before leaving home. Lions I would know but separating Impala from Thomson's Gazelle at distance was going to be difficult, especially in a black and white viewfinder.

When the others returned, we lunched at the hotel and a minibus took us to Nairobi's Wilson Airport for the forty-five-minute journey to Governor's Airstrip in the western heart of the Mara. The flight in a twin-engine Otter took us over the Great Rift Valley, above huge herds of

Wildebeest constantly on the move in search of fresh feeding grounds, across Maasai Villages – manyatta – with their distinctive geometric shapes and, finally, to the airstrip a mile or so to the south of the Musiara Marsh. From there a convoy of Toyota Landcruiser's, less sophisticated and easier to maintain than Land Rovers, took us and our luggage to the Mara River Camp ten miles north and outside the official boundaries of the reserve.

The Mara River Camp is not the most expensive or luxurious of the organised accommodation available to the tourist in the area, it's probably in the lower half of the luxury scale, but I was amazed at how well organised and comfortable it turned out to be considering where we were. It is built right on the east bank of the Mara River with cultivated lawn down to the river's edge. There is a paved patio outside the dining area where lunch is taken, and drinks around the fire before dinner, which is taken inside because not long after dark, it can get quite cold. For the four weeks I spent a hundred miles south of the equator daylight was from six-thirty a.m. to six-thirty p.m.

The accommodation was in individual tented chalets reached by yet more paved paths that meandered through trees along the riverbank. The chalets had a concrete base with two-foot high side walls the length of the tent, out the back doors of which was the private shower, flush toilet and wash hand basin enclosed by a four-foot high brick wall and a thatched roof. The sleeping tent contained two single beds and two bedside tables with electric reading lamps. The camp's generator provided electricity from approximately five a.m. till about nine a.m. and again from six p.m. until eleven p.m. Hot water produced by wood burning fires under a massive oil drum was available in the evenings but took five to ten minutes to reach my chalet. I soon got into the habit of turning on the shower immediately I returned at night so that by the time I had unpacked the kit from the day's outing, the warm water had started to come through. The front of the tent had a small concrete patio with a table and chair under an awning and the whole chalet had a second roof of thatched branches so that it merged with the surrounding vegetation. Having unpacked my luggage and found my way around, I sat down at the table on the patio feeling very "Hemingway" and stared at the Mara River just ten yards in front of me and at the bloat of Hippos.

Over dinner, always three courses and usually soup, meat and two veg and a pudding, mercifully washed down with half a bottle of Bardolino, I found myself asking if the hippos came ashore at all? Keith Scholey assured me that they did. Every night.

"You'll hear them grazing on the grass outside your tent," he said.

I didn't sleep much that first night.

Sunday morning was spent unloading the equipment from the Land Rovers that had driven down from Nairobi, checking that the Ikegami HL79 camera that I was to use had survived the journey, fitting the Nikon lens to the camera, (there hadn't been time to try it before leaving England) and setting up the battery charging facilities and Video Tape editing area in a spare room in the Camp's wooden reception hut. Bob Lassiter, the Sound Recordist with whom I was to work, and who was to be instrumental in our achieving some remarkable footage during the second week, checked out the BVW35 tape recorder and his associated sound equipment. I had an extremely nerve racking ten minutes when the HL79 refused to work when switched on. My first thought was that the battery must be flat, unusual because it is normal for them to be issued fully charged, but after trying three I really thought there must be a serious problem with the camera. It was only when I tried the fourth Anton Bauer battery and the camera sprang into life, that I worked out that the fuses, in the three batteries I had previously tried had all broken in-transit. Fortunately, they came with spares.

In the afternoon, we became tourists for two hours and went for a game drive around the area of the Musiara Marsh to familiarise ourselves with the landscape and to get used to spotting the animals. With the vast area of straw coloured grasses, I quickly realised why Lions are the colour they are. In that short trip we saw Olive Baboons, Buffalo, Wildebeest, Zebra, Topi, Thomson's Gazelle—known locally as Cheetah food—Impala, Giraffe, and many birds that I'd never heard of, let alone seen before, such as Augur Buzzard, Bateleur—a very distinctive, almost tail-less bird of prey, Crowned and Wattled Plovers, Black Shouldered Kite, Woodland Kingfisher—one of seven types resident in the Mara, the majority of which do not feed on fish, and three species of Vulture—African White-backed, Rüppell's, and Lappet-faced. Huge, ugly and ungainly on the ground, we were to learn how useful these birds were in directing us to feeding predators. Numbers of circling Vultures can be seen from miles away across the plains and are indicative that fresh meat is on the ground below them.

Back at the Mara River Camp, we checked that everything was ready for the first day's shooting. Plenty of charged batteries and a box of ten thirty-minute Beta format video tapes, we were to average three tapes a day for the next fortnight. One last check of the door mount before dark. I say door mount, but in reality, the passenger door of the Land Rover 110 had been removed and replaced with a similar sized piece of three-quarter inch thick plywood, the top of which was nine inches lower than the windowsill of the original door. This was strengthened by dural struts to minimise flexing and bolted to the top was an Arriflex 150mm bowl to take the camera panning head. This allowed almost half the camera to protrude outside the Land Rover and gave about a 160 / 170-degree pan. It also meant that the operators head, left arm and shoulder were outside the vehicle.

Over dinner we were introduced to Jonathan Scott, a zoologist, writer, wildlife artist and award-winning photographer who was to co–host, with Julian Pettifer, the live television transmissions in three-weeks' time. He has written and illustrated with drawings and photographs, three books about the wildlife here and, if I'd got up earlier on that first morning and bought them in that bookshop in Nairobi, I could have got them autographed. It was fascinating to hear him talk about the ecology of the region. The Masai Mara Reserve is only bordered by lines on a map and is but a small part of a much larger ecosystem that includes the immense Serengeti region to the south in Tanzania and parts of the Loita and Aitong plains to the north. It's an area of some ten thousand square miles, encompassing the yearly movements of the migratory Wildebeest population. The Mara receives the most rain in the ecosystem, about fifty inches a year at Musiara, and plenty of grass remains here after the Serengeti has dried up. The Wildebeest population, now about one and a half million, together with two-hundred thousand Zebra and half a million Thomson's Gazelle, form a vast assemblage of plains game, whose annual movements through the ecosystem are known as 'the migration'. Also, over dinner we learnt from one of the Camp's local drivers, who was out on the plains everyday taking tourists on game drives, that a lone male cheetah that looked as if he had not eaten for two or three days, had been spotted in the small ridge of hillocks that spreads eastwards away from the northern end of the Marsh. We agreed to start there in the morning.

I needn't really have bothered to set the alarms on both my watch and travelling clock, as I was awoken at four-forty-five a.m. by the camp's generator. This gave me plenty of time to make the call time of five-thirty a.m. at the dining room for coffee and to collect our picnic breakfast and lunch. Did I say coffee? I am absolutely convinced that the Kenyans must export their entire bean production because I have no idea what this stuff was made from. I could not argue with Keith's description of it; "death on the plains". Both the picnic boxes contained a hard-boiled egg and two slices of bread. The difference between them was a piece of cold bacon in the one marked breakfast and cheese in the one for lunch.

Finding the Cheetah was relatively easy, it already had three or four Safari trucks around it and it was there to stay. We withdrew after an hour and set off north to the Loita Plains. We stopped quite often to shoot basic portraits of solo animals even if they were just browsing, or in the Lion's case sleeping. It was money in the bank. As the week went on and we managed to shoot more interesting behavioural sequences, we became more discriminating. Apart from a half minute sequence of a female Warthog with two piglets, difficult to do much with, as Warthogs keep themselves further away from the vehicle than most of the other animals, we recorded two sequences which did finally make the transmission. At about two miles range, Keith spotted some circling Vultures and when we arrived, a lone Spotted Hyena was finishing its meal on a juvenile Wildebeest carcass. There was no telling whether Hyenas had killed it themselves, it was unusual for there to be only one, and it was soon to be harried off by ever-increasing numbers of Vultures and Maribou Storks. A Jackal skittered about nervously in the background looking for the opportunity to dive in for a morsel, but the chance never came.

We moved on, this time in a westerly direction across the northern edge of the plain. The landscape changed from mixed grasses and Acacia scrub to more open rolling countryside. On the skyline we spotted a white Suzuki

Jeep. Through the binoculars it was possible to distinguish a camera mount on the roof of the car.

"It's Hugh," said Keith.

It was then that I learned that this was a very economically efficient trip for Keith Scholey as he was the Assistant Producer on two documentary films being made for the Natural History Unit, here in the Mara, and both were based at the Mara River Camp. Owen Newman was shooting material for a film about Cheetahs, and a film about Wild Dogs was being made by Hugh Miles. For anybody, like me, who has sat in awe of some of the Wildlife Camerawork in films such as 'Kingdom of the Ice Bear', 'Darkness in the Grass' and 'Hunters of the Skies', Hugh is the master.

Returning to Camp via the Marsh itself, we stumbled across a group of twelve to fifteen Banded Mongoose playing in and around a fallen dead tree trunk. They were chattering away to each other, playing what seemed like tag, scent marking the tree and scratching in the earth for insects to eat. Continuously, at least one Mongoose was standing on its hind legs, on sentry duty. Once back at camp, at around seven p.m., we cleared out the Land Rover, put batteries on charge and looked at the 'rushes'. Then a quick shower and a slow cool drink before dinner and bed by about ten p.m.. With five-thirty a.m. starts and thirteen hours in a Land Rover—I was going to say at a stretch but stretching was an impossibility—late nights were not in order at this stage of the trip.

We left the Camp in the dark, and headed north across the Loita plains towards Aitong, Keith picking a route along the rutted track using dipped headlights. The East African dawn when it comes, is quick and dramatic. It is virtually monochromatic, at times red and black, the sunlight shafting between black rain clouds, Wildebeest and Acacia trees silhouetted on the skyline. By seven-fifteen a.m. we had recorded several dawn shots, portrait sequences on Jackal and Bat Eared Foxes, and found a group of three young male cheetahs. From the size of their stomachs, and their casual, almost arrogant gait, it was easy to see that they had recently fed and would be unlikely to seek food again today. We decided to stay with them for the rest of the day in the hope of picking them up again the following day. Knowing where they were the night before can only be a rough guide as they are constantly on the move, even at night. We recorded several sequences of scent marking—like lions they urinate on trees—and grooming. Towards evening, the three cheetahs ran amok in a herd of Wildebeest, harassing the younger ones. It seemed a half-hearted affair—practising, I suppose, but we recorded it anyway. That night, for the first time since arriving in the Mara, I slept right through until woken by the camp generator at just before five a.m..

From dawn until about nine a.m. we quartered the southern Aitong plain, vainly searching for any clues as to the whereabouts of those three cheetahs. We had told Owen Newman about them the night before over dinner and had agreed a head lamp flashing signal if either crew found the Cheetah and could see the other vehicle. We never saw Owen again that day until we met over dinner. After about three hours of searching, we retired to a slight rise that over-looked the plain. Another essential requirement was that it be covered in short grass, so that one at a time we could get out of the vehicle for relief, while the other two kept watch. We half-heartedly ate our hard-boiled eggs and cold bacon, one or other of us scanning the far distance for any signs of life.

We decided to amble south again, having one last look around the area. We stumbled across a family of Bat-Eared Foxes playing around their burrow and set about recording the sequence. Peaceful family life was shattered when Keith yelled,

"Forget that, hang on and keep the camera running".

About half a mile away to our right he'd spotted agitation amongst a small herd of Wildebeest. We hurtled across the plain, the camera still on its mount, (up to now I'd taken it off for travelling), arriving to find our three cheetahs still in the process of despatching a Wildebeest they had just brought down. It struggled to get to its feet one last time, but instantly one of the cheetahs whipped a paw across its nose and brought it crashing to the ground again. While that cheetah smothered it, the other two ripped into its rear end, the most efficient in terms of food gained for least effort. It seemed only a matter of minutes before the cheetahs' stomachs were visibly bulging to bursting point. In a ragged circle about six yards in diameter and centred on the carcase were thirty to forty Vultures and Maribou Storks, with more circling over-head. There literally is a pecking order, the various species of Vulture have differently designed beaks to enable them to get at different parts of the carcase. From the moment we arrived, to the point where there was a bright white skeleton of a Wildebeest, with everything that could possibly be eaten gone, took just ninety minutes. Although the cheetahs were pressured into leaving the carcase by the sheer numbers of Vultures, they were not far away, having retired to the shade of some acacia scrub. We eased the Land Rover over to them, recorded a few peaceful shots of three very fat cats settling down to sleep off their big meal, and decided to treat ourselves to a proper lunch back at the Mara River Camp.

Keith said that there was not much point in going out again until around four o'clock, so after lunch I sat on the patio outside the dining area and settled down to write a letter home. (The letters were basically a diary of events and are the bones of this chapter). A monitor lizard about a metre long strolled along the river bank in front of me and elephants browsed on the acacia scrub the other side of the river. Some species of iridescent yellow Weaver, I couldn't work out which—there are more than ten—rushed up and down the opposite bank building its dome-like structure of a nest, at the end of a very flimsy branch over-hanging the water. Robin Prytherch, the ornithologist I'd worked with on previous live 'BirdWatches', used to give himself a half hour break after lunch to look at the birds around the Camp. He'd never been to Africa before and was like a dog with two tails.

At four o'clock we set off for the Marsh and came across the pride of Lions whose territory is centred on it.

Locally each pride is known by the name of the area they inhabit. This pride is known as the Marsh Lions and were the subject of Jonathan Scott's first book. As we arrived, they were just emerging from the Marsh and heading for the trees that border the Mara River, and the exact location of 'Crocodile Camp', the temporary accommodation that was to be built by the weekend after next, to house the forty or fifty of us required to transmit the live programmes. We followed them into the woods and recorded a lovely sequence of the lionesses and six or seven cubs scrabbling up and down various tree trunks. They were in a very playful mood. After about ten minutes, one of the lionesses decided to lead the group out of the woods again and set off pretty much towards my camera but heading to pass the rear of the Land Rover. Two yards short of passing the rear door she swung sharply to her left and proceeded to rub her back along the side of the vehicle, under my lens and left elbow and on round the front of the truck. There are a few moments in life when time does appear to stand still and that for me was certainly one. I passed on the beer before dinner that evening and opted instead for a very large gin and tonic.

The lionesses that we had seen the day before, at play with their cubs, had not looked very full. Keith thought it well worthwhile trying to find and stay with them. They were going to have to look for food sooner or later. To the eastern side of the Marsh, lay open grass land, virtually featureless except for two huge Termite mounds and a lone acacia tree. This almost square mile of two to three-foot high grass, spreads east as far as the Musiara Gate, and is bordered to the north by two ridges of undulating hillocks, and to the south by a long, meandering lugga, dry now but a fast-flowing stream in the rainy season. Headed for those plains, we went around the northern end of the marsh, stopping at the spring which not only feeds it, but was to be the source of washing water for 'Crocodile Camp' in the third and fourth weeks of the trip. We recorded some of the various birds that feed in and around the area. Egrets, Herons, Saddle-bill Storks, Crowned Cranes, African Jacana, even a Greenshank on a visit from Europe or maybe even England.

Once onto the grassy plain, the pride was not difficult to spot. Currently there were fifteen lions in the pride, four adult females, a couple of cubs about a year old, five that were probably six months and four more about three months. The lionesses were stretched out on top of a termite mound, mostly on their backs with their paws in the air, intent on sleeping their way through the hottest part of the day. The cubs, however, had yet to learn to conserve energy in the heat, and would jump on each other and tumble down the side of the mound locked together as one ball of fur. Occasionally the fly swishing tail of a lioness would prove too tempting a moving target, and one of the younger cubs would pounce on it and sink its teeth in, only to be firmly rebuffed with a very large clip round the ear. We recorded several sequences of the cubs at play, suckling the females—mothers and aunts share the feeding duties—and the occasional little fights that broke out. It was so easy to compare them to domestic cats, until an adult yawned and exposed huge, lethal teeth. Towards evening the pride moved on across the plain and settled down under the lone acacia tree. Wildebeest and Zebra herds had passed within half a mile and had been ignored, so it seemed unlikely that the lions would feed. Just to be sure, we sat with them until it was too dark to 'film', before returning to Camp.

Next morning, (Friday and only a week since leaving home), we set out at five-forty-five a.m. to find the lion pride once more, determined to sit out the day with them in the hope that they would need to find food. They had moved away from the acacia tree up onto the ridge at the north of the plain and were hidden in amongst the bushes and scrub on the top of the hillocks. This not only provided them with cover so that they were difficult to see, but also furnished them with a grandstand view of the plain stretching away to the south. Alan Hayward's team had come along side during the morning to see how we were getting along. We agreed that it was inefficient for both crews to sit with the pride all day and they went off towards the Mara River to record material of Hippos in the river and the Olive Baboons that congregate in the trees along its edge. We had brought some 'Storno' two-way talk back sets for truck-to-truck communications, but they were unreliable over anything further than about a mile, so they agreed to come back to us later in the day so that they could join in the coverage if anything happened. We settled down to watch and wait.

Very little did happen. Occasionally a lioness would get up, stretch and settle down again, exposing sufficient of its body for us to see that she looked lean around the midriff, thereby keeping our spirits up, which was more than could be said of the lunch we ate around one p.m.. It was still the same, hard-boiled egg, bread and cheese. Having decided that the coffee did us more harm than good we were keeping our liquid intake up with Cokes and Sprites which we kept in a cool box at the back of the truck. The weather pattern had changed since our arrival, and the days were getting hotter, so we were very glad of the extra fluid. We had positioned the Land Rover at the bottom, and parallel to the ridge, passenger and camera side facing the lions. This enabled Keith to keep an eye on the plains to the south for any signs of the herds of game that might tempt the lions into action. Between lunch and about three p.m. a few straggly columns of Wildebeest wandered in a south-westerly direction about a mile to our right, provoking one of the lionesses to stand and gaze in their direction. We, in turn, would power up the equipment and try to control our pulse rates by breathing deeply, only to switch off and relax seconds later when she lay down again.

Suddenly the 'Storno' crackled distortedly into life.

"--re --t -f --el" .... "-ohn t- -eith, -o pet—l".

We deduced from this that the 'B' team were stranded without fuel. We asked them where they were, but we guessed that they could not hear us as their message never changed. We had to try to find them. We could not leave it to chance that some other vehicle would pass them, but which way to go? And what appalling timing. Having sat for nearly two days with a pride of lions, almost certain that they hadn't eaten for three, we were most reluctant to leave. For no other reason than it was the direction that they had left us in, we headed for the river, comforted by the fact that they could not be more than a mile away, or we would have never heard them at all!

We'd chosen well. After a short while the radio signal became stronger and we were able to establish that they were near the Kitchwa crossing. It was not long before we spotted them. Just above the grasses we saw John Downer standing on the roof of their Land Rover, the Storno set at arm's length, as high as he could get it. After an exchange of unprintable, but good-natured jokes, we set about the serious business of trying to work out how to get fuel from our Land Rover into theirs. The result was that Alan got under our vehicle, broke into the fuel line, and using empty Coke bottles we transferred about five litres of fuel to their tank. Hoping that this would get them back to Camp, six or seven miles to the North, we set off back to where we had left the lions, praying that we had not missed the action we had waited so patiently for. Our luck had held up, the lions were still where we had left them, and we positioned ourselves once more and settled down to wait.

Between about five p.m. and six p.m. the herds of Wildebeest and Zebra, in ever increasing numbers and still tramping towards the Serengeti, were stopping to graze on the grasses in the plain to the south of the lugga. The frequency with which the lionesses got up to have a look increased in proportion. Earlier in the day they would be up for seconds at a time, now they would spend minutes erect on top of the ridge looking down their noses intently at the game about a mile away.

It was on the dot of six p.m. that the hunt started. Three lionesses rose to their feet at the same time and strode purposefully down the side of the ridge about one-hundred-and-fifty yards apart. Keith started up the Land Rover and drove us about six-hundred yards south towards the lugga and the unaware game and parked side-on to the lions' direction of travel. All three of us strained through our binoculars to try and spot a lion in the long sandy-coloured grass. From behind they are easier to spot as the back of their ears are black so that other lions can see them, but we were as disadvantaged as the Wildebeest. I don't recall which of us picked it out first, but it wasn't long before I'd trained the camera on the top-half of a lion's head moving steadily, and resolutely, straight towards our Land Rover. It was about one-hundred-and-fifty yards away when we first started recording, and it just kept coming straight at us. At the point where its head was beginning to fill the frame, I clearly saw its jaw tighten and the eyes steel in deathly concentration. Intensely aware of the silence, I knew then what it must feel like to be on the menu. Hardly daring to breathe, we let the lion pass behind the truck, waited patiently for it to proceed a further fifty or so yards and started up the engine. Sweeping round in a large semicircle we crossed the lugga and placed ourselves as near to the Wildebeest as we could without disturbing them.

Parked now with the Land Rover pointing at the Wildebeest and parallel to the lion's direction of travel, we sat, pulses racing, binoculars trained on the grass for the slightest sign of movement. Dusk was falling fast, and I switched two stops worth of electronic gain into the camera. The lioness showed herself briefly as she slipped into the lugga. Was she going to go left and behind the truck? Should we move and risk the possibility of panicking the Wildebeest into stampeding? We decided to sit tight and hope she went to our right and would reappear camera side of the vehicle. It seemed an eternity before we regained contact with her again, until scanning the grass with the camera, I picked up the tell-tale slinking black ridge on the back of the lioness about twenty-five yards in front of me. Intermittently she would stop dead in her tracks as a Wildebeest raised its head from grazing for a look around. When it returned to graze, unaware of the impending danger, she would stealthily move forward, just the tips of her shoulders and the brow of her forehead visible above the grass.

Minutes ticked by as the lioness inched ever nearer to her prey. Not daring to stop tape, praying that the batteries would last and with my temples thumping, I sat like a coiled spring with my eye glued to the viewfinder. Suddenly, all hell broke loose. Like a sprinter from the starting blocks, she was off, charging into the scattering Wildebeest. Panicking Zebra barked as she ran amok among the mixed herd. It was hard to tell which animal she was after, it almost looked as if she was going to fail, until one adult Wildebeest broke stride and turned fatefully to face the lioness. She sprang straight at its throat, hooked a paw over the back of its neck and with one twist of her body brought it crashing to the ground. Knowing that they'd survived another day, the herds of stampeding Wildebeest and Zebra slowed to walking pace and resumed grazing. The barking stopped, the thundering of hooves died away and the silence hurt.

The following morning, all except Alan Hayward's crew of three, arose late and took breakfast at the camp. It was totally unmemorable, but if pushed, I'd say it was the same as the picnic breakfast except that the bacon was warm, and it was on a plate. Alan, John Downer and Tony Briscombe had left the Mara River Camp at five a.m. to recce the balloon flight. Arrangements had been made with the company that operate dawn flights over the Mara from Little Governors Camp for a crew to fly on both Saturday and Sunday next. The previous evening, we had learned that there were three spare places in the eight-man basket and a recce was offered. Apart from the stunning views of the landscape, on landing passengers are treated to a full, freshly cooked, English breakfast with champagne. One look at the smiles on their faces when they returned, showed that they had enjoyed their trip to the full!

Bob Lassiter, Keith and I spent a leisurely morning cleaning out the Land Rover, dusting off the equipment and reviewing material with Robin and Dave. We agreed that the 'Lion hunt' sequence could do with some cutaways of blissfully unaware Wildebeest, so later that afternoon we went back to the scene of the previous day's excitement and recorded a few shots in similar light. Just for fun, I hung out of the side of the vehicle with the camera dangling at arm's length, to get the lens down into the grass, but not for long.

Robin Hellier was to return to Nairobi the following day to meet with people from Kenya Broadcasting who were to handle the last part of the outgoing radio link. So, the middle of the day, either side of a sit-down lunch, was spent rapidly writing postcards home for Robin to take with him. I gave up the good intention of trying to write something different on each card and hoped the recipients were never going to compare them.

The seating arrangements for dinner had gradually changed over the week we had been here. When we first arrived, the tables had been set up for fours and sixes. Now the staff at the Mara River Camp had aligned three tables so that all the 'filming' crews were able to sit down together. We learned that Hugh Miles had been following the Wild Dogs for several seasons and that recently, the Aitong pack had been dying from some unknown disease. It had been reduced in number from about thirty to about six and all the signs indicated a kind of rabies. Hugh had no idea if he was going to end up with enough material for a story, or how that story would turn out.

Sunday, we set out at five-thirty a.m. again in search of more atmospheric shots and general views of the surrounding terrain. We spent some time at dawn break recording Elephant and Wildebeest herds silhouetted along the skyline. It was a gentle, unhurried morning with no great pressure to record material. We had been very lucky in the first week and were confident that we had plenty of interesting behavioural sequences to slot into the live transmissions. Between the two teams, we had lions mating and hunting, we'd recorded various animals scent-marking their territory in different ways, we'd seen cheetah hunting, vultures clearing up the carcase, elephants and giraffe feeding. The only event we hadn't recorded, and the one the Natural history experts back in Bristol had said to Robin Hellier that he was very unlikely to get in two weeks pre-shooting, was a 'crossing'. The annual movements of the Wildebeest herds, northwards in spring towards the Mara and the plains beyond, and south again in autumn, back to the Serengeti, is one of Africa's most amazing sights. To achieve their goal, the herds must cross the Mara River, a task they do not take lightly. It can happen any time between August and October and is completely unpredictable. Film makers have recorded this event before, and Robin was advised to bring out previously recorded material, to guarantee showing the experience which is so dramatically part of the Mara. As the programmes were going to be live, using video cameras, with pre-recorded video inserts, Robin chose not to bring filmed material of a crossing. Throughout the previous week we had kept our ear to the game drivers' grapevine for any clues of a build-up of animals at any of the traditional crossing points, but there had been no news at all.

Lunch on Sundays at the Mara River Camp was always curry, and it would seem to be a custom amongst natural history film makers that it is never missed. Long may the tradition continue as it was the best meal of the first fortnight in Kenya. Afterwards, with no feelings of guilt at all, I sat and soaked up the sun's rays. Letters and postcards written the day before, I felt completely at ease looking over the river, watching the birds about their business, the sun shining onto the lower slopes of the Siria escarpment that rises to the west beyond, antelope picking their way precariously amongst the boulders and elephants browsing in the acacia scrub. I was very reluctant to leave the peace and comfort, when late in the afternoon news came of a female cheetah with cubs moving north across the Loita plain. When we eventually found them, Alan's team had already spent some time with them and had recorded a wonderful sequence of the mother shepherding her cubs across the plain, calling to them to keep up. During this tranquil family sequence, she shot off, without warning, into the scrub and returned seconds later with a Spring Hare for their tea. As dusk fell, we were able to shoot two camera coverage of them settling down under a fallen tree for the night. The cubs though, remained very playful right up until we left, hiding behind branches and pouncing on their brother or sister and grabbing them by the throat just as an adult would its prey. The cubs were about six weeks old.

Eighteen of us sat down to dinner together that night. The Discovery channel of America had started its build-up to the live transmissions by flying in four technical TV Journalists and Eric, the Channel's public relations man. Between them, the four journalists had to file stories on how the programmes were being made to the Los Angeles Times, the U.P.I. news agency and the American equivalent of the British trade magazines 'Broadcast' or 'Television Week'. Part of the co-production deal was that each pre-shoot crew would take a journalist out with them for the next two days.

Before dawn broke, the four of us, Keith, Bob, the American Journalist and I, headed north to try and find the female cheetah and her cubs. They were nowhere to be found. The cheetah had moved off during the night and two hours of searching in ever-increasing circles provided our guest with nothing to write home about. The morning had started brightly as we recounted the highlights of the last week. Now an embarrassed silence had descended over the Land Rover. To make matters worse, Bob had turned a whiter shade of pale and was suffering from severe stomach pain and we decided that we should return to camp to get him some medical attention.

It was about eleven a.m. when our team, containing one very sick Sound Recordist and one saddle sore and unimpressed American Journalist, pulled in at the Mara River Camp to be greeted with the news that large herds of Wildebeest were gathering on Paradise Plain. We left Bob in the capable hands of Robin and Dave, moved the BVW 35 video tape recorder into a position on the floor where I could get at the controls, brought the portable 'SQN' sound mixer into the front seat so that Keith could monitor sound levels, and set off south. This time, as we wanted to be on the south side of the river so that if a 'crossing' developed the animals would be coming towards us, we left the camp in a westerly direction and crossed the river at Mara Bridge. We turned south on the C13 road that winds along the lower slopes of the Siria escarpment towards Tanzania, past Kitchwa Tembo Camp and into the reserve via the Oloololo Gate. After some seven or eight miles the terrain became much softer and greener as we negotiated the fringes of the Olpunyata Swamp.

We slid along for another three miles or so until, rounding a corner of the riverine forest, we were confronted by a large lugga, still running with water, and standing on the bank opposite, and directly in our path, a Hippopotamus. Fourteen feet long, five foot high and probably weighing anything up to a ton, the old male hippo stood its ground. We could see that the lugga wasn't completely full, the water level was two feet below the bank, but we had no idea how deep it was. We had three choices. Find another way across the lugga, retrace our steps almost back to the Oloololo Gate and take the fifteen-mile-long way round the swamp to Mara Serena lodge, or wait for the Hippo to move and gamble on the water not being too deep. We backed up, turned right, away from the Mara River, and drove along beside the lugga to see if there was a more viable crossing point.

After half an hour of meandering, we'd found nothing worth attempting. The safe course of action would take at least an hour and a half, and, in all probability, we would miss the 'crossing'. We counted the number of cold drinks we had left, realised that with four lunches and a breakfast between us we could survive for at least twenty-four hours if we got stuck and decided to gamble. We got everything off the floor onto seats just in case. Keith checked that the Land Rover was in low ratio four-wheel drive and eased us over the edge of the lugga. The nose dropped away at about forty-five degrees, and it looked as if we were about to drive straight under until just as the water broke over the top of the bonnet we started to level off. Water was coming in around the wooden door panel and glancing outside I could see that the tyres were completely submerged. Slowly, steam rising from the engine, we climbed out of the other side, vowing that when the time came, we would take the long route back to camp. As we approached the south side of the Serena crossing, we were extremely relieved to see no sign of Wildebeest. That at least meant that we hadn't missed anything.

Within half a mile of each other. there are two traditional crossing points that the Wildebeest that have gathered in Paradise Plain have used for centuries to continue their journey south, Paradise and Serena. The former is open, with good visibility where the river flows quickly, white water foaming over black rocks, the other a narrow strip of open ground, hemmed in by the river and an impenetrable thicket of cover, and known locally as the cul-de-sac. The banks, some five metres high, are steep on both sides except for one stretch of muddy terrace on the north side where the Wildebeest come first to drink. So many factors are involved in creating the right conditions for a 'crossing'. The lack of forage, the desire to drink, the right numbers to push the lead animals into overcoming their fear of predators, even exposed vehicles on the opposite bank can spook the early animals into turning around before the pressure from behind is great enough.

We eased the Land Rover quietly into position behind some bushes, attempting to keep ourselves hidden but affording a view of the entrance to the cul-de-sac and the plain beyond. There wasn't a Wildebeest to be seen anywhere. We pulled quietly away from the river and in a large loop approached Paradise crossing. Still there were no Wildebeest to be seen, only a crocodile, twelve to fifteen feet in length, basking at the water's edge. Logic was telling us that this had been a wasted trip, but it 'smelt' right. Vultures were sitting in high branches overhanging the river, a Fish Eagle was noisily patrolling up and down and every so often a pair of eyes would break surface for a few seconds and then slowly, oh so slowly, submerge. There was an air of expectancy everywhere.

It was one p.m. when we decided to return to the cover of the bushes on the south side of the Serena crossing and wait. We took it in turns to peer through the trees to the entrance to the cul-de-sac and pick at our lunches. The sun, vertically overhead, beat down on the roof of the Land Rover and if we spoke at all, it was in whispers. We kept looking at our watches, as if it was going to help, but if anything, time slowed down. That hour until we saw the first Wildebeest at the top of the opposite bank seemed to take forever. Then there were ten, almost instantly hundreds. The occasional hoof beat became a tumultuous thunder, intermittent bleating became a cacophony of bellowing and barking, as a mixed herd of thousands of Wildebeest and Zebra poured in from the plain to the narrow, constricted access to the river. Bumping and barging into each other, the mass of game became denser as the cul-de-sac filled up and the lead animals teetered at the water's edge.

Keith, his hand on the ignition switch, me with my thumb on the tape recorder start button and the American Journalist holding the microphone, sat and waited for the first splash denoting that a Wildebeest had launched itself into the river. When that happened, we were to back the vehicle out from behind our cover to the top of the muddy, Hippo-eroded gully that would be the herd's exit route, twenty-five yards downstream, and with a clear view of the opposite bank. Then for reasons we'll never know, the herd turned, fled away from the river, out of the cul-de-sac and departed out of our sight onto the plain. We sank back into our seats, damp and dejected.

Keith was the first to speak.

"It'll be alright. They will come over at three".

Call it fieldcraft, intuition or just plain jam, he was right. As before, the build-up was sudden and swift. This time the balance between fear and the urge to move south tipped in favour of a 'crossing' and the first animals took the plunge. As planned, we backed the Land Rover out into the open and started recording. Within seconds the river was black with heaving Wildebeest, desperately treading water, their horned heads held above the river. Thousands of animals poured through the cul-de-sac and leapt into the river, trampling others in the panic, the weaker ones swept downstream to drown. White eyes bulging, lips stretched back revealing clenched teeth they struggled to reach the southern bank. Focussing on an individual animal in midstream, I saw its head snap back as it was violently pulled beneath the water by a crocodile. The successful ones raced past the Land Rover only feet away, mud splattering onto the bonnet and the doors, while on the far bank still more animals poured off the plains, and dust from thundering hooves rose like a funeral pyre encouraging still more Wildebeest to follow. Amidst the confusion of thousands of grunting and bellowing animals, calves were separated from their mothers, who stood helplessly on the bank looking back at the river while most of the herd headed off into the distance. For a full fifteen minutes they poured over before the exodus abated. The pressure eased, the beasts on the far bank had time to consider and turned away. Bloated carcasses drifted down stream, exhausted and injured animals littered the bank, Vultures circled overhead, and the river was striped with blood. Having foolishly endowed the Wildebeest with human emotions, it was with a lump in my throat and tears in my eyes that I stopped the tape.

The remainder of the second week of pre-shooting was much more relaxed. To broadcast from the World's most important wildlife sanctuary and not show its greatest spectacle would have been disappointing. Now we could spend time looking for bonuses. So far, we had only recorded material of three of the 'big five', Buffalo, Elephant and Lion. During the latter part of the week both Alan and I, on separate occasions managed to find and record a sequence of a rhinoceros and her baby, but two days of trying, failed to produce a Leopard. I added Kori Bustard, Ostrich and Secretary Bird to my personal list, bringing the total to seventy-one birds I had never seen before. While searching for Leopard, Keith took us to the appropriately named Leopard Gorge, a unique rocky gully where we saw Rock Hyrax, a thick set, tail-less animal looking like a giant grey-brown guinea pig, and unbelievably, the Elephant's closest relative. Friday, we called in at the half-built Crocodile Camp, two rows each of about twenty tents in the edges of the riverine woods facing out to the Marsh.

For me it was the beginning of the end. The atmosphere was changing. No longer did our little band of three have that awe-inspiring landscape and the magnificent animals to ourselves, we were going to have to share them. No longer the peace and tranquillity as we sat alone on the plain with a pride of Lions for company. From now on it was going to be data, digits and multilingual talkback, scripts and schedules, tech runs and transmission times. The unreal world of television was on its way from Nairobi.

We had our last Sunday curry lunch at the Mara River Camp after helping to transfer four and a half tons of technical equipment from two DC-3's into huge trucks for the final two-mile journey to 'Wireless Ridge'. After moving our personal equipment down to Crocodile Camp, we went to Governor's airstrip to await the arrival of the rest of the team. Standing on the tarmac, I re-ran in my mind the privileges of the last two weeks, torn between the sadness of having my Mara invaded and the joy of knowing the treat that was in store for my colleagues from West London, when out of the silent sky crackled the twin-engined Navajo, carrying fellow cameramen Rex Palmer, Martin Wyatt and James Day.

Chapter Five
At Sixties and Seventies

I didn't realise that the sixties swung until I read about it a decade later, and sex didn't discover me until the latter part of the seventies, so this period was mostly spent learning my craft, honing my camera skills and acquiring the range of experience needed for the different types of programme; the anticipation required for good sports coverage that came from being able to read the game, be that game Soccer, Rugby Union and League, Cricket, Tennis or Bowls; from being up-to-date with the key players and personalities within each of those sports, and the contrasting requirements of the concert hall, the knowledge of the layout of the orchestra, the need to feel the phrasing of a musical theme so as to be able to start and finish camera moves in complete empathy with the piece. These skills could not be learnt quickly. The very variety of output, the infrequency with which the same type of programme that one was allocated to work on, determined that to become a competent cameraman. took years. To become a very good one took decades. Not that our masters ever appreciated the fact. Always a constant bone of contention and often an inhibition to our recognition, was that Cameramen saw the role as a vocation, and success in it, as an end, while most other jobs in the BBC were seen by those in them as a stepping-stone to somewhere else, some more powerful, some more prestigious position in the hierarchy.

The department's output over the course of any one year, at its most intense during the summer months, would include the two weeks of Wimbledon, the Cricket Test Matches from Trent Bridge, Old Trafford, Edgbaston, the Oval and Lords, Golf Tournaments including the Open, and weekly horse racing coverage – peaking for the Grand National and the Derby. Saturdays for nine months of the year it would be "Match of the Day"; midweek during the Winter there was floodlit Rugby League on cold, windy and often snowy Tuesday nights and "Sportsnight" to service on Wednesdays including, what was for me the grubbiest of all sporting competitions, the 'Sportsnight Greyhound Derby'. The Five Nations Rugby Union Championship, but only from Twickenham, the BBC national regions clung fervently to Cardiff Arms Park and Murrayfield. Athletics from Crystal Palace and the track at White City now buried under a pile of BBC offices. Motor Sport from Silverstone, Brands Hatch, Crystal Palace and the half-road, half-mud of Lyddon Hill. With the introduction of colour, Snooker, - "*he's going for the yellow ball by the side pocket - and for those watching in black and white, it's next to the blue*", a classic from Ted Lowe on "Pot Black" and with more and more airtime to fill and the increasing competition from ITV, Bowls and Darts appeared on our schedules. But there was more to Outside Broadcast coverage than sport.

The annual state occasions—Trooping the Colour, The State Opening of Parliament, where we cameramen had to dress in morning suits, and the Act of Remembrance at the Cenotaph. Classical Music Concerts from the Festival Hall and the Royal Albert Hall, including selections from the Promenade Season, "Young Musician of the Year", "Come Dancing", "Jazz 625", "Rock goes to College", "Sight and Sound in Concert", the occasional opera from the Royal Opera House at Covent Garden, "Songs of Praise", "Gardener's World", they were all part of the mainstream of Outside Broadcast Department's output. And at the very end of the seventies, drama series and serials, single plays, children's drama, "The Clothes Show", and "Tomorrow's World". The limiting factor for most of this period though, was the physical size, weight and complexity of the Television Camera. Requiring two men to carry it, a hosepipe of a cable to send and receive signals from its control unit, and electronics engineers to maintain and monitor its technical performance, the Television Camera for most of this period went nowhere without its associated Mobile Control Room.

Staffing was based around the needs of this basic building block of any Outside Broadcast, the M. C. R. (from 1967 onwards, following the introduction of colour, the C.M.C.R.). These vehicles, built on coach chassis, were designed to contain the electronic equipment that received the pictures from the cameras down multicore cables, send control signals to those cameras and allow the producer to select which of the cameras, usually four, that should be sent to the nation either down a land line or, via another radio link vehicle, out through the ether to a receiving site on masts such as that at Crystal Palace. (A not dissimilar process happened for the accompanying sound). Crews were formed then, in the sixties, on the basis of a Senior Technical & Lighting Engineer, STLE, and the technical contact with the production team, three systems engineers – known as "racks" engineers, a Senior Cameraman in charge of three other cameramen and often a trainee, and a Sound Supervisor, responsible for controlling the quality and level of the mixture of incoming sounds that went to make up the outgoing audio signal as well as the audio communication systems, and his, (hers didn't appear in OBs until the mid-eighties) two Sound Assistants. To complete the typical Outside Broadcast Unit there were two more trucks, the Camera Van that transported the cameras, the lighter camera mounts, the microphones, monitors and talkback systems, and the Tender, usually an articulated lorry, for the miles of cable and the larger camera mounts. These three vehicles were driven everywhere by the unit's band of Rigger / Drivers whose other jobs included cable rigging, camera tracking and that most valuable of functions, making tea.

***

Once the three months of theoretical training was over, there was only one place a television cameraman could continue to learn and accumulate experience. At the controls of a camera, on a programme, often live. Nothing

I had read, nothing that I had been told, quite prepared me for my first live television transmission, "Come Dancing" from the Lyceum Ballroom in the Strand with the Joe Loss Orchestra. In consultation with the Producer, my first Senior Cameraman, Jack Hayward, had decided that I should operate the camera in the balcony. It's primary function for the programme was to offer either a wide shot of the whole ballroom floor, or a full shot of the Joe Loss Orchestra, and I was to be told which, and when, and to be given time to swing lenses. This, of course, was before the arrival in television of the zoom lens. The cameras could be equipped with four lenses, from a range of six or seven, to suit the programme need. With a rotary handle at the back of the camera it was possible to rotate the turret of lenses in order to place the required lens in front of the picture -taking tube.

All in all, then, a nice simple start to live television for yours truly, except for one thing. "Come Dancing" with the Joe Loss Orchestra started in a particular way. BBC television would be handed live to the Outside Broadcast, which would be showing a blank, black screen. Within a second, up would come a white circle of light almost filling the screen and containing the figure of Joe Loss on the dance floor. As soon as the light was upon him, he would strike up the band, and conducting as he went, would run up onto the stage to his position in front of his orchestra, whereupon the rest of the hall lighting would be brought up along with the programme title caption. This opening shot was to be on a forty-inch lens, the longest in the kit, from the balcony camera. National, network television would that evening be coming live to my camera, which would be showing a black picture and, even though I couldn't see, Joe Loss was supposed to appear in the spotlight in the centre of frame.

Of course, we rehearsed it. I framed up the shot of Joe in the spotlight and ten seconds before the transmission the spotlight is switched off. Everybody keeps still and when the spotlight comes back up, off we go. What could be simpler? Now add first time ever nerves, the pounding pulse moving adrenaline through my system, tiredness – it's ten-twenty-five p.m. and we'd been working since eight that morning—and that I am the only person in the hot, dirty and condemned part of the building and that I can't see if Joe Loss has moved or even if the camera has drifted off to one side. That ten seconds in total darkness with nothing visual to relate to, listening to Network Control count us down, had to be, at that point in my life, the longest in living memory and the relief when the spotlight came on, in frame, was probably audible.

Network countdowns remind me of a time later in my career when the crew were to transmit a concert live from the Royal Festival Hall, but only to Northern Ireland. I forget the detail, I think it was a Northern Irish Orchestra that were playing, but they had sent over their Producer and his assistant to direct the programme and see it on and off the air in the province. Just before the concert was about to start, the Belfast Network Control talkback called out,

"One minute to transmission Festival Hall",
to which our assistant replied,

"Would that be a full minute or sixty seconds?".

But back to the "learning curve", certainly a contradiction in terms in my case, because learning has been a series of bloody great steps. With no control over the frequency, or number of times, one might work on a particular programme type, the discussion amongst camera crews, in breaks while rehearsing on a show, or in down-time between programmes, played an extremely important part in training and building a wealth of stored, almost innate data, about the right and wrong way to present information visually. What was being handed down was the evolved visual grammar that had grown up with the film industry and had been adopted by television. In the same way as the spoken and written language had rules that governed the way that people communicated, so it was with communication through the two-dimensional moving image. These rules, a combination of the guidelines for composition in art and still photography, modified and amended to take into account the added dimension of movement, often continuous movement, both within the frame and of the frame. Key parts of an image on the thirds, looking room, pivot points, the way humans move as cues to adjust framing – such as anticipating a sit or rise – and the basic rules of editing or cutting between camera shots – matching shot sizes and perspective and not crossing the "line", were just a small part of that language in which I needed to be totally fluent.

The "line" was one of the most difficult concepts for several cameramen, and I have to say, directors, to grasp.

In its simplest form the concept is best explained in the example of two people having a conversation while sitting at a table, opposite each other. The "line" is that which you would draw in space between the noses of the two people. With two cameras on the same side of that "line", one camera by each person's shoulder photographing the other person across the table, even with no sound, cutting between the two pictures would give the viewer the impression that the two people were in conversation with each other. Put one camera the other side of the "line" and both people will be looking out of the same side of frame leaving the viewer with the impression that both people are talking to an unseen third person. Now put twelve or more people round a dining table in animated conversation and it becomes easy to see how important it is to make sure the camera is the right side of the "line" so that the viewer remains comfortable with who is sitting where and who is talking to whom.

Most programmes I worked on in the sixties and early part of the seventies were sport and the concept of the "line" was rarely tested. Cameras were placed at horse racing tracks, athletic stadiums and motor racing circuits to ensure that the horses, runners and cars continued to travel in the same direction as each camera was cut to. Anybody who saw the John Frankenheimer film "Grand Prix", will remember what effect breaking the rule can have. After three or four minutes of going around a racetrack travelling in the same direction, the camera along-side, or in, several cars, Frankenheimer intentionally cut to a shot of a car coming straight at camera from the opposite direction. Half the audience grabbed the seat in front of them and stood on an imaginary brake to stop the cinema!

At football and rugby grounds cameras were placed so that whichever camera was cut to, team A was always attacking towards the same end – in the first half anyway, and before Kerry Packer's Channel Nine got hold of cricket coverage in Australia and it migrated to the UK, you could tell which end the bowler was bowling from at Lords, the Oval or any other cricket ground for that matter.

***

Those were the days before I kept notes or took a laptop with me to record my recollections of events, people and places and, even then, only on unusual projects. But, in amongst the weekly diet of sports coverage, I can still recall the most memorable programmes.

My colleagues and I were standing next to our control van in the grounds of Buckingham Palace. We were there to record the Queen's Christmas broadcast – still in black and white, I think. We were outside a side door waiting for the signal to take our equipment into the palace. The side door opened and out stepped a short woman, wearing a headscarf, accompanied by two corgis. We all fell silent, stood up straight, and said, "Good Morning Ma'am.".

I've also had this recurring visual image in my head of sitting on a Vinten 'Falcon' dolly, at the controls of (I think), a Pye Mk VI black and white camera, waiting to record a shot of actors approaching a brick storeroom, with a wooden door and that it might have been inserts for "Z-Cars". And the other thing I remember was that John Woodvine was in it, and that I'd recently read a review of a play he was in that had just opened, Alan Plater's "Close the Coalhouse Door". I've Googled the play and found out that it was premiered in 1968. Then I put Z-Cars and 1968 into the search function on the BBC Genome project Web site, which has Radio Times entries going back to 1923, and found that, not only was it two complete episodes but a first for the programme.

It was shot entirely on location, and it was the location that provoked the story. A deserted factory shell earmarked for demolition. Having decided it would be a great location, director Gerald Blake took writer Allan Prior to the atmospheric and deserted place which inspired him to write "Will he ... won't he," a story of a young man on the run and armed with a gun. So, the four camera Outside Broadcast unit that I was part of, recorded the entire story. Something I should really have remembered.

The story was in two parts, transmitted on Monday 9th and Tuesday 10th December 1968 and starred James Ellis, John Slater, John Woodvine with Paul Angelis, Ron Davies, and Bernard Holley. A nice thing to know I was part of.

***

In 1971, a decision was taken to do a forty-five-minute broadcast of a Royal Navy exercise, live, from the flight deck of the aircraft carrier HMS Ark Royal. There have been many Ark Royals since the C16th, but this was the 4th, launched in 1950 and decommissioned in 1979. It was also the ship on which the 1976 documentary "Sailor" was filmed, with its title music of Rod Stewart's cover of the Sutherland Brothers song, 'Sailing'. My crew, with cameramen colleagues Frank, Selwyn and Simon, were to spend five days aboard the aircraft carrier. The ship was just finishing a three-month tour of duty, so extending it by five days didn't go down too well with most of the ship's company, especially as they had to dock at Plymouth to allow our C.M.C.R., Tender, Camera Van and a Radio Link truck to be winched aboard. The vehicles then went down to the hanger deck via the massive lift that usually raised the Buccaneers, Gannets and Phantoms to the flight deck, and once all the production team, engineers, cameramen and sound staff were aboard the ship, it set sail for Lime Bay. We were shown to our bunk beds, where the heads were, the galley and the Chief Petty Officer's mess, where we could socialise. We were told that like the CPOs, we were limited to two pints of beer and two measures of spirits a day. Once we discovered that the navy crew members wanted more beer and less spirits, we were able to trade, and so made friends very quickly. I remember being on the flight deck after dark, watching Phantoms being launched. With flames out of the back of the engines, the aircraft would disappear out of sight below the end of the flight deck before re-appearing and climbing into the night sky. What a heart-stopping moment that must have been for the pilot.

My three camera colleagues had camera positions on 'the island', the narrow superstructure above the flight deck, that contained the bridge and flight control. I had a camera position on the flight deck. Very exciting to be so close and to be looking up at the pilots as they signalled to the deck crew that they were ready for take-off. On one occasion during the live transmission, a bit too exciting. A Buccaneer had a so called 'bomb hang-up', which was where the pilot had pressed the button to release the bomb, but it had stayed attached to the aircraft. Normal procedure when this happened on an exercise in UK waters, was for the aircraft to return to a RNAF land base such as Yeovilton. But because we were live and it would make for a more dramatic story, the decision was taken to bring the aircraft back on board. I followed the aircraft down onto the flight deck, zooming in on the hung-up bomb as the aircraft got closer. After the programme had finished, the flight deck crew came up to me and said,

"Didn't you get the message? We were all told to clear the deck as the bomb could have released as the plane was caught by the arrester cable. You could have been wiped off the deck".

The control tower had told the flight deck crew, but my producer, Dennis Monger, didn't tell me. Any respect I had for him up to that point completely evaporated.

The day after transmission was spent putting the equipment away and standing on the flight deck as the ship sailed back to Devonport. I was offered, and took, the chance, to sit in the pilot's seat of one of the Phantoms that was parked on deck,

"Don't touch that red handle between your legs, it's the ejector seat",

and I was quite moved as Ark Royal pulled into the harbour and I could see all the wives, girlfriends, sons and daughters waving to their returning relatives.

***

In 1972, the year of the Munich Summer Olympics, about half of BBC Television Outside Broadcast staff and equipment went to Germany to assist with the coverage of the many events at multiple locations. My colleagues and I were not one of those crews. Cricket, the Promenade season from the Royal Albert Hall, Songs of Praise and many other programmes continued through the summer months. At quite short notice at the beginning of November, *'Televisión Española',* Spain's national television service, (hereafter TVE), contacted the BBC to see if we could send a colour OB unit to Barcelona. TVE were contracted to televise the Commercial Union Assurance Masters Tennis tournament, (later known as the ATP Tour Finals), and had promised that it would be in colour. Unfortunately for them, the company who was providing them with their first new colour Outside Broadcast Unit was not going to deliver in time. My unit and crew were allocated the job. The C.M.C.R., Camera Van and Tender were to drive to Barcelona, which was scheduled to take five days and the crew were to fly out on the 26th November. The tournament was to last five days from 28th November till the 2nd December.

My colleague Simon thought that, as we had nothing to do while the equipment was being driven to Spain, or even while it was coming back, why don't we drive there instead of flying. We negotiated with our local accounts department to pay us the equivalent of the return airfare and we set off on an adventure.

We took the overnight ferry to Le Havre, Simon driving his British Racing Green Renault 4, I as navigator, as at that stage I couldn't drive. We were off the ferry before dawn and headed down the west side of France, mainly on 'N' roads. Simon managed to get us to an overnight stop near Arcachon, South of Bordeaux; we were not going straight to Barcelona but were heading for Madrid. As well as navigating, I was studying a Spanish phrase book. As Simon was dealing with the French conversation, I was going to do the Spanish. We stopped the following night at a Spanish 'Parador', one of a large collection of government hotels, often in restored historic buildings, and always reasonably priced. We were just outside Burgos, about two hours' drive north of Madrid.

The drive to the Spanish capitol was spectacular, as ahead of us was the plateau, two thousand feet high where Madrid was located and from where we were on the plain below, it looked like a vertical wall of rock. As we got ever closer, we could detect vehicles winding their way up what was a steep incline. Simon had booked two nights' accommodation in a cheap hotel in the centre of Madrid so that, after parking the car, we could walk to all the major sites of interest, especially the Prado Museum. We spent a long time there, looking at works by El Greco, Velazquez,

Goya and many others, but there comes a time when the senses become overloaded and we needed to get outside for some air, a drink and something to eat. That evening we dined at a restaurant that I'd seen recommended in the Sunday Times, located in the Plaza Mayor. We arrived at eight, p.m. to a complete lack of enthusiasm to give us menus or take an order. Later we realised that Spanish people do not eat until much later in the evening.

The journey to Barcelona took us around eight hours to complete the three-hundred and ninety miles, passing Zaragoza and Tarragona. No time to sightsee, as we were to start work the next day. When we met up with the rest of the team, we discovered that our Senior Cameraman Frank and colleague Selwyn had decided to follow our example and drive down to Barcelona, but directly. The only thing about the story of their journey that has stuck in my memory is that Selwyn couldn't understand why there was no accommodation at the *Hôtel de Ville*.

We spent the morning putting the cameras into the arena where the tennis tournament was to take place, checking that everything worked ready for a production check of all facilities, our Producer/Director being Slim Wilkinson, a veteran of many summers spent at Wimbledon. Then the TVE Camera crew turned up with their Director, thanked us for setting up the equipment and said they would take over from here.

As a crew we were taken aback by this and told Slim Wilkinson that we didn't think this was part of the deal, or that it was right. TVE's response was to say that they would get the police to enforce the removal of our equipment and vehicles and would bring in their black and white equipment for their crew to operate and that they would pacify the sponsors. It became a minor diplomatic incident that made the back pages of the 'Red Tops' back in the UK. We came up with a solution. We suggested a compromise where the camera crews did alternative matches. The Spanish cameramen agreed, as long as they did the final. So, we stayed, and Commercial Union were so pleased that they provided dinner with wine for all television personnel every night. From then on, both crews became great pals, dining at nine p.m. with the tennis starting at ten-thirty p.m., with two matches a night that often did not finish till two-thirty a.m.. The week passed in a bit of a haze, ending after the final (in which Ille Nastase beat Stan Smith), with an England v Spain football match in the street, using traffic lights as goal posts.

Simon and I drove back via Chartres to visit the Cathedral, stayed for two nights in Paris visiting the Louvre, (Mona Lisa √, Venus de Milo √), Notré-Dame Cathedral and Sacré-Cœur Basilica with its panoramic views over Paris. On the way back to Le Havre for the overnight ferry, we called in at Versailles, taking the internal tour, exploring the gardens, and walking out to Petit Trianon, completing my first ever trip to France and Spain.

***

Other multi-camera Outside Broadcasts I will never forget, were two weddings and a funeral.

At the end of January 1965, as a trainee cameraman, I assisted with the installation of cameras into St. Paul's Cathedral for the funeral of Sir Winston Churchill. The most taxing camera to get into position was in the Golden gallery, the smallest and highest of the two external galleries that encircle the dome. We carried the Pye Mk 6 camera up the five-hundred and twenty-eight steps, stopping at the Whispering Gallery to test its acoustic properties (an excuse to take a rest), and once at the top, eighty-five metres above the floor of the Cathedral, we were astounded at the views over London. We could easily see as far away as Battersea Power Station, as well as along the route the cortège would take down Ludgate Hill and the Thames along which the coffin would be transported, accompanied by military salutations, to Waterloo station, (probably the last mainline station you'd start from if going to Oxfordshire, but Churchill just wanted to remind the French). In the afternoon he was buried at St Martin's Churchyard at Bladon, just outside the grounds of Blenheim Palace, the resting place of his ancestors and his brother.

***

I was back at St. Paul's in July 1981 for what was described as the wedding of the century, that of Prince Charles to Lady Diana Spencer. It was then, the biggest colour outside broadcast the BBC had undertaken. The Corporation managed to muster seventeen Mobile Control Rooms with a little help from the independent facilities companies, TVR and Trilion. At St Pauls there were eighteen cameras covering the service inside, as well as the exterior shots around the Cathedral. Supporting the BBC's Central Colour Control Room, equipped with forty-two black and white monitors, were two BBC Type 5 C.M.C.Rs., each with eight cameras and another two-camera unit. In total the BBC used over sixty cameras.

On the big day, the broadcast started at seven-forty-five a.m., and we all had to be at the Cathedral by six-thirty a.m., so I booked into the Waldorf, on the Aldwych, for the night before. In the morning, I walked the mile along the Aldwych, the Strand, Fleet Street and Ludgate Hill, the pavements on both sides of the road already packed with happy, cheering and flag waving families awaiting the cavalcade of cars and carriages that were to pass along the route. Fortunately, my official pass allowed me to walk in the road.

I was fortunate enough to be operating the camera inside the Cathedral, just in front of the couple and to their right, so I had the "two shot" as they exchanged vows, thankfully unaware, that it was being watched worldwide by an estimated audience of seven-hundred and fifty million.

The other wedding of national interest in the nineteen eighties, was of course, that of Prince Andrew and Sarah Ferguson which took place at Westminster Abbey. My camera was positioned just outside the Great West Door, spotting the arrivals of the good and the great and eventually the happy couple. At one point, a young couple came over to me and said,

"Hello again, what on earth are you doing here?". It was Mr. & Mrs. Jonathan Coltman-Rogers whom I'd last seen over dinner at their home, Stanage Park in the Welsh Marches, but that's a story for a later chapter.

Much later, in the late nineties, I was asked by a neighbour in our village if I had a Video camera, and if so, would I kindly record his son's wedding. I said that I could, but I would like to see the couple beforehand, so would they pop round for a drink. I asked them if they were sure they wanted me to do this as,

"I've only covered two weddings before, Charles and Diana and Andrew and Fergie and you do know what happened to them".

***

The Wimbledon Tennis Championships were a constant in the summer schedules for Outside Broadcasts and I, with most of my cameramen colleagues, have spent many a sun-soaked three weeks in SW19.

The Championships in the Summer of 1967, that were shown on BBC Two, marked the beginning of regular colour television in Britain. Journalists who attended a special viewing at Television Centre were impressed with the new technology and the quality of the picture. David Attenborough, then Controller of BBC Two, announced that the channel would initially broadcast in colour about five hours a week. By December, eighty percent of programmes were in colour.

The original December launch date was brought forward to the 1st July so the BBC could claim to be the first colour broadcaster in Europe. France, Germany and Holland, who had planned an autumn launch of their colour services, were all beaten to air, but in Britain, with fewer than five-thousand colour sets in circulation, the audience was very small.

The 1st July was the middle Saturday of Wimbledon fortnight. The new colour cameras had been installed on Centre Court, alongside the usual black and white cameras. The new Colour Control Room had been brought into the BBC compound and a viewing area set up for the BBC Heads of Department to watch the transmission.

The match that afternoon was between the South African Cliff Drysdale and Britain's Roger Taylor. I didn't see it, as it was my turn to man the camera in the compound that covered the pre-match introductions by the various sports presenters. So it was, that the first shot in colour, live on BBC that day, was my shot of a vase of very colourful flowers and a gentle zoom out to include Peter West, who introduced the programme.

***

London Television Outside Broadcasts had colour cameras and mobile control rooms probably a year ahead of the studios at Television Centre getting their colour equipment, so we inherited programmes that would normally have been recorded in the studios. My crew and I recorded several "Sight & Sound in Concert", current music shows where the pictures were on BBC2 and synchronous stereo sound was available on Radio2. The venue was the Golders Green Hippodrome at Temple Fortune, a theatre the BBC had taken a lease on while the T.V. Centre studios were being converted to colour.

An interesting variety of musical groups and artists from The Chieftains, the Irish folk band, through Elkie Brooks, Jethro Tull, and a band formed from the ashes of Deep Purple called 'Paice, Ashton, Lord'. These programmes were usually live, starting at around ten-twenty p.m.. Rehearsals ended around five-thirty p.m. to six p.m., so by transmission time artists, the director and crew had spent a couple of hours in the pub. So, most of these "rock and pop" concerts were shot, successfully I might add, in a state of gentle inebriation. One such concert was a special from Farnham Maltings in Surrey, featuring Rick Wakeman. As we were hurrying back from the pub for the ten-twenty p.m. transmission on BBC2, we met the director coming towards us yelling,

"They're coming to us ten minutes late, we've got time for another one!"

Other programmes we picked up from the studios were "Crackerjack" at the BBC Television Theatre in Shepherd's Bush and the annual BBC Children's Christmas Pantomime, the most memorable part of which was the camera crew's first meeting with the director from the studios. He started by asking if we'd televised a pantomime before. Our Senior Cameraman for this programme was Maurice, a laconic chap in his fifties and nearing retirement, who inhaled on his hand rolled cigarette and said,

"Every show we do is a fucking pantomime".

***

Towards the end of 1970, our large colour television cameras were used on location for a BBC drama serial. Drama location recordings were up to this point shot on film, but for "Jude the Obscure", the television serial based on Thomas Hardy's novel, the director, Hugh David, (real name David Hughes, but had to change his name because there already was an Equity member called David Hughes), wanted to use video cameras so that the pictures were a better match with the studio shots. It starred a young Robert Powell, Fiona Walker and Alex Marshall, and was first broadcast on BBC Television in early 1971. Briefly, Hardy's novel describes the attempt of Jude (Robert Powell), an orphan brought up by his working class aunt, to get to university. He starts to work as a stonemason, falls in love and is tricked into marrying Arabella (Alex Marshall). Their marriage falls apart and Arabella leaves for Australia. Jude goes to the university town of Christminster, has his application to university rebuffed, meets his cousin Sue Brideshead (Fiona Walker), falls in love, only to find she is engaged to be married to Phillotson, his old town schoolmaster.

We took our caravan of trucks up onto the Ridgeway, Britain's oldest road, following a route used since prehistoric times by travellers, herdsmen and soldiers, moving from Wiltshire towards the Thames passing Wantage and Wallington, Oxfordshire towns down across the plain below. Hugh wanted shots of Jude walking the Ridgeway and views down across the plain towards Oxford, Hardy's Christminster. We couldn't see the gleaming spires, but Hugh would mix a still photograph onto the horizon in editing. We also recorded sequences in Oxford of Jude walking through the streets, looking very much like a tramp and a scene in a Catholic Church in Jericho, north of the city centre. Robert Powell was easy to get along with and came with the camera crew to the pub at lunch times. On one occasion, still dressed as a tramp, he stayed at the pub door saying,

"I'll be in shortly".

We got to the bar and were ordering our drinks when this tramp shuffled up to us and said,

"Please, guv, can you spare us a drink, just a half will do, I ain't got no money, see".

The bar went very quiet.

We also recorded the exterior shots of the marriage of Phillotson to Sue Bridehead in a small country village with a delightful little church. Extras of all ages were required to populate the village and Hugh's wife Wendy brought along their two little sons aged six and eight.

Unlike the studio camera crew, we were invited to an end of shoot party at Hugh and Wendy's house in Windsor, so I guess we must have done a good job.

***

It's the one-off programmes that I remember the most, multiple Football or Rugby matches, Golf Tournaments or Cricket Test Matches blur into one and most memories are incidental to the programme being televised. My crew and I were doing Indoor Bowls at Alexandria Palace in North London a few weeks after we'd televised an outdoor tournament at Beach House Park in Worthing. During a mid-afternoon break for a cup of tea, the sports producer came up to our table and asked how we were enjoying the games. My colleague Derek said,

"OK, but I prefer covering the outdoor tournaments".

When asked why, he replied,

"At least I can watch the grass grow".

A week spent covering bowls in Worthing would mean the O.B. crew would have to stay away from home and the different camera crews split into roughly two camps when it came to booking accommodation. There were those who preferred a pub with rooms, because they wanted to drink beer, play darts and eat whatever was available and there were those who preferred to find a good restaurant, preferably with rooms, and spend the evening having good food, wine and conversation. My first crew were of the former persuasion, but as someone who didn't really enjoy beer, I and a like-minded colleague would seek out different places to stay. Luckily, when I was promoted to Camera Supervisor in the early eighties, my camera crew were all the same mind.

The half tarmac, half mud Rallycross events at Lyddon Hill, halfway between Canterbury and Dover, were, as well as fun to televise, a source of memories incidental to providing Grandstand with exciting races on Saturdays. The normal routine was for the crew to arrive at two p.m. on Friday, install the cameras, effects microphones and the commentary position with monitors, microphones, noise cancelling headphones and talkback facilities, in readiness for a full production facilities check at four-thirty p.m. Once the producer, in my era, Ricky Tilling, and Murray Walker, assisted by the stage manager, was comfortable in his commentary position, we'd return to our pre-booked accommodation for the night.

One unforgettable evening was had when the camera crew, Ricky the producer, Andy Tallack the stage manager and Murray were all booked into the same pub, with rosettes for its food, in Fordwich a couple of miles Northeast of Canterbury and we all dined together in a side room away from the rest of the pub's clientele. Murray was able to relax, and we enjoyed a wealth of stories – a lovely man and as enthusiastic about much more than just motor sport.

During the Summer months the demand on outside broadcast crews was a lot heavier. At Wimbledon, for example, we crewed to have one and a half cameramen per camera and organised a rotation to have three cameramen operate two cameras on a two on, one off basis, to allow for coffee, lunch and pee breaks. To cope with the increase in staffing levels, we had cameramen from London Television Studios attached to O.B.'s for three or four months over the Summer.

On another trip to Lyddon Hill, this time a two-day event, we had a young cameraman from the studios on the crew. He was a bit surprised when we told him to bring his passport. We organised to get to Lyddon Hill early, at about ten-thirty a.m., so we could finish the rig by two p.m.. This time the production facilities check was not until Saturday morning. We'd booked two nights' accommodation at a small hotel, with a night porter, very near the passenger terminal for the cross-channel ferry. We went to Boulogne for dinner. *Assiette de fruits de Mer*, the multi-tiered stand of shellfish, with *aioli*, washed down with copious bottles of Muscadet, and we were back in Dover by one a.m..

On the Saturday night we ate in an "Italian" restaurant in Dover. I still have an oil painting I bought off the wall for £25. This was before real Italian restaurants started to open in the U.K., like The River Café or Locanda Locatelli, as it was more like the ones often described as a *"Trattoria Phallocraticus"* because of the three foot high, wooden pepper mills, and with a menu that was pan-European. When most of us had chosen what we were going to eat from the menu, my colleague Pete Hill and the young cameraman from the studios had yet to decide. Pete asked the young chap if he would like to share the Chateau Briand, to which he replied,

"Only if it's white".

Still a lot to learn about life on the road.

Held on 24th April 1982, the 27th edition of the annual Eurovision Song Contest took place in the Convention

Centre in Harrogate, North Yorkshire. It was the UKs turn to host the show, and the BBC's turn to televise it, because Bucks Fizz had won in Dublin the previous year with the song "Making Your Mind Up". I had the dubious honour of being the lead Camera Supervisor on the programme. I say dubious, because the show has far greater security than any event other than Royal occasions, plenty of hype and media coverage and it's a four-day slog with so many countries to rehearse, each with their own orchestral conductor. Most of the cameras in the hall and behind the scenes were in fixed positions, but as the lead Camera Supervisor I had no choice but to operate the main camera which was mounted on a crane. I think it was a Chapman "Nike", but I can't be sure. It consisted of a heavy base on wheels, with a counter-balanced arm, the front end being a platform with a mount for the camera and a seat for the operator and is three and a half times longer than the back end which has a large, square bucket to contain the lead weights required to balance the arm. These lead weights were thirteen kilograms each and a considerable number were required to balance me and the camera. Two Rigger Drivers from my crew were to man the back end of the crane, which involved moving the crane along the isle from one side of the hall to the centre and elevating and lowering the arm to rehearsed positions for different shots. They very rarely had the opportunity to do this type of work and were very nervous. On the full dress run on the Friday evening, they'd had too much "Dutch courage" and we missed a shot and received a massive bollocking from the Director, Michael Hurll.

I can't remember whether it was Thursday or Friday, but everything stopped for a visit from the Chairman of the BBC Board of Governors, Lord Howard, who'd popped across from his home, Castle Howard. He was brought over to see me and requested an explanation of the workings of the crane. After explaining that we balance out the arm with lead weights he asked what we used to fine trim it if the addition of another thirteen kilograms was too much. I know I probably shouldn't have, but I couldn't stop myself saying,

"We use the Rigger Drivers' wallets".

To save you looking it up, the German entrant, Nicole, was the winner with the song *"Ein bißchen Frieden"*.

A couple of music programmes that were more fun and less pressurised to work on were the 1988 Young Musician of the Year competition, and Jazz at the Philharmonic, which a combination of Google and my memory thinks was in 1967 at Poplar Town Hall and included the musicians Dizzy Gillespie and Clark Terry, both trumpeters, tenor sax players Zoot Sims and James Moody, pianist Teddy Wilson, bassist Bob Cranshaw and drummer Louis Bellson. Can't remember the music, can't remember which camera I did, or its position relative to the stage, but I can vividly remember the evening meal-break. Getting a meal at five-thirty p.m. or thereabouts in London in the sixties and seventies usually meant eating in "ethnic" restaurants. Indian, Chinese and later, Thai, were the only options. This evening, between rehearsals and the recording, we went to a Chinese restaurant—not the entire crew—just the cameramen. We'd just got our meal, when four of the musicians walked in and sat the other side of the central isle from me. Ten or so minutes later, after their food arrived, Dizzie Gillespie leaned over to me and said,

"Do you wanna help Anglo American relationships?".

"Of course," I replied.

"Then pass the salt."

Working on the BBC Young Musician of the Year was a joy. The biennial competition was established in 1978 by Humphrey Burton, Walter Todds and Roy Tipping, then members of the BBC Television Music Department. Entrants were under nineteen and entered in one of four categories, Keyboard, String, Brass and Woodwind, (Percussion being added in 1994). In 1988 we were at the Royal Northern College of Music for the category finals where the top five in each category competed for the chance to play a concerto for their instrument with a full orchestra. Shortly after, we were back in Manchester, this time at the Free Trade Hall for the final concert where the entire camera crew fell in love with Elgar's Cello concerto played by Paul Watkins, who didn't win, but two years later was appointed Principal Cellist of the BBC Symphony Orchestra. We asked Humphrey Burton, who as well as being a respected classical music television director, was to introduce the programme, which would be the recording he would recommend. He came up with two, I can't remember the other one, but I bought the Jacqueline

Du Pre recording with the Philadelphia Orchestra conducted by her husband Daniel Barenboim.

I've worked several times for Humphrey, on concerts at the Royal Albert Hall, Royal festival Hall and a rare treat, Leonard Bernstein conducting Sibelius 5th Symphony and Stravinsky's "The Right of Spring", at the then, just recently opened (and acoustically superb), Fairfield Halls in Croydon.

Recording, or occasionally transmitting live, several ballets and operas from Covent Garden, have been challenging, where opera coverage can contain three-to four-hundred shots, shared amongst four, sometimes five cameras. It was during rehearsals at one opera there, that Humphrey announced that he was going to be away a little longer this lunchtime as he had accepted an offer of a lunch given by Chateau Mouton Rothschild, with a vertical tasting of their wines. I jokingly said,

"Please bring back a bottle of the '45, it's my birth year."

At about half past three p.m., Humphrey returned and handed me a half-full bottle of the '66.

"It's the best I could do," he said.

Even at nearly midnight, when I got home, it tasted wonderful.

Chapter Six
The Closed Show

Out there, on the cusp between the last Sunday and Monday of April 1997, as they had done every lunar cycle since 1957, a small, devoted bunch of insomniacs gathered in front of their television sets, to watch the 40th Anniversary edition of the world's longest running television programme hosted by the same presenter. The "Sky at Night", introduced without a break by that undiminished enthusiast Patrick Moore, celebrated its achievement with a forty-five minute special on the story of the telescope, entitled "Eyes on the Universe".

I shouldn't think many people noticed, because the grey suits in charge of what we saw on our screens gave it all the advanced publicity of a change in the cover price of the Radio Times. (At a small celebratory gathering at the Planetarium, one grey suit praised Patrick's contribution to Astrology!). If that appears a little cynical or bitter, it was meant to. Having worked on the programme, as location cameraman, for a relatively short ten years, I've been privileged to meet many scientists who work in or around astronomy, who started out because of the "Sky at Night". I've lost count of the number of times we watched as Patrick autographed a dog-eared copy of one of his early books for a scientist who had just said, "This book got me started". Wherever in the world the team has turned up to record a programme, be it North American or European Space Agency establishments, observatories like the Keck in Hawaii or the rooftop observatory at Taunton school, the programme has been welcomed with open arms and with gratitude for the work it has done in publicising and popularising astronomy. It is a unique programme that has a special place in British television history and, to my mind, a sad reflection on the state of the industry that it let the programme's achievements slip by with little or no recognition.

The majority of the thirteen programmes a year are recorded close to transmission day, in the studio, with Patrick either talking through a topic on his own or with a guest astronomer. Occasionally, perhaps twice a year, the programme is made where the science was being achieved. They, along with the two specials, the 35th Anniversary programme, "Space for Astronomy" and the aforementioned 40th, have been my passport to some fascinating locations around the globe. Given my own penchant for the juice of fermented grapes, I somehow feel that it's probably more than a coincidence that the Astronomical Observatories in Australia, Chile, California and South Africa that we visited were also very near some magnificent wine-growing areas.

It was in 1985 that Producer Pieter Morpurgo decided to use video instead of film for the location shoots. Doug Whittaker, the sound recordist, probably knows the exact date as he has worked on the "filming" for the programme since then. Until the middle of 1989, Alastair 'Mitch' Mitchell was the cameraman and I picked up the job on his retirement. The programmes invariably consist of interviews with scientists sitting in front of their computer terminals, their voices laid-over pictures of the telescopes and instruments they use and the scientific results they achieve. It's not been the challenge of the camerawork that's made working on the programme such a joy.

I was broken in gently by the "Sky at Night" team. The first location I worked at was in Birmingham (Warwickshire not Alabama), at the University, where we made a programme explaining to aspiring astronomers what courses they should take and what subjects they should consider studying. It wasn't long before we ventured further afield though, to La Palma in the Canaries, to the top of the extinct volcano of Los Muchachos, where there is an international observatory. British involvement with the site began with the transfer of the 100inch Isaac Newton Telescope from Herstmonceux in Sussex but now included the much newer and larger 165inch William Herschel reflector telescope, and the main reason for our visit.

In the year and a half running up to the 35th anniversary programme, "Space for Astronomy", which transmitted in April 1992, it was necessary to record material illustrating the contribution to astronomical research that had been achieved since man had been able to put probes into space. So, the team went to Noordwijk in Holland, the Headquarters of the European Space

Agency, and to Darmstaad in Germany where ESA has its mission control, and in 1991 the programme made two very culturally contrasting trips. To the USA in the August, but before that, in the March of that year, and five months before the downfall of Gorbachev, the 'Sky at Night' team went to the Soviet Union.

There were two very good reasons for trying to get into the Soviet Union to make programmes about astronomy and space exploration. Firstly, May 11th was to be a special day for Helen Sharman from Surbiton who was due to become the first Briton in Space, joining a Soviet crew for a short stay on the Soviet's "*Mir*" orbiting Space Station and, secondly, Producer Pieter Morpurgo had obtained departmental financial approval for the thirty-fifth anniversary special, "Space for Astronomy", an essential part of which would be the Soviet achievements over this period. After all they started it with Sputnik back in 1957.

Despite recent programmes in the "Horizon" series entitled "Red Star in Space", mainly consisting of edited stock footage, it was hoped that we could gather some original material. So for the trip to be of value, we needed to see the Soviet's Mission Control, their Space Research Centre, Star City, where they train their Cosmonauts and hopefully get to Baikonur, the Soviet Launch site in Kazakhstan. People to interview were also required if the programme was to hold together. We needed a Space Hardware specialist, someone responsible for Cosmonaut training, an Astronomer or Space Research Scientist, all of whom should preferably speak English to avoid the formality of translations, and we needed to talk to Helen Sharman.

Now this was not the sort of trip to be found in the latest 'Winter Sun' brochures, but fortunately Pieter had discovered a travel agent, based in Windsor, who specialised in minority interest and scientifically based trips. They had taken parties to Cape Canaveral for Apollo launches, to the Philippines for a total eclipse of the Sun and even organised train journeys across the remoter parts of South America. Now they were canvassing in the specialist press to see if there was sufficient interest in a 'Scientific' trip to the Soviet Union to include Baikonur.

This travel company had established a contact in the Foreign Relations Department of the Astronomical Council of the Soviet Academy of Sciences in Moscow, who seemed to indicate that there would be "no objection" to a party visiting all the locations on Pieter's hit list, including being at the Soviet launch site at the right time to see the Russians let one go. After numerous phone calls and fax's back and forth between Pieter, the tour organiser and Nikolai Kuznetsov, the PR man in Moscow, all the indications were that there would be "no objection" to a television crew on the trip and that we would "probably" be able to talk to all the right people.

With absolutely no knowledge of where we were to stay in Moscow, or even where in Kazakhstan the Launch Site was, and exactly how we were to get between the two, Doug, Angela, Patrick, who was well below par due to the very recent death of his devoted housekeeper, Pieter and I, joined the other sixteen members of this unique and trailblazing party at Heathrow for the Sunday lunchtime Finnair flight to Moscow via Helsinki. Pieter had decided that, as we were part of a party of twenty-one, it would be impossible to make a programme without seeing, or making reference to, the others in the group and that we should make it plain that Patrick was part of the first western tourist group to undertake such a trip. To that end, we started work almost immediately after take-off and interviewed eight of the group about what they expected to see or hoped to learn.

As we came down below the cloud on our approach to Helsinki airport it was getting dark, and my first sight of Finland was reminiscent of a chess board. It was squares of black and white, the dark pine trees standing up amongst the snow-covered fields. The hour-long wait in the transit lounge, which looked like any other, passed uneventfully and we reboarded the same plane for the onward journey into the Soviet Union.

It was night as we circled over Moscow, a sea of minuscule gold and silver lights looking like hundreds and thousands on a dark chocolate cake. I don't know why, but just like crossing into east Berlin, something I had done on a whim two years before the wall came down, getting through Soviet immigration was a very nerve-racking experience, made worse by the fact that I was asked if I smoked. My first reaction was to say no just in case it had recently been made a civil offence, but I decided on the truth and said yes and was then asked if I had any cigarettes that I could let the officer have. Passing over a half-finished packet of Marlboro, I was let in with a smile.

We were met by Irene and Sergei of Romus Tours and bussed through the blackness, past innumerable slab-sided tower blocks of flats to the Salyut hotel, which we later discovered to be in the outer southwestern suburbs of Moscow and completely the opposite side of the city to the airport. It was a massive utilitarian block twenty-four stories high, (we were quick to realise that it was at least that high as the sign to the bar said twenty fourth floor), with a large soulless reception area. We were all thankful that we were expected and allocated rooms, in my case 931, and given room cards which we were to hand to the concierge on our floor in exchange for a room key. Fortunately, we had managed to successfully communicate the need for a room on the ground floor to store the five boxes of camera kit and, as it was just after midnight and the bar closed at twelve, we retired to our rooms. On the way up in the lift we noticed that the lift only went to the twenty-second floor. Odd!

Once in my room, I didn't bother to unpack as we were to leave again in the morning for Kazakhstan. I opened the duty-free Armagnac, made up a litre of water with a sterotab and, after all the warnings about taking a universal sink plug, I was surprised to find that the room had one. It didn't fit either the sink or the bath. The black and white television had some slow, turgid filmed drama with overlong close-ups of the person not speaking, so I went to bed wondering what tomorrow would bring.

The group met at the allotted time and place for breakfast. The hotel had three huge rooms that served food, each of which could probably seat a thousand people, but there is no choice as to where you sat or when you ate. "Party X will breakfast at nine-fifteen a.m. in the third-floor restaurant". Breakfast consisted of a nondescript fruit juice, sweet dark brown dried bread, butter, cheese and smoked fish, a very large pot of tea, some milk, but there was no sugar available. As with all parties or groups, it very soon became clear which one of the group was going to get up its collective nose. Anthony was ours. An overweight Mancunian with unkempt hair, bottle glass spectacles on the end of his nose, hiking boots, webbed trousers and a blue, Peter Storm cagoule. He carried all his possessions in a rucksack. All the time. He wore it on the plane, on the coach, even to breakfast. He had a Collins Russian phrase book and would accost total strangers in the foyer of the hotel and try to start up a conversation.

We were due to leave at ten a.m. for the internal flight to Kazakhstan. We were all herded on to a coach and then, after a whispered conversation in Russian with Nikolai, Irene told us that we couldn't leave until some 'military personnel' had joined us, and that they would not be here for an hour or so. To fill in the time we were to be given a short tour of Moscow. We were shown the exterior of the university, twenty-eight-thousand students, five-thousand teachers and postgraduates, and the panoramic view of the city from the Lenin Hills which allowed us to look down on the Lenin Stadium and the Moskva river. This was quite obviously part of the normal tourist circuit as teenagers would sidle up and ask if you wanted to change money, or you could have your photograph taken, against the

Moscow skyline, shaking hands with a cardboard cut-out of Gorbachov.

Back at the hotel carpark, the "military" arrived. Two of them, one in dark blue denim jeans and a matching bomber jacket, the other slim, dark, sullen and dressed in a long black leather trench coat that almost reached his ankles and slotting perfectly into every cheap spy novel's description of a KGB agent. We were now allowed to proceed across Moscow to the airport, the same airport we had arrived at, only this time, we were marched to the military terminal while we watched our equipment and luggage disappear onto the back of an army lorry. The terminal was not unlike any other small airport, off white tiles, a few black plastic pseudo leather bench seats and, at the far end of the waiting area, a closed café. We had been told that we were to take off for the three-and-a-half hour flight at two-twenty p.m. so a small snack wouldn't have gone amiss. At two o'clock, and without warning, the café opened. The group piled into the small room to be confronted by a large coffee machine in the "Gaggio" mold, a great transparent jar of coffee beans, a small plate of cake and a very large Russian lady who was only allowed to sell bottles of Pepsi.

Two-thirty p.m. and we finally got onto the plane, a Tupolev Tu-134, not dissimilar to a DC-9. We were the only people on the aircraft, our party of twenty-one plus Nikolai, the two 'KGB' chaps and the flight crew who were all in air-force uniforms. This was quite clearly a military flight, and the closest we got to cabin service was when the 'KGB' man in the denim casuals came round with paper cups of juice. We took off fifteen minutes later and, flying east away from the sun, it soon got dark. Before night fell. we all strained to see some of the countryside out of the aircraft windows, but all we managed to see was endless snow covered, flat, barren tundra. We landed at seven-forty p.m. local time in pitch darkness. There was a coach on the tarmac which pulled right up to the side of the aircraft, and we were shepherded straight onto it. We sat and watched as army personnel loaded all the camera equipment and personal luggage into the under-seat storage lockers and we were bussed out of the airport and into the night.

About thirty minutes passed before we entered the town of Leninsk, a purpose-built conurbation constructed, powered and fed entirely by imported goods and materials. It had a population of over one-hundred thousand and everyone who lived there worked at the Soviet Spaceport. There was no sign of people, no buses or bicycles, just one or two cars. Turning left, turning right and once doing a complete 'u' turn, we passed through street after street of dark, square, slab-sided apartment blocks, with only the occasional dim light behind net curtains. Finally, after a route than none of us could retrace, we pulled up outside the Baikonur hotel.

The hotel was a pleasant surprise. The rooms were small suites with a lobby, containing a large fridge, albeit empty, with two doors leading off, in one direction to the bathroom and in the other to a lounge with three chairs, a table and a single bed. Off this room was the main bedroom with double bed, wardrobe and chest of drawers.

When all the group had gathered back in the foyer, we were shown through to the dining room where we were again surprised by the spread laid out on the tables before us. There were plates of mixed cold meats and salamis, smoked fish, caviar, sauced cabbage and cucumber. Liberal quantities of bottled water, Kazakhstan brandy and Pepsi were set out on the table and when we had finished the *hors d'oeuvre* course we were given steak and potatoes and coffee to finish. After the meal, we were told that the eight a.m. breakfast was delayed until nine a.m. and that we would not now be leaving for the spaceport until ten a.m.. As the rest of the group drifted off to their beds, Doug and I went to our rooms and unpacked the equipment and prepared the kit for the next day's shooting. Lying in bed I wondered why we were the only people in the hotel, why would anybody come to this god-forsaken part of the world, why were the rooms so spacious and why was the food so good. Then it dawned on me, this was, of course, a military hotel designed for visiting generals when they wanted to come down from Moscow to see the Space Centre.

Doug was late down to breakfast, and I went up to knock on his room to see if he was up. He replied immediately. He was locked in. He had left the room key in the lock of his exterior door, had shut the inner door to the lounge area and the door had stuck shut. Turning the handle had no effect on the latch. I returned to the breakfast table and managed to get Nikolai to understand the problem and translate to the hotel management that we needed some assistance. They managed to poke out his room key from the lock and open the exterior door with the pass key, and then left me. Doug managed to pass out a small screwdriver from his toolkit under the door and after five minutes or so I managed to prize back the latch, and Doug came down to breakfast. Cold meats, cheese, grape juice, sweet bread and a tortilla-type omelette, bottled water and coffee.

We boarded the coach and I suggested that we commandeer the back of the coach as it had a back door, and that if we could get the driver to open both the front and back doors when we stopped, we stood a chance of getting off at the same time as the rest of the party. As we set off, Nikolai said that he understood that Helen Sharman was going to be at Baikonur for the next launch, so we were hopeful of getting both an interview with her and a shot of a rocket going up. We were driven for an hour across miles of barren snow-covered tundra. Here and there snow had melted, but as the ground was still frozen, great pools of water formed on the road and the flooding caused a few problems for the coach. There were no signs of habitation, no animals, just the occasional crow-like bird and one bedraggled forlorn and lean-looking bird of prey which sat on a clump of soil that stood proud of the snowy wasteland. In the distance, we could just discern the outline of derelict buildings and one or two electricity generating stations. The Spaceport site was spread over an area 400 km square, that's more than London to Manchester along each side, and like Leninsk, every requirement including food had to come here by train. The road we were taken along ran parallel to, and on occasions crossed, railway lines and we passed several trains, both passenger and cargo, occupied but standing motionless. It appeared that when there had been a failure or an accident, the Soviets just bulldozed the train or carriage to one side and left it, because we passed innumerable rusting hulks laying on their sides.

Eventually we arrived at the *'Proton'* launch site, an immense grey girder tower construction surrounded by an irregular and somewhat chaotic mess of low buildings similar in appearance to a disused cement works. We were told that we had ten minutes here. While the rest of the group had the launch complex explained to them by a five-star general, we rushed around like headless chickens shooting wide angles, close ups, shots of the group and three pieces to camera from Patrick. Fortunately, he was word perfect, and we recorded the links in 'take one' each time and the battery Paglight, just put a hint of sparkle into the close ups in an otherwise uniformly grey scene.

Back on the coach and we drove for another ten minutes through more grey featureless landscape, past more rusting hulks of trains. Occasionally, in the distance, almost merging with the grey sky, we could see some sort of indefinable construction. We pulled up in front of a large slab-sided building, a hanger or large hall, the outside was crumbling and cracked. Not knowing what we were to see inside, we lugged in the camera, tripod, recorder, lights and as much power cable as we could carry. We were, apparently, still in part of the same complex, and this was the hanger where the Soviets assembled the *'Proton'* rocket. The building was huge, with small windows at the top near the ceiling some sixty to seventy feet above us, and probably two- to three-hundred feet long. Totally unlightable with three 500watt lamps, I just switched on some electronic gain in the camera and recorded some general views, pans and cutaway close-ups.

The morning continued in the same manner. Ten minutes in or at each of the soviet's launch or assembly plants, interspersed with similar amounts of time spent driving across barren grey wasteland. We went to the 'Energia' launch pad, again grey, again huge, with a great, grey articulated tentacle that snaked from the top of the structure to the ground. This was the Cosmonauts escape tube. The entire structure looked like European post war low tech even though it had recently been rebuilt after the first launch of the *'Energia / Buran'* combination, which had blown the pad apart. We went to the 'Energia' assembly hanger, where we were rushed around, but mostly under, towering rockets and boosters on their sides in the latter stages of construction. We were taken to the *'Buran'* complex, the Soviet equivalent of the American Space Shuttle and, apart from the lettering on the vehicle, it looked to my untrained eye an exact copy of the American space craft. The shape, the heat resistant tiles, the black and white paint work, all just as we had become used to in the many news shots we had seen of the American shuttles. Then it was back on the bus and off to lunch in a building near the Leninsk museum.

At one end of a room large enough to house a badminton court, we were served the usual mixed meat starter, a thin soup with a chicken bone in the bottom of our bowls and tongue and mashed potato. After the food, I moved away from the group and joined the coach driver for a smoke. We attempted to converse, he in Russian, me in pidgin English. Why I thought he was more likely to understand I don't know! I gave him the remains of a packet of Marlboro cigarettes and from then on, the back door of the coach opened before the front one thereby giving us a head-start every time we stopped.

We were then taken into the Leninsk museum, where the exhibits that we saw and recorded shots of, included a full-size model of *'Sputnik'*, the first ever space craft launched just thirty-three and a half years previously. It was a shiny stainless-steel ball about fifteen inches in diameter, with thin aerials about five feet long radiating out from its circumference. I was amazed at how small it was and in awe of how quickly the two superpowers had built upon their first tentative probes into space and were now hurling man and equipment carrying vehicles weighing tons into the heavens with confident regularity. We saw a Russian space capsule of the type that took Gagarin into space. It looked so frighteningly low tech. It reminded me of the inside of a nineteen-fifties radio hams den, with the electrical equipment having large hand sized rotary faders and big key switches.

After the museum, we returned to the coach and moved on to the *'Soyuz'* complex, where in one corner a Progress capsule was being prepared for a future launch to carry supplies up to the *'Mir'* space station and at the other end of the building two 'Soyuz' manned capsules. These two were part of the Juno project, one a backup vehicle, the other the capsule that Helen Sharman was to take off in. Then at about four-thirty p.m., we were ushered hurriedly back on to the coach and taken to a large car park in the middle of a collection of buildings, most of them two to three stories high and bristling with radio aerials and dishes. The car park was full of army vehicles, black army police cars and numerous black limousines. ('Zil' I think they are called, but they are the classic party chief car that roars down the centre lane in Moscow streets). The group was hurriedly led single file, with Pieter, Doug and I scurrying on behind, loaded up with camera, tripod, two recorders, tapes, batteries and paglight, through between the buildings and onto a six-foot high covered podium, where just less than a kilometre away out in front of us, with a 'Progress' supply capsule on top, was an *S4 Soyuz* rocket gently emitting smoke. We were to witness a launch.

Watched unsmilingly by dozens of five-star generals, dressed in gold braid covered blue grey uniforms, we recorded a Patrick piece to camera with the smoking rocket in the background. Fortunately, one of our party knew his Russian numbers and was able to interpret the countdown being announced to the assembled military personnel over the tannoy. We had fifteen minutes to wait for the launch, during which all the people in the party drifted over to tell me their experiences of previous trips to see American launches. They told me how noisy it was going to be and how fast it was going to roar heavenwards. Doug and I had decided that we would feed the output of the camera to both recorders, we couldn't afford a failure and, if anything went wrong with the launch, we were sure the Soviets would confiscate the tape. So, we had the larger BVW 35 standing quite obviously beside the tripod and the smaller, dockable BVV 5, connected by a separate video cable, on the floor under Doug's waterproof.

It didn't matter that the final countdown was in a completely unintelligible foreign language, we all were able to sense to the second when it was going to go; with one minute to lift off we ran both recorders and, with the two times converter switched into the Fuji 14-1 lens, the rocket almost filled the frame. It was the mounting excitement in the announcer's voice that finally prepared us, the escaping vapours increased around the pad and then the support arms craned away from the rocket as full power came on. Flame and smoke billowed out from the bottom of the rocket as it slowly lifted off from its mooring. For a few seconds it seemed to climb in silence and then we were hit by a crackling, rumbling wall of sound that vibrated our bones. Skyward it roared, arching away from us and not quite as quickly as I had been led to believe. I hung on to a usable shot up until the point where the boosters separated away from the main rocket and then it was all over. We were then told that it was time to go. There had been no sign of a Cosmonaut, let alone Helen Sharman, and no mention of where she was or when we were going to be able to see her. We collected up the equipment and moved back to the coach. Twice we were ushered to one side out of the way of the rapidly disappearing staff cars whisking the five-star generals off to goodness knows where.

Back at the hotel, the group was bubbling over with excitement at seeing the Soviet launch, all that is, except for the 'Sky at Night' team. We were very aware that a rocket launch, some wide angles, a collection of close-ups of hardware, and a few links to camera do not make a programme. The promises of the British Cosmonaut, an Astronomer and a Space hardware man to talk to, were fast disappearing and Pieter was very concerned that we might return without a programme. One of the group that we were travelling with was a Dr John Mason, Scientist, Computer expert and Astronomy buff extraordinaire, and a friend of Patrick's. He had collaborated on several books with Patrick in the past and seemed to be spending more time with us than the rest of the group. Over dinner Pieter decided it would be worth interviewing John first thing the following morning so that we had some reaction to what we had shot so far. Dinner was another splendid spread, although the Russian meal was beginning to become rather monotonous. A great selection of tastes for the first course, an average to poor main course and usually a non-existent pudding or dessert. Tonight's meal was cold meats, salami and what looked, and tasted, like cold black pudding, cucumber, cabbage, sardines and red caviar. The main course was again a sort of steak, but nobody was taking bets as to what animal it came from, potatoes and cucumber. As the night before, the table was liberally dotted with bottles of drink, this time they appeared to be Pepsi, Beers and water. Pieter topped an unlabelled bottle of clear liquid and poured himself a large glass, feeling particularly dry after a tense day. He took two large gulps, and for a moment he was quite still, and then one could almost see steam coming from his ears as he flushed very rapidly and let out a low resonant gasp.

"This is Vodka!"

The first few hours of Wednesday morning were rather fraught. The coach was due to leave for the airport at nine-thirty a.m., breakfast would be served at eight a.m. We had an interview to do with Dr John Mason on the steps of the hotel, and Doug and I had all the equipment to pack into the flight cases for the return trip to Moscow. I met with Doug at seven-thirty a.m. and we packed everything that we didn't need and got the cases to the front door of the hotel. We rushed through breakfast as quickly as our hosts would allow and were set up outside the hotel in the snow by eight-thirty a.m. where we recorded for half an hour. John was very lucid about his reactions to his visit to the Russian Spaceport and their current Space programme. It was an interview well worth doing as it made the final cut. Also, this was the first time we had been able to look around outside the hotel. It seemed to be set apart from the rest of the town, surrounded by a wire mesh, eight-foot-high fence with armed military personnel marching up and down just a few yards away. Not that anybody ever confirmed our suspicions, but we all left Leninsk convinced, as I had thought on our arrival, that we had stayed at a military hotel.

On the coach to the airport, we managed to get clearance through Nikolai to record some material at the airport of the group as they boarded the plane. Even though

Doug and I had decided to carry the camera and recorder in a ready-to-shoot condition, this permission came as somewhat of a surprise to us especially after the non-availability of the interviewees. What was even more surprising was that, just before take-off, one of the air force crew came and ushered me forward to the cockpit where I was able to record the take-off from the jump seat of the Antonov 72. After this initial excitement, we settled down to the boredom of the four-hour flight back to Moscow. The military Antonov 72, described by Doug as a 'dustbin with a small roman candle strapped to each side,' had only one window on each side near the back so it was impossible to see any of the terrain below. Still struggling for material, we recorded a Patrick piece to camera, phrased as if we were on our way to Baikonur. Once we had finished, Doug, who was sitting in the row in front of me, slipped a plastic cup, half-full of a clear liquid, through between the canvas seats. It was a mixture of Dry Martini and Gin he had concocted and kept in his hip flask,

"Thought you might like some wide spectrum mouth wash and nerve tonic" he said.

Away to my left, another of the party reached down into his holdall and brought out a small screw top ginger beer bottle and poured himself about half an inch into a paper cup.

"Whisky," he said. "Cheers".

Pieter was still fretting about the programme content. The more he talked to Nikolai and the tour organiser, the more he realised that it was likely that the interviewees that we had hoped to record at Star City, the Space Research

Centre and Mission Control were going to be 'unavailable'.

As the plane slowed to a halt, a coach came across the tarmac to meet us. While the military loaded all the personal luggage for the entire group and the two-hundred kilograms of kit we had brought onto the coach, we were still reeling at the thought that we had been allowed to record material at a Soviet Military Airfield and on one of their planes. All the media reports we had ever seen or read indicated that anyone taking photographs at an Eastern Block Military Establishment had usually ended up in jail, or at the very least, being deported. The journey to the hotel took just a few minutes. It was the same hotel but this time we had landed at a different military airfield in the southwest of Moscow. We all booked into the hotel again, very quickly and into the same rooms. As far as the hotel was concerned, we had never left.

We lunched at the same tables in the same restaurant as we had breakfasted two days earlier. The food continued in the same vein as previous meals, mixed meats and cabbage starter, bottles of beer, only this time, the main course was a piece of chicken, which looked as if it had come off a bird that had spent three years in Dachau. Our courier, Irene, who had not gone to Kazakhstan with us, re-joined us at the hotel on our return and I lunched at the same table. I asked her to explain how the black market in hard currencies worked. I couldn't understand how the Russians could give away so many Roubles to the pound. The official exchange rate was 1.1 Roubles to £1.00, and the tourist rate, available at hotels was 11 Roubles to

£1.00. On the streets the black marketeers were offering 40 Roubles to the £1.00, and about 25 Roubles to $1.00 US. Irene explained that it is illegal to take Roubles out of the country when you leave and that there are wealthy Russians who wish to travel abroad who are prepared to pay more than the 'official' rates to buy hard currencies. There are also Hard Currency shops selling western goods that are unavailable anywhere else, and people need the dollars and pounds to be able to purchase those items. I then asked what the average wage of a Muscovite was. Irene said, "about 300 Roubles a month". That equated to about £7.50, or $12.00, at black market rates. To confuse the issue even further, the listed room rate at the hotel was 27 Roubles a night and a packet of Marlboro cigarettes in the hotel shop was 90 Roubles.

That afternoon, Romus Tours had organised a sightseeing coach trip for the group to see Red Square, the Kremlin and finishing up at a famous shopping area called Arbat Street. Pieter declined the offer on our behalf because he was hoping, with Dr Mason's help, to be able to set up some interviews. At four-thirty p.m. he gave up on the possibility of shooting that day and Angela, Doug and I were released. We stepped outside the hotel and negotiated with a taxi driver to take us to Arbat Street. For $10 he agreed to drive us the half hour trip into the centre of town, wait and bring us back again at six p.m.. The three quarters of a mile long street didn't have that many shops as such, but it is lined on both sides for almost the whole of its length, by temporary stalls selling hand painted artifacts and icons, the majority of which were 'Gorby' dolls. There were thousands of them. Built on the traditional Russian doll principle they were updated to reflect the current interest in Glasnost. As each doll opened, it revealed an earlier political leader, Khrushchev, Brezhnev and, in the better and more expensive ones, on back to Lenin. They ranged in quality from tatty to exquisite, and from $10 to $25. What was amusing, after the event, but at the time slightly scary, was that if you wished to purchase one with hard currency you were told to go down a side alley, out of view of the main street where the exchange was carried out extremely furtively. True to his word, our taxi driver was waiting for us dead on six o'clock, and we went back to the hotel. Dinner was at seven p.m., so there was just time to wash my hair. Unfortunately, it wasn't a very pleasant experience as the hot water in my bathroom ran rust-coloured.

There was a shock awaiting us at dinner. There was no alcohol on the table. This was the first time at any meal, other than breakfasts, where this had happened. Doug decided to try and order some beers. After a couple of attempts a waiter who understood a little English was brought over to our table. Doug put the question which he seemed to understand, but then he went away. Five minutes later he came back and said,

"No beer".

We asked if they had anything alcoholic for sale. He went away again. Another five minutes passed before he returned.

"We have Champagne," he said.

"How much?" we asked.

"Three dollars," was the reply.

Although we had eaten most of our food, we asked for two bottles and were careful about slipping the waiter the money. Loosened up by the bubbly, which was Russian but, from where we couldn't work out, we decided to find the bar.

We walked round the ground floor looking for signs until eventually we spotted a long dark corridor leading away from the back of the reception area. At the far end a dimly lit sign indicated that the bar was somewhere off in that direction. Down a few more corridors we eventually found a lift which just had an up and a down button. We were shot skywards at a great rate and lurched out into virtual darkness on what we assumed to be the twenty-fourth floor. The bar was dimly lit to the point where it took several minutes for our eyes to become accustomed to our surroundings. The room was longer than it was wide with the service counter at the far end, hanging in the top left corner of which was an appallingly mis-coloured TV set playing western pop videos. The decor was sixties student union with very dark blue walls and black furniture, low tables and bench seats. They were serving Champagne by the tumbler full at 5 Roubles a shot. Over several glasses Pieter let slip that the next 'Sky at Night' trip was coming together. He hoped to be visiting Baltimore, Cape Canaveral, Pasadena in California and Hawaii sometime in the summer. It was enough of a carrot to keep us going. At ten p.m. I called it a day and retired to my room which involved plummeting to the ground floor in the 'bar' lift, walking round three sides of the check-in block, showing my key card to the security men at the entrance to the lobby containing the 'accommodation' lifts, going up to the ninth floor and swapping my key card for the room key at the concierge's desk. Once in my room, I opened the window for air, and I noticed that the view appeared much prettier looking than it was in daylight. The lights twinkling in the apartments belying the drab greyness of it all. Dogs prowled the streets and howled.

Thursday morning was to be an early start. We were all to leave at eight thirty a.m. sharp to go to Star City, the Soviet's Cosmonaut Training Centre, an hour and a half's drive to the north of Moscow at a place called Kaliningrad. Doug and I cut short our breakfast in order to get all our equipment down from the ninth floor and not to delay the coach on our behalf. We of course left late at eight-fifty a.m.. After several wrong turns we arrived at ten-twenty a.m. to be met by a well-prepared military public relations man who conveyed Helen Sharman's heart-felt apologies that she would not be able to meet us today as she was training. Unfortunately, it will also not be possible to interview anyone responsible for Cosmonaut training. Pieter finally conceded that we did not have the programme we came for, scheduled to be transmitted just a few days before Helen Sharman's launch. A 'Sky at Night' programme about Soviet Space achievements going out that close to the launch, without reference to her, would be a disaster.

Dejectedly, and not at this stage overly interested, we sat in a first-floor lecture room overlooking a full-scale mock-up of the '*Mir*' Space Station, while the public relations man droned on about its construction and the functions of its different parts. In one corner of the room was a five-foot square display board with a block schematic diagram of how they recycle urine and make it drinkable again, a subject that the public relations man got quite excited about. What was worse, was that we ended up shooting five or six shots of it. They were desperate times. Towards the end of the lecture, we were introduced to a short stocky man in full army dress uniform, covered in medals, who was announced as a Soviet Cosmonaut, and was prepared to answer questions. This, of course, had to be done through an interpreter, the only one around being Irene, the Tour guide, who had trouble understanding some of the more technical Russian words let alone being able to translate them. We were allowed five minutes to shoot a quick piece to camera from Patrick with the '*Mir*' mock-up in the background and some wide angles and cut-aways. We were then taken to another part of the 'City' to see the water tank they use for weightlessness training. It was huge, very dark and almost perfectly still. We managed to get some technicians to turn on some lighting, though it still looked like a black hole, but we shot it anyway. We were then bused quickly away to lunch at the public canteen in the attached museum. On arrival we were told that lunch itself was not to be for half an hour so, while the rest of the group went round the museum, we recorded a few pieces to camera for the thirty-fifth anniversary programme. There was a biting wind blowing and we quickly got very cold. At two-thirty p.m., the visit was all over, and we were whisked away back towards Moscow.

Kaliningrad was outside the Moscow equivalent of the M25, and the road marked a dramatic change in the architecture. Inside this arbitrary boundary all the living accommodation seemed to be in large soulless grey concrete apartment blocks, but outside there were individual smallholdings, each somewhere between a quarter and a half of an acre in size. Centred on each was a wooden bungalow, about two feet off the ground on wooden stilts and with louvred shutters to the windows. They were once brightly coloured but now rather faded and dilapidated. As we sped past in the coach, I caught glimpses of rotund, darkly dressed women in head scarves, carrying buckets, chickens scurrying about, smoke wisping up from chimneys and men sawing wood.

At about four-fifteen p.m., somewhere near the centre of Moscow, the coach came to a standstill outside a run-down, pale green and white, pre-revolutionary building in its own fenced off piece of land. Much to our surprise, this was the headquarters of the Astronomical Council of the Soviet Union and we had been granted an interview with Professor Alexander Boyarchuk, President of the Council and Director of the Institute of Astronomy at the Academy of Sciences. The coach carried on back to the hotel with the rest of the group, and while Patrick and Pieter talked to the Professor, I got Nikolai, who had stayed with us, to try and establish what power rating the domestic wiring in

Boyarchuk's office was. This was the first time since we had arrived that I had needed to use the mains lighting kit and I didn't particularly want anything to go wrong. Something must have got lost in translation, because after a very good interview lasting almost half an hour, the wall sockets were far too hot to touch. Had the recording lasted any longer I think there might have been a bit of a disaster.

We were back at the Salyut Hotel by six-fifteen p.m.. The coach had come back for us, which gave Doug and I forty-five minutes to get the kit up to our rooms, put the batteries on charge and get cleaned up in time for dinner at seven p.m.. The food seemed to be getting worse, in both quality and quantity. It may of course have been hotel policy to reduce the amount of food they gave out the nearer to the guests' departure date, on the other hand, paranoia might have been setting in. Either way, that night's meal was a very small plate of smoked fish followed by a little piece of meat, the committee decision on what kind of meat resolved that it was pork, and some beetroot. Fortunately, our table was now heavily into Russian Champagne even to the point where we were getting particular about whether we got dry or medium. Our waitress was obviously aware of the dollars we had and openly offered to change some money. Giving us twenty-three Roubles to the dollar we all changed ten dollars' worth. What we were going to spend it on I don't know but it seemed a good idea at the time. On the downside, Anthony made a heavy play to gatecrash our table. You remember him, Mancunian with bottle glasses and webbed trousers. He had really wound Patrick up because he was always trying to engage him in conversation. Tonight, we had made a mistake and not ensured that all the places were taken at our table and Anthony had sat with us. As soon as we realised that there was going to be no more to eat, we made a great play on the fact that we needed a strategic planning meeting to work out our programme movements for the following day and left the restaurant for the twenty-fourth floor. I have no recollection of what we talked about, but everybody bought a couple of rounds of drinks, usually Champagne, sometimes Vodka. Well, Vodka was what we ordered but it was the same colour as dark navy rum. At eleven thirty p.m. I left for my room. When I got to the concierge on the ninth floor I asked if it was possible to put through a telephone call to London. She told me in pidgin English that there was a problem and that I should ask again the next day. Back in my room it crossed my mind that I should go back and offer her dollars, but I opted for sleep.

Friday was to be the last scheduled Scientific tour. It was to take in the Soviet Space Research Centre in the morning and their Mission Control in the afternoon. I don't recall where in relation to the centre of Moscow these buildings were, but it was at least an hour's drive from the hotel, and the only thing that distinguished the Space Research Centre from any other grey apartment block was the lack of washing hanging from the windows. The group was given three illustrated lectures on the current Soviet research satellites by two of their project directors. These lectures took place in three different, dim lecture rooms at opposing ends of the building, which felt to Doug and me, to be a quarter of a mile long. Each time we moved, of course, we had to lug the camera, tripod, recorder, lights etc. with us, just in case. We were always last to arrive and had to sit at the back, from where we would record some dingy wide angles of the event and, hopefully, a few cut-aways of the projected slides and the lecturer. After two hours at the Research Centre, half of it spent walking endless corridors, we were back on the coach heading for lunch, supposedly somewhere on the way to Mission Control. Unfortunately, neither the coach driver nor Irene knew exactly where the restaurant was. After we had stopped a couple of times for the driver to ask, we eventually arrived. We were taken upstairs right through the public eating area to a back room which had been laid up especially for us. The only thing that was memorable about the meal was the vegetable with the main course. Bowls full of whole bulbs of boiled garlic still in their skins.

At two-thirty p.m. we left the restaurant for Mission Control, or more correctly, the Soviet Space Flight Control Centre. Although he had lunched with us, Nikolai was not on the coach anymore and we wondered if his disappearance was significant. This was the last chance for the Soviets to produce somebody for us to interview. We were met by one of the Centre's public relations men who spoke very good English and we were taken to a large lecture room where we were given an introductory speech. He said that we would be going into the main operations room and that we would be allowed to take photographs, but no professional filming! We were to leave our equipment in this room, it would be perfectly safe, and we could collect it afterwards. Pieter was livid. Steam was coming from his ears, and he only just managed to retain control of his voice, when politely asking the public relations man why this should be, as we had been led to believe that there would be no objections to our filming here. The reply was that the correct arrangements had not been made and that we ought to know that this (Russia) was now a market economy. So now we knew. The right palms had not been greased. Where had the money run out? Nikolai? Our tour operator? Wherever, Pieter felt absolutely conned. Pieter is a small, gentle, polite man, who seems to consider carefully what he is going to say before speaking, but there is Latin blood in his ancestry and, at this moment, it showed. He roared into the tour operator in front of the whole group, a totally understandable reaction, but, in retrospect, probably mistimed.

Gloom clouds hung over the 'Sky at Night' team as we walked, a few paces behind the rest of the group, to the main control room, where we were introduced to an expert who was going to explain it to us, interpreted through the public relations man. I eased my way to the centre of the balcony overlooking the rows of workstations and the main tracking screen, took out my still camera and proceeded to expose one slide at about a second. As I was about to try another shot at a different exposure the expert came up to me and rattled off something in Russian, pointing at my camera. Being extremely twitchy about what we could or could not do I put the camera away, and the public relations man ushered the expert away. Later I was told that the expert wanted to know if I was using slide film, and did I have any to spare as it is very difficult to get in Russia. Luckily the one exposure turned out to be perfect. We were shown videos of *'Buran's'* first flight and of the inside of *'Mir'* when the Japanese paid the Soviets for one of their journalists to train and fly with them. We were also shown material of a Mars Rover vehicle that they claimed to be developing and then we were ushered back to collect our equipment, out of the building and onto the coach.

I was down for dinner sharp at the allotted time of seven p.m. I was hungry but the meal didn't help a lot. That night was the smallest meal that we had been presented with, the starter being a cabbage salad and a few bits of dried-up meat, probably beef, although Patrick was convinced it was Yak. The main course was supposed to be chicken and rice but, if it was, it was the darkest, toughest piece of chicken that I had ever experienced. Our humour returned as we tested the four different types of Champagne that was on offer, Dry, Semi Dry, Medium Sweet and Sweet. Pieter decided to see if it was possible to change some more money. The man who appeared to be the head waiter asked how much Pieter would like to change. Ten dollars was agreed upon and the waiter went away. Some five minutes later he returned with a clean white napkin, smartly folded into a cone, on a silver salver. Pieter took the napkin, placed it on his lap, removed the two-hundred and thirty Roubles, placed a ten-dollar bill inside his old napkin and put it on the table. Sometime later it was casually collected up. What a farce. As Doug observed,

"This country is going to be in a mess if they ever decide to devalue the napkin."

After dinner, the six of us (Dr Mason has become part of the team) negotiate two taxis to take us to see Red Square at night. Even with only about one fifth of the floodlights on, it still looked spectacular, especially St. Basils. We all found walls to lean on, or trees to support ourselves against to get some still photographs with long exposures. A group of children realised that we were English and engaged us in conversation. One of them explained that he came from Kazakhstan and when I said that we had just returned from Baikonur in Kazakhstan they all laughed. I wasn't aware that I could crack jokes in Russian, but then maybe they knew something we didn't. As we returned to our taxis, exactly in the place we had left them an hour and a half ago, we were harassed by a young couple who tried to sell us bottles of Vodka and tins of Black Caviar. Irene had told us that you can buy as much Caviar as you like, but it is illegal to take it out of the country, which was a bit of a shame as Angela had already bought a few tins from one of the waitresses in our hotel.

Patrick, Pieter or Dr Mason, I'm not sure which, had managed sometime during the day to establish a contact at the University and we were to spend the next day recording some more material. In the morning we were to shoot pieces to camera and in the afternoon, with any luck, some interviews. Irene had offered a minibus from the coach company that could be put at our disposal, at ten dollars an hour, so, with a full day ahead of us, we retired early to bed.

Saturday started in the by now accustomed Soviet fashion. The minibus failed to turn up. Fortunately, it was very easy to get two willing taxis to take us and our gear into Moscow to the University, wait while we recorded Patrick's links, and then take us on to Red Square and finally back to the hotel for $15 and a packet of Marlboro. Looking back, shooting the closing link for the programme in Red Square was funny. Neither Irene, nor Nikolai would say whether it was necessary to get permission to 'film' in the Square. We knew that we had seen many news reports on Television back home with the BBC's correspondent backed by the walls of the Kremlin, but maybe the BBC's Moscow office had a season ticket. We also knew that if we'd set up a camera without permission in Trafalgar Square, we'd probably get nicked. So, when we arrived at the bottom of the short road that leads up to the Square at the opposite end to St. Basils, Pieter and I left the others in the taxis and walked up to recce exactly where we were going to put the camera. Having made the decision we returned to the cars, where Doug and I collected the minimum kit together and we walked to the location with the other four trying to surround us so that we wouldn't be spotted. They formed a circle while we set up the camera and then, when we were ready, they fanned out leaving just Patrick facing the camera. He rattled off two quick pieces, stepped out of the way while I recorded a couple of wide angles and then the circle reformed while we stripped down the kit and beetled back to the waiting taxis. Lunch back at the hotel was another farce. The rest of the group was out for the whole day on another sight-seeing tour and, although we had asked Irene to confirm with the hotel that it would be all right for us to dine there, I don't think we were on anybody's list. We were shown to one table by a waitress when we first arrived and for some minutes nothing happened. Then we were ushered to another table, three over to the right, and served instantly. At two p.m. our faithful taxis were waiting outside to drive us back to a part of the University, where we met our contact Edvard, a senior professor at the faculty, and his seventeen year old daughter Katarina. They were thrilled to see us and made us tea and offered us cake. While Pieter and I recce'd the possible locations for the two interviews, Angela spent time chatting as best she could to Katarina. At the end, Angela handed her some chewing gum and a few BBC pens and the poor girl's eyes ran with tears of joy.

Pieter and I decided that, although it would be quite difficult to shoot in, we would use the so called 'offices' of the two gentlemen we were to interview. In a room about thirty feet long and twenty feet wide we saw benches of Russian computer technology. None of it worked, all of it looked to the western eye to be nineteen fifties, state of the Ark technology. Down the long wall of this room, keeping out the daylight, were heavy black cloths from ceiling to floor. In the five-foot gap between these cloths and the windows, were cubicles about eight feet long. Each cubicle had a bench to write at, a few shelves for books, a lamp and a phone. These were the 'offices' of the Soviet Union's top Astronomers. The first interview was with a Professor Lazoff, and he was understandable, but the second chap's English was untransmittable. The only thing he said that was intelligible to all of us, was that the Soviets had no plans to develop a Mars Rover vehicle. So, who were we supposed to believe? It was three and a half hours after we arrived that we stepped out of the University again to find our taxis still parked in the same place that we had left them. In any other town in the world, taxi drivers would have fitted in a dozen other jobs, but not here.

Dinner that night was out of the ordinary. We had taken up the option, arranged by Romus Tours, to be taken by bus to a famous Moscow restaurant for a banquet, for the princely sum of $22 or nearly two months' wages for the average Muscovite. After a week in Russia, we were not going to turn down a banquet at any price. The restaurant was the Slavyansky Bazaar, an amazing pre-revolutionary building, with an ornately decorated domed ceiling, tall columns supporting the balustraded second floor. In the past it had been the meeting place and watering hole for many of Russia's greatest poets, writers and musicians. Tchaikovsky, Rimsky-Korsakov, Chekov, Gorki, Stanislavski and many more – they had all eaten here – and as we entered the huge restaurant, the foyer area was hung with portraits of many of them. We were escorted, by waiters in Cossack costume, to an immense table, laid up for over twenty people, groaning under the weight of plate upon plate of hors d'oeuvre, breads, bottles of Champagne, white wine and Vodka. The room was packed. Every table full of Russians, talking, laughing and eating as if they hadn't a care in the world. On the table there was caviar, smoked salmon, ham in aspic, eggs, varieties of pickled cabbage, salad with tomatoes, salamis, cold meats, and more types of smoked fish. Each place setting had four sets of knives and forks, a dessert spoon and fork, and three different size glasses. The cabaret, we were told, was continuous. Different troupes would bound on to the low stage and give demonstrations of regional dances and, in between acts, a different band would keep the music going. We had finally cracked it. Moscow was not all dullness, drabness and gloom.

Doug, Pieter, Angela and I were at one end of the table, while Patrick and Dr Mason were at the other with Edvard, whom they had invited from the university, Irene, who could translate, and Nikolai. We were glad to be away from Astronomy for a bit, and it wasn't long before we had demolished our two bottles of white wine, our bottle of Champagne, and our bottle of Vodka. We managed to get a repeat order of drinks, but, surprisingly, they wanted the money in Roubles. It came to just over one-hundred and eighty Roubles and we gave the man two-hundred and told him to keep the change. We also decided to slow up a bit on the starters otherwise there wouldn't be any room left for the other courses. The waiters asked if we'd finished and took the plates away. The band started to play 'Strangers in the Night' and we were then presented with a small bowl of ice cream. That, apparently, was it. They'd done it again. Doug poured a large slug of Vodka on the ice cream, tasted it, said it was wonderful and so we all followed suit. It was time to leave. We returned to the hotel and retired to the twenty-fourth floor for a planning meeting, where Patrick proceeded to get very depressed. He said he didn't know how he was going to manage without Woody, his housekeeper and that he was thinking of retiring. We took it in turns to try and cheer him up, and the last thing I remember is being locked in conversation, our foreheads virtually touching, talking about the art of spin bowling, which is something I know very little about.

The following day the flight to Helsinki was not until ten-fifty p.m. so we joined the coach trip to Zagorsk, one of a collection of old villages known as the Golden Ring. These villages, about forty miles outside of Moscow, are founded on Monasteries, and the collections of churches that huddle together, usually on the top of a hill and surrounded by a high wall, have gleaming golden, onion-shaped spires. Today there were rows of coaches in the car parks, the souvenir shops were doing great business and the children in the street were offering for sale, postcard sets, badges, and, if you were that interested and shopped around, you could buy a complete Russian Army uniform, including the watch, from the various kids. The problem was that they wouldn't take no for an answer and continued to follow us wherever we went.

On the bus to the airport, the tour organiser from the travel agency in Windsor, decided to make a speech to the group. He thanked Irene and Nikolai for what he said was an amazing trip and then proceeded to say that he would never entertain a BBC crew on a trip in the future as we had been obnoxious and got in everybody's way. I don't know how, but Doug must have sensed something like this was coming up, because he managed to record the speech and gave the tape to Pieter. We were all seething but refrained from saying or doing anything. We had gone out of our way to be as pleasant as we could with the other members of the group. We were only too aware that they were paying for, what for some would be, their holiday of a lifetime. We were never aware of getting in their way or holding them up. We always worked within their schedule. The man was quite clearly getting back at Pieter for his explosion at Mission Control.

Getting through the airport was another farce. Firstly, we had to get through customs, where we were required to declare how much foreign currency we were taking out of the country, and that we were taking no Russian money with us. Then every piece of luggage had to go through the x-ray machine. The machine spotted several small round tins in Angela's suitcase, the caviar, and the soldier pointed to the screen and in halting English asked what they were. Doug quickly interjected; "Film," he said, as the soldier pointed at each tin. The explanation was accepted, and we all collected our luggage and then went to the Finnair check-in desk. Once we were booked in, we then went through passport control and were officially out of the USSR. But they had one more laugh instore for us. We went to the cafeteria to get a drink while waiting to be called for the flight, and the only currency they would take in payment was roubles!

The flight was bliss. Amongst the 'Sky at Night' team the champagne flowed. We floated through Helsinki airport on a sea of bubbles, onto a coach and five minutes round the corner we booked into the Rantacipi Airport Hotel, an absolute haven of western civilisation. We were allowed to store the equipment in a room behind reception, the barman came to us at the table and offered to bring us drinks, the rooms were clean and bright, there were hot showers, there was CNN on the television and people spoke English. We christened the hotel the "anti-Soviet decompression chamber".

From the bubble of contented conversation at breakfast, everyone in the group had wallowed in a bath or under the shower for some considerable time. Breakfast was a wonderfully long, almost sensuous affair. There was bacon, eggs, cold meats, different kinds of breads, fresh fruit juices, various fruit and cereals, a bottomless coffee pot, fresh milk and sugar. The group spent almost an hour and a half, gently wandering up to the buffet for another fresh taste and revelling in the continuous coffee. We hadn't quite finished work though.

We left the hotel three hours before the flight departure time as we had a couple of Patrick pieces to camera to do at the Airport, out on the tarmac. Finnair, with whom we were to fly back to Heathrow, were extremely helpful in getting us airside and putting a plane at our disposal so that we could record Patrick climbing aboard. The piece was to go at the beginning of the programme, as if on the way into the Soviet Union, so we finished off by shooting a couple of take-offs and that was it. We packed the kit for the last time, checked in, and headed for Duty Free. It was there that I spotted our tour organiser, and I decided to tackle him about his speech on the coach to Moscow Airport. I said that I was outraged at his totally unjustifiable verbal attack on me and my crew, and that even if he felt he had a grievance with the programme's Producer over the arrangements for the trip, he had no right to publicly accuse us of being obstructive and offensive, and that I wanted an apology. I expected him to launch into another diatribe, but he just meekly said that he apologised and walked away.

The short flight into Heathrow was long enough to get giggly on champagne and memories. We recalled the laughs over the Vodka that Pieter thought was water, Doug being locked in his room, the farce over changing money and being conned over the seven-course banquet. What was not mentioned, but will remain with us longer, are the mental snapshots of the drab streets, the grey featureless apartment blocks, the working conditions of the top Soviet scientists, the blank landscapes, the wooden bungalows on the outskirts of Moscow, the fading, crumbling pre-revolutionary buildings, the food queues and the grey, the relentless, endless grey.

***

May 1977, and I am very happy jogging along on Alec Wright's crew with Keith, Robin, Graham and John. We were working on a good mix of programmes, sport, including several Sunday Cricket games at grounds around the country, much more enjoyable than test matches – they only lasted a day, and they were in more attractive locations than Lord's or the Oval – and they were graced with the commentary of that poet and wine connoisseur, John Arlott, as he sipped his way through a bottle of Chablis.

We did several light entertainment shows including, memorably, a 'Steeleye Span' concert, from Penshurst Place in Kent. Formed from ex members of 'Fairport Convention' they played medieval songs combined with 20th-century electronic instruments, loosely termed 'folk rock'.

The production team said they had laid on an evening meal at the local pub, so we went along only to find that it was pie and chips, for which we were required to pay rather more than our evening meal allowance. Alec Wright, our Senior Cameraman said that he was not having that and said we should leave and go to the other pub in the village. It did not serve food. We had four rounds of 'Brandy Doms', (half Cognac, half Benedictine). Back in the 14th-century Baronial Hall, the audience was being served a medieval banquet, including glasses of mead. I accepted the offer of a tumbler of mead, and the glug of

Chapter Seven
Sent to the Devil

In the March of 1987, I was at the gala dinner and award ceremony that the British Academy of Film and Television Arts staged for the Film and Television Craft Awards. In previous years, the event had taken place at BAFTA headquarters in Piccadilly, London, and although Princess Anne graced the evenings, they had been low-key affairs, with heavily edited highlights shown late at night on Channel Four. This year, for the first time, they were to be broadcast live on network television and, as the BBC were to broadcast the Production Awards for the artists and directors, ITV were to broadcast the Craft Awards. So it was, that somewhere around ten twenty p.m., Julie T. Wallace walked across the platform in Granada's Manchester studio, curtsied to Princess Anne, who was there to hand out the bronze masks, and go up to the microphone to announce the nominees of the craft award for best video cameraman for 1986, and introduce clips from the programmes. After an interminably long eight minutes, Julie said,

"And the winner is..."

***

Around the middle of the seventies, smaller, lighter colour television cameras were being introduced, and they were becoming physically comparable to 16mm film cameras. Plays and drama serials that had scenes that were both indoors and out, had used the television studios' video cameras for indoors and shot the location sequences on film. There was a noticeable difference between the pictures recorded electronically and those recorded on celluloid. The two systems had different contrast handling abilities, and the colour rendition was different.

Drama department negotiated with Outside Broadcast department to develop a small, two camera Mobile Control Unit, with a simple vision mixing desk, an on-board video tape recorder, a sound desk and a radio communication system so that the director could talk to cameramen, floor managers and production managers without them being limited by cables. The unit would allow complete scenes to be recorded on location, to be edited into the studio scenes with no noticeable difference in technical quality.

Very soon after using the unit, drama producers and directors wanted to shoot entire productions on location because of the realism of location shooting, especially the more authentic sound quality. The first unit of this type was named the Location Production Unit One, (LPU 1), which soon became fully booked and very quickly prompting the building of a second similar unit, which for reasons I never fully understood, was not called LPU 2, but LMCR.

brandy proffered by Maddie Prior, the lead vocalist. Amazingly we got all our scripted shots, apart from one slip-up from Alec.

Then out of the blue, I am called into the office of the recently appointed Head of Cameras, David Jones, and told that I am to do a two-week attachment to the LPU, with senior cameraman Frank and his number two, Alan Hayward. Frank, my senior cameraman from back in the days of the Ark Royal and Barcelona, was tall, extremely thin, (if female, he would be described as anorexic), and seemed to exist on a diet of cigarettes and alcohol, preferably Guinness. Before lunch he was the equal of any of the cameramen of his time. Rather than take the location catering, he would insist on leaving site and going to the pub and his camerawork and demeanour suffered for it.

The unit was booked to record a BBC 2 'Play of the Week' entitled "Shooting the Chandelier", written by David Mercer, with a cast including the actors Denholm Elliot, Alun Armstrong and Edward Fox, and directed by Jane Howell. The location was Melton Constable Hall, a few miles south-west of the Georgian town of Holt, in North Norfolk. It was the same location that Joseph Losey used for the 1970 film "The Go-between" starring Julie Christy.

The first few days on location were spent watching what went on, who was who and who did what. There was the Production Designer, responsible for the look of the sets, ensuring that everything was of the same period, and his team consisting of a Property Buyer, Set Dressers, who moved furniture and wall hangings etc. in and out of position, and Chippies, who were around to build, mainly, wooden supports, and to put blocks of wood under furniture to raise them into shot as required. They also carried a selection of small wedges to tilt a painting or mirror to avoid unwanted reflections. The Costume Designer with their assistant and a team of dressers, who were responsible for ensuring that actors, and at times tens of extras, were all in the correct costume for every scene, even though, on most location shoots, scenes were shot completely out of sequence. They also had to set up a room, or rooms, to hang up the costumes and for the actors to change in. Repeat this for the Make-Up department. If there are no rooms available at the location then large vehicles are brought in to create the dressing rooms, make-up rooms and costume storage. Often, a large generator is required to supply electrical power for the O.B. unit, the lighting, the dressing and make-up rooms and, not forgetting, the most important vehicle of all, the catering truck!

To many, location catering would appear to be an extravagant luxury. It is more than cost-effective. It was usually hoped to be able to record for eight hours a day between nine a.m. and six p.m. with an hour's break for lunch. Actors, Costume and Make-up would have to be on location at around seven-thirty a.m., sometimes earlier if many extras are involved. They would have had to leave their accommodation way before breakfast. Then, if cast and crew were to leave location and try and find eating establishments that could feed a minimum of forty people lunch in under an hour, let alone having to get actors into their 'civvies' and then back into costume, ready to record again. Impossible. The amount of time saved, the maintenance of cast and crew morale, more than makes economic sense.

After a few days, even though I was not operating, I already felt part of the team. Up to this point in my career, apart from a few producers, there had always been a sense of 'us and them' between production teams and the technical crew. For example, Light Entertainment Department, whenever they left the comfort of the studios to work on location with an O.B. Unit, referred to us as 'the welly boot brigade'.

Four days into the shoot and Alan Hayward had to return home because his father has taken ill, and I had to step in. Another big step on the learning "curve". Exhilarating, testing and exacting camerawork and the adrenalin rush was back.

This location shoot was also the start of my love affair with the North Norfolk Coast. On the Sunday off, my long-term friend Peter Belcher, the recording engineer on the unit, and I, spent a day at Cley Marshes, the North Norfolk Wildlife Trusts premier bird reserve. We were privileged to see not only adult Avocets, which returned to Norfolk in the 1940's after an absence of over one-hundred years, but just-hatched chicks, the first successful hatch at Cley. It was Victorian hunters and egg-collectors who drove the Avocet to national extinction in the nineteenth century, and the specie's fortunes have changed radically during the years since the end of the Second World War. I've returned to North Norfolk nearly every year since.

But I digress.

On my return to Base, (have I mentioned it was in Acton, West London), I went to see David, Head of Cameras, and let him know that I'd enjoyed the attachment and that I had learned a lot.

***

It was probably twelve months later, and the regular shuffling of camera staff between units took place. Frank Hudson was relieved of his position as Senior Cameraman on the LPU, a decision he contested, to be replaced by Trevor Wimlett, and I was to be his number two. Trevor and I spent eighteen months together, and we were able to form great working relationships with the unit's two Rigger Drivers, Phil Bunker and John Cowling, whose roles became that of 'film grips'. They were the cameraman's righthand man. If a track needed laying, a dolly needed moving, a camera mount needed changing, they were on it. Phil worked with Trevor and John, known as 'grey cloud' because of his mop of wild grey hair, worked with me. John was a rough diamond if ever there was one. He loved being right up at the sharp end 'on the floor'. He looked like he came from gypsy stock, probably sired more children than he knew about; women adored him; he loved his drink and was very easy-come-easy-go with money. He would take a thousand-pound cash advance against his expenses claim and put it on a horse;

if it won, he would buy everyone champagne, if it lost, he wouldn't think twice about sleeping on the floor of the camera van.

Trevor and I worked on at least seven dramas together, there may be more that I have completely forgotten, but many had moments that added to my understanding of the process of creating good drama, and a few times when I was tested.

We first worked together on "Malice Aforethought" directed by Cyril Coke. Briefly the plot centred around Dr Bickleigh, (played by Howell Bennet), who for over a decade has been despised by his wife, Julia Bickleigh, (played by Judy Parfitt). He wanted romance and dreamed of escaping with Madeleine, (played by Cheryl Campbell), with whom he was having a passionate affair. But his wife refuses to divorce him so he is reduced to more drastic means.

Shot on location near Longparish in Hampshire, using both cameras and recording complete scenes with a pre-determined shot list and a vision mixer, John Barclay in the control van, it was not unlike working in a studio environment.

But my test came in the last week of the shoot. Trevor had pre-booked his holiday long before the unit was booked for the programme, and it was accepted that I would finish the shoot as the lead cameraman. Spoiler alert. We were shooting the courtroom scene, where Dr Bickleigh is found guilty of murder, in a courtroom in Winchester. There wasn't really room for two cameras, so we shot everything from the judge's point of view looking at the defendant and the legal teams first. Then we reset to shoot shots of the judge. Cyril, the director, came into the courtroom from the control van, and said,

"OK this is where the camera goes,"

and we recorded the judge's occasional lines. I was unhappy. I was convinced that for the pictures to cut with those we had already shot, the judge should be looking out of the other side of the frame. I said over talkback to Cyril and John, the vision mixer,

"I think we're the wrong side of the line and these shots won't cut".

There was a whispered conversation and then a chorus of,

"No, it's OK, let's move on."

I had a problem. If I just shrugged my shoulders and moved on, and when the sequences came to be edited, and they saw the problem, it could cost an expensive re-shoot. I decided to push my novice luck and over talkback said,

"Please let me have a few minutes to do the shots from the other side of the line, and then you'll have it both ways to look at in editing."

There was a reluctant,

"OK"

from the van. Much to my satisfaction, as we were recording the shots, I heard someone whisper,

"He's right you know".

There and then I learnt never to do a shot unless I was convinced that it would cut with what went before, and what was to come next, even if it's days or weeks later.

September 1978 and Producer Inness Lloyd had a script which he believed could be completed in two weeks using the LPU with its ability to record complete scenes. The problem was that the director contracted to the piece, Don Taylor, said he wanted to shoot it the way he'd worked when using film, one shot at a time. This would have taken twice as long, and Inness was not prepared to double the budget. So, Don Taylor wrote a completely new script that could be shot on one camera in two weeks. It was called "In Hiding" and was the first of a series of four plays featuring Denholm Elliott. The story in this Playhouse Special was about a boy, Mark, who is sent to his Aunt's house in the country for the summer holidays because his father is absent and his mother too busy. He creates his own little dream world in a derelict house, until one morning he discovers another occupant.

Obviously, Trevor was going to have to operate, and I just assisted where I could. But most importantly, I learned a few good reasons why a director prefers to shoot one shot at a time. It is far easier to get the lens virtually on someone's eyeline, so the person talking is almost, but not quite, looking at the viewer, who will feel more powerfully connected when they can see both eyes clearly. Additionally, if each actor's lines are recorded separately, pauses in conversations can be shortened or lengthened for dramatic effect in editing. The play was well-received, especially in the Evening Standard.

We recorded two further plays in the Playhouse Specials featuring Denholm Elliot. "School Play" by Frederic Raphael was the third of four, also starring

Jeremy Kemp, Michael Kitchen, Tim Pigott-Smith, and Jenny Agutter and directed by James Cellan Jones. Described as an unerringly biting and witty satire, it was made all the funnier because the actors, all in their forties and fifties, wore shorts, school blazers and caps.

The last of four plays featuring Denholm Elliott was "Gentle Folk" a play by Alexander Baron and directed by Rodney Bennett. This time a period drama set in 1911 and centred around a country house party with guests from literary circles, business and politics. Also there, a young man who has premonitions.

We recorded it at Socknersh Manor, a Grade II-listed country pile in Etchingham, near Burwash, East Sussex, and not far from Rudyard Kipling's Jacobean house, Bateman's. Then, Socknersh Manor was co-owned by Englebert Humperdink and (Sir) Tom Jones and bought by the chart-topping singers in their heyday, although they never lived there full-time. Not that I can confirm, but allegedly, the Manor boasted a pool, cinema, party room, tennis courts, stables, sunken spa, separate self-contained apartment and even a private underground petrol station. Singing for your supper would seem to pay extremely well.

The play was shot using both cameras, achieving complete scenes, but the next drama Trevor and I worked on, Shakespeare's rarely staged Henry VIII, was recorded in a very different way.

Between 1978 and 1985, the BBC televised the entire Shakespeare canon of thirty-seven plays, lauded as a remarkable technical and dramatic accomplishment, and Henry VIII was part of that series. As was "As You Like It", which I worked on first. It was recorded in Scotland at Glamis Castle, six miles West of Forfar, and the childhood home of HM Queen Elizabeth, The Queen Mother and the birthplace of Princess Margaret.

I was there as number two to Senior Cameraman Don Oliver, (Trevor was away on another project). Known to us as 'Tonka Tester' for his ability to break things, and by our Sports Producers as 'a legend in his own lunchtime', I don't believe he'd ever worked on a drama before, so I was not looking forward to the two weeks. So it proved, as many a time I had to whisper in his ear that we must match shot sizes when doing cut dialogue sequences, and that camera height above ground is dictated by eyeline, e.g. when recording a conversation where one person is sitting and one standing, your camera should be at the same height as the head of the person next to you - you don't just place it where it's most comfortable to operate.

We recorded in the castle and its grounds with a wonderful cast. The play starred Helen Mirren (Rosalind), Brian Stirner (Orlando), Richard Pasco, James Bolam, Angharad Rees – affectionately known as angrenade -, Tony Church, Clive Francis and David Prowse, (the Green Cross Code and, later, Darth Vader), who played Charles, the court wrestler.

It was the wonderful Helen Mirren who subtly helped solve another problem that can arise when recording two camera cut sequences. In a very intimate scene between the lovers Rosalind and Orlando, Helen and Brian were standing very close together, facing each other, and it was proving impossible for both cameras to get clean close ups of the two actors. If it wasn't Brian's out of focus left ear in the right side of frame in my shot of Helen, then it was Don's camera in the left. If we backed the cameras away from the eyeline to avoid those problems the shot became a one-eyed profile shot and lost all the intimacy. Helen suggested to Basil Coleman, the director in the control van, that he record the sequence and then play it back to the monitor we had out for the lighting director. This we did, and when we went for another take, Helen gently threw her weight from one foot to the other, to be out of the way of Don's shot of Brian, and back for my clean shot of her. Brilliant! But another important reason for shooting one shot at a time.

Director Kevin Billington had a different idea on how to use a two-camera set up when we recorded Shakespeare's Henry VIII. The recording took place, mostly at Leeds castle in Kent, with a few scenes shot at Hever Castle. Another stellar cast, with John Stride as Henry VIII, Ronald Pickup as Cranmer, Barbara Kellerman, as Anne Bullen (Boleyn), Timothy West as Wolsey and Claire Bloom as Katherine of Aragon.

Kevin's idea was to have two recording machines on site, with each camera recorded separately, and to have the two cameras side by side, one offering a two shot, the other a single shot. This way he would have the play totally uncut and have all options open in editing but achieve it in half the time it would take to shoot one shot at a time. And again, this came with compromises. The camera offering the two-shot had to be nearest the eyeline to get a clean shot of both actors, and consequently, the single shot on the other camera was way-off eyeline. Trevor and I were always trying to put our cameras in the same place.

I worked with Trevor on the first of two stories in a series called "A Question of Guilt", which were reconstructions of famous historical cases of three female murder suspects, shot mainly using both cameras to achieve cut sequences. The first, "Constance Kent" shot mostly in North Somerset and a bit in Dorset, is memorable for a couple of reasons. The series starred Joss Ackland, and, on one occasion, Trevor and I were chatting to him and asking what he was going to do next. He said that between the periods when he was required to be here on location, he was rehearsing a play with a Chinese director. He said it was proving a little difficult,

"Because after four hours you want another one".

On the Dorset part of the shoot, a few of us including Joss, went to a good restaurant for dinner, and as part of the cheese course were offered the then very rare Dorset Blue Vinny, which was once made in nearly every farmhouse in Dorset until the Second World War when production almost died out entirely. As the cheese became increasingly difficult to source after the war (some even say it was once made illegal), it made way for opportunists to sell other blue cheeses under the guise of Dorset Blue

Vinny. Legend has it, if you whispered in the right person's ear in the local pub and left money on your doorstep, in the morning a piece of cheese would appear! In the early 1980s, Michael Davies resurrected Dorset Blue Vinny using a three-hundred-year-old recipe.

The other play in the series, 'Mary Blandy', was shot mostly in Herefordshire and partly in Kent. Trevor was on a lighting attachment, so I was acting Senior Cameraman and joined by Neil Cameron. The Kent part of the shoot was two weeks, but with Saturday and Sunday off in the middle. I can remember vividly one sequence, the hanging of Mary Blandy, which we shot in a field which sloped up to the towering Saltwood Castle, the then home of the MP and diarist Alan Clark. The castle was near Hythe in Kent and Alan Clark had inherited it from his father Lord Kenneth Clark of the art and architecture series "Civilisation".

Trevor's lighting attachment included visiting the Mary Blandy shoot to follow our lighting director, Hu Cartwright. On the 'wrap' on the Friday evening, somebody said why don't we go to Boulogne for lunch tomorrow? ('Wrap' by the way, is what the Production Manager calls out to signal the end of the days shooting. It comes from the early days of the film industry and means 'Wind Reel And Print'. The camera assistant would rewind the film, take it out of the camera and get it processed so that the 'rushes' could be watched the next morning in case anything needed reshooting.)

Saturday morning and around fourteen or fifteen of us boarded the ferry, although for some reason, Trevor took his car. We ate in a quayside sea-food restaurant, the obligatory *Assiette de fruits de Mer*, the multi-tiered stand of shellfish, with *aioli*, many crunchy baguettes, and multiple bottles of white wine, most probably Muscadet.

At about three o'clock, as we stepped out into the sunshine, someone said,

"Paris is just down the road".

Trevor said,

"I'm game".

So, Neil and I, plus three ladies from the make-up team, shoe-horned ourselves into Trevor's Lancia and headed south. One-hundred and seventy miles and three and a half hours later we made it. We managed to acquire a couple of three bedded rooms in a small hotel, got ourselves something to eat, and then drove around Paris looking for an open *pharmacie* as one of the ladies was in desperate need. The following morning, Sunday, with the car safely in an underground car park, we did the obvious sights. Having stopped in Paris on my way back from Barcelona seven years before, I had a rough idea where everything we should see was, and how long it took to get between them. I took control of the tour, starting at Notre Dame,

"OK team you have fifteen minutes in here", moving on to the Louvre to see the 'Mona Lisa' and the 'Venus de Milo',

"Meet you outside in thirty minutes",

some lunch just off the Place de la Concorde, then the metro to Abbesses for Sacré-Cœur and the stunning view over Paris. Then we were back to the car for the drive to Boulogne for the ferry, which returned us back to blighty mid to late evening.

We all reported at the allotted time on Monday morning to be given a dressing down by the Production Manager, who said that it could have gone horribly wrong and could have put the whole shoot in jeopardy. I think she was jealous really.

I recall spending a day at The Anna Scher School of Performing Arts to record one of their productions.

In 1968, Scher started an extracurricular performing arts school at Islington's Ecclesbourne Primary School. Seventy pupils came the first week. In 1970, the classes moved across the road to a council hall in Bentham Court on Ecclesbourne Road. By 1975 she had one-thousand pupils and five thousand on the waiting list, so moved to the custom converted mission hall on Barnsbury Road in 1976, which is where we went.

Described by one ex pupil,

"She was just this whirlwind of energy. I was like- 'What the hell is that?'- I'd never met anybody with that drive".

Her methods combined improvisation, discipline and professionalism with the natural talents within the local community, which made for highly able, confident actors that delivered natural performances every time, and she has produced household names for generations including

Kathy Burke, Phil Daniels, Natalie Cassidy, Gary and Martin Kemp, Patsy Palmer, and the future *Birds of a Feather* stars Pauline Quirke and Linda Robson.

And it was Pauline and Linda, aged about nineteen at the time, who stood out in the little production they'd put together, which we were there to record.

Also, that part of London availed me of another new dining experience, which was a supper of pie, mash and liquor in a long-established traditional shop with floor to ceiling white ceramic tiles on the walls.

Between dramas, the LPU was used as additional cameras to main unit programmes. One such was the 'Bobby Bare Music Show' at the USAF base in Mildenhall. We were allowed to use the canteen on the base for food and coffee. They took GB pounds at the till, but the change was given in US dollars. Gee thanks guys!

Trevor was going through a phase of wearing bright checked trousers, as were a few other cameramen in the department, and this day he was wearing yellow check. When the director, Rick Gardner, met with us he pointed at Trevor's trousers. I jumped in and said,

"Sorry, Trevor thought it was the Rupert Bear Show".

With lightweight cameras that were capable of being carried on the shoulder or under the arm, Trevor and I were on each side of the stage, almost amongst the instruments, our role being to give close-up shots of hands and faces of the musicians. Early on I had to offer a close-up of the violinist, a tall, leggy blonde in an immaculately tailored trouser suit. When she had finished her solo, I looked over the camera at her and she nodded in the direction of the steel guitar player. I gambled and offered a shot, and shortly was cut to, as he started his solo. When he finished, I again looked at the violinist and she nodded towards the lead guitarist. This went on for the entire gig and won me many plaudits from Rick the director. Afterwards I went to the artists' caravan to say thanks and goodbye. The tall blonde rushed out of the van and said,

"You're not going, are you?'

"Yes, we're heading back to London"

"Aren't you staying at the Hotel?'

"I'm afraid not. We must get back".

Had we been staying, which technically we should have, there might have been more than another paragraph to the "Bobby Bare Show" story.

We also joined a main OB unit for the opening of the Tate Gallery extension by H.M. Queen Elizabeth II on 24 May 1979. We'd seen the rehearsal schedule and the transmission times a few weeks before, and we were to be free between one and five-thirty p.m., so, we booked into the Rex Whistler Restaurant for lunch. At the time, the restaurant was in the 'Good Food Guide', not only for its food, but for its extremely affordable wine list. I have absolutely no recollection of what we ate, but the wine was Chateau Leoville Lascases, and we had half a bottle of Malmsey with dessert. At four-thirty p.m. we were the last two people in the restaurant and were very politely asked if we wouldn't mind leaving, as they had to lay up for afternoon tea. For the Queen.

***

In September 1980, I applied for, and was successful in getting promotion to Senior Television Cameraman. Head of Cameras, David Jones, said that I had to do a stint back on a main OB unit, so for a while I was back doing the sport and events, concerts and light entertainment shows.

Happily for me, I was back as Senior Cameraman on the LPU by the middle of 1982 and straight into a fascinating play for which we shot around half on location.

The Child Growth Foundation (CGF) was founded in 1977 by Tam and Vreli Fry following a discussion between six sets of parents whose children were being treated at Great Ormond Street Hospital for a variety of growth conditions. Through connections Tam Fry had at the BBC, he worked then in current affairs, a television drama called 'Being Normal' was commissioned. It transmitted in July 1983.

The drama starred David Suchet and Anna Carteret and highlighted the story of one of the parents' daughters who had Growth Hormone Deficiency. Given different names, Bill and Jody, this was Tam and Vrali's story written first as a play and then as a television drama by Brian Phelan. I'd met Tam twice before, once at his house and again in Blackpool when we were covering a party conference. We shot scenes of Bill and Jody (played by David and Anna) arriving at the writer's cottage in the country to discuss turning their story into a play/TV drama. We also shot scenes in and around Addenbrook's hospital in Cambridge, and in a house nearby, supposedly in London, where Bill and Jody lived. The piece was directed by Peter Smith and he, David and Anna couldn't decide how the next scene to be recorded should be played. Jody had come back from the hospital with the news that the treatment their daughter was now taking was successful and she had grown. Bill was at work. When Bill came home, the scene we were about to shoot, did he not know, or had Jody phoned him at work with the news? Peter turned to me and said, "What do you think?" After a few moments of thought, I said, "As this is such a massive breakthrough, I don't believe Jody could have kept it to herself and would have had to share it with Bill but would have told him not to let on that he knew, so that their daughter could tell her father when he got home". And that is the way David and Anna played it.

By June 1983 I had been joined on the LPU by Johnny Johnson as my number two. The first show we did together was 'Maybury,' for which we recorded location inserts in the Twickenham area of London. Produced by Ruth Boswell and Directed by Barry Davis, Patrick Stewart played the lead role of Dr Eddie Roebuck, Head of the Psychiatry Department at Maybury Hospital, and each episode in the series dealt with the individual case of a sufferer. In this case, the story 'New Gods for Old' ran to two episodes and was about a young man with epilepsy. The character, Robert Clyde Moffat was played by a twenty-two year old actor, just out of drama school. We shot scenes where he lived, and at the hardware store where he worked and where he had an epileptic fit which was frighteningly realistic. I also shot a scene of him walking towards camera through a crowded street on a long lens, so that sometimes you could see him in amongst the out of focus crowd. When we finished the shot, the young actor came up to me and said,

"Can that shot be played back on your viewfinder?"

. "Yes", I said, and asked the guys in the truck to play it back.

After watching it, he said,

"Thanks, I'm going to be a director one day".

That twenty-two year old was Kenneth Branagh.

A black comedy by the writer Andrew Davies was the next project that we worked on. Best known for the later works of *House of Cards* and *A Very Peculiar Practice*, and his adaptations of *Vanity Fair*, *Middlemarch*, *Bleak House, Pride and Prejudice*, and *War and Peace,* 'Heart Attack Hotel', gave viewers the first glimpse of the characters, Dr Stephen Dakar, and his girlfriend, Lyn, who later became the central characters of *A Very Peculiar Practice*.

The Doctor and his girlfriend book into a luxury hotel which serves rich food and encourages guests to use all the exercise facilities, the gymnasium, the pool and the sauna, with deadly consequences.

The owners of the hotel, played by Michael Gough and Madge Ryan, can't let the gift of protein go to waste. Hence my favourite line from Michael Gough,

"My wife has found something new to do with Brill".

We shot it all, apart from one scene of two drunks attempting to play golf, in a large house on the outskirts of Hay on Wye (so quiet, we said it was closed Monday to Friday and shut at the weekends). The house had all the exercise facilities the script required and which the crew were allowed to use at the end of the day after recording was finished. Stephen Dakar and Lyn were played by Hugh Fraser and Amanda Hillwood. Hugh went on to play Captain Hastings in multiple episodes of 'Poirot', and Amanda continued her portrayal of Lyn in *A Very Peculiar Practice*.

There are only three or four times when I have collapsed laughing when operating, and one was on this shoot. The sequence started with a wide shot at the bottom of the broad baronial staircase, which the two drunken chaps, who were off to play golf, were going to descend. Dressed in tweed hacking jackets and plus-fours, wearing flat caps and struggling with bags of golf clubs which got entangled with the balusters, the staggering descent was hilarious, and I couldn't stop the camera from shaking. We had to shoot it again. I set up the shot, locked off the camera and turned my back on the scene.

One of the most enjoyable shows Johnny and I did together was the comedy drama series called "Cockles". It was produced by Ruth Boswell and directed by Barry Davis with whom we had worked on "Maybury". Written by Douglas Livingston in six fifty-five minute episodes, it was shot on location in Herne Bay on the North Kent coast, with studio inserts.

Very briefly, Arthur Dumpton (James Grout) returns to his childhood holiday resort of Cocklesea, now a run-down, faded destination of times gone by. With a large redundancy pay-out, he wants to return the town to the glory days of his memories. He tries to get old friends from his boyhood to help his rejuvenation project. Instead, along with other residents of the town, they fleece him of his money.

Each of the six episodes was a complete story in its own right, with Arthur trying to re-establish the local theatre in one and bringing a national fishing competition back to the Cocklesea beach in another, while shady deals were being done behind his back. One of which was importing 'blue movies' on VHS tapes, which not only involved a night shoot at a nearby harbour as the small boat struggled to dock but required one of us to shoot a 'blue movie' (tastefully of course), that would be seen on a TV in another scene. I let Johnny do that one.

We, the camera crew, cast and production team, often gathered of an evening to watch what we had recorded in the last few days, and we all fell about laughing, convinced we had a classic on our hands. How wrong we were. When it transmitted it fell completely flat, and as far as I can ascertain, was never repeated. That was all down to the editing. Barry Davis, who should have overseen the editing, unfortunately, died before the edit, and whoever took over didn't really have Barry's take on the piece.

The next drama I worked on was not so much fun, not because of the work, but because colleague Johnny threw a serious wobbly. The six-part drama series was called "Johnny Jarvis" to be directed by Alan Dosser. Before moving on to directing TV dramas, Alan was artistic director of the Liverpool Everyman Theatre from 1970 to 75. He nurtured the careers of many future stars, including Julie Walters, Pete Postlethwaite, Bill Nighy, Antony Sher, and Jonathan Pryce. For reasons that were never satisfactorily explained to me, the first three episodes were to be shot on video, and the last three on film. When shooting on film Alan would be working with one cameraman, and he wanted to do the same on video. Just as Trevor had done on 'In Hiding', back in September 1978, it was down to me to work with Alan, and hope that Johnny would watch and learn. Unfortunately, he couldn't accept my decision, and phoned Head of Cameras and asked to be taken off the programme and be allocated to some other job. Couldn't see why he should sit around and not operate. For me, collaborating with Alan for four weeks in and around Hackney, was very satisfying.

Johnny was back and in a better frame of mind when we recorded most of the location scenes for 'The Box of Delights'.

John Masefield's enchanting children's fantasy, dramatized by Alan Seymour in six thirty-minute episodes, tells the story of a young boy whose chance meeting with a Punch-and-Judy man leads him to a world where almost anything is possible. The BBC brought the series to life on the small screen with a (for then) massive budget of one million pounds. Described by some critics as capturing the true spirit of Christmas better than any other children's drama and surpassing *The Lion, the Witch and the Wardrobe* as the ultimate winter's tale, 'The 'Box of Delights' begins with Kay Harker's train journey to 'Seekings' near Tatchester, where he will spend his Christmas holiday from school. On the journey he meets Cole Hawlings (Patrick Troughton), an old Punch-and-Judy man who tells Kay (Devin Stanfield) that,

"The wolves are running,"

a warning that evil is close at hand.

Producer Paul Stone had come across Masefield's book some ten years before he managed to bring it to television. The BBC then managed to sell it to two-hundred-and-fifteen American PBS stations where it was shown at prime-time viewing hours, the six thirty-minute episodes being shown as three sixty-minute broadcasts. Most of the budget was spent on special effects which today look very dated but, at the time, were the best and most ambitious attempted for a British TV series.

Johnny and I recorded scenes at Bridgenorth station on The Severn Valley Railway, who put a steam engine and coaches at our disposal for the day, and on the train while it was moving. Also, scenes at a house used as 'Seekings', where Kay was spending Christmas. We also recorded scenes in the Dudley Canal Tunnel and Limestone Mines, and a night-shoot at a canal lock where Robert Stephens, who was playing the evil Abner Brown, foolishly, as he was drunk, insisted on doing his own stunt of drowning in the icy water.

As great as Special Effects Department were, vast tracks of snow-covered landscape were beyond their capabilities. We had to go where there was snow. Only one camera was needed for the scenes we were to record in the Cairngorms, so the single camera unit, SCU4, was sent on its way north. We were to fly and pick up hire cars at the airport, which I think was Inverness, but it might have been Aberdeen. SCU4 was Alasdair (Mitch) Mitchell's unit at the time, but I went with him to make sure every sequence was shot in the same style.

An aside about Mitch – he liked a party. I went four or five times to his house where I was aware of his daughter Erika. Later, I heard she had married, and she was now Erika Leonard. Unfortunately, Mitch passed away before Erika published her first novel under the pseudonym – E.L. James.

As we took off from Heathrow, Mitch said,

"Breakfast in London, lunch in Inverness, luggage in Frankfurt".

As it turned out, it was prophetic. We'd packed thermal underwear, down-filled jackets and trousers, warm socks and hiking boots, and on landing at Inverness, Mitch's case did not show up. Fortunately, on the flight Mitch had gracefully said that I should shoot the sequences, as it was my show.

It didn't get any better. On arrival at the location, it was so bitterly cold, the generator could not be started, so no electrical power, and worst of all, the gas bottles were so cold, the catering truck couldn't function. There was nothing for it but to sit in the pub lounge, heated by a roaring fire, and sip whisky, and hope for warmer weather the following day. Some 'filming' days can be tough!

Fortunately, it did warm up enough to get powered up and we got on with recording the scenes - wide shots of snow-covered landscapes with two evil characters, associates of Abner, struggling to walk through knee deep, pure white drifts. Then I had to shoot a wolf's point of view of a horse's back legs as it trotted through virgin snow. Running, bent over with the camera close to the ground was tough, and after three takes I was 'cream crackered'.

The six weekly episodes ran up to Christmas Eve 1984, with me being credited as the location Senior Cameraman, and Colin Reid as the studio Senior Cameraman.

In early 1985, I was announced as one of the four nominees short-listed for a BAFTA craft award for Best Video Cameraman 1984. Johnny had another wobble because he wasn't on the nomination and said that I should have complained to BAFTA. As if.

All the nominees in Camera and Editing categories were invited to a celebratory dinner at The Howard Hotel in London by Kodak, who having realised that video was about to overtake celluloid as a recording medium, were publicising the fact that they were starting to manufacture video tape. I also went to the presentation ceremony at BAFTA headquarters in Piccadilly. I didn't win but the after-show buffet was very enjoyable.

Probably due to Production Department pressure, there was a change of policy and Head of Cameras started to allocate cameramen to programmes, rather than whoever was attached to the equipment doing the programme. So, my next drama assignment was the location sequences for a contemporary drama called 'The Detective'. Dramatized in five parts by Ted Whitehead from the novel by Paul Ferris, it was directed by Don Leaver, Produced by Sally Head, and starred Tom Bell as Crocker, who stumbles upon evidence of criminal activity that could threaten the government, but upsetting politicians won't put him off.

We shot many little scenes in and around London, using the single camera unit, SCU4, and Sally Head must have been pleased with the sequences, as I was invited to an after party at her house in Chiswick. Ted Whitehouse, the script writer who dramatized the Paul Ferris novel, was also there, and they were discussing their next project, an adaption of a novel by the feminist author Fay Weldon, who, by the way, is commonly thought to have coined the slogan,

"Go to work on an Egg".

Early Spring 1984, and Head of Cameras was getting together a list of those cameramen who he thought would be suitable to go to Los Angeles for the Summer Olympics. When asked, I said,

"I'd rather not".

A paid-for trip abroad is not something I would normally turn down, but the job would not be covering the actual sporting events but rushing hither and thither to then sit and wait for someone to interview.

"In that case", he said,

"You'll just have to re-join the LPU and do 'Blott on the Landscape' then".

Result!

Adapted from Tom Sharpe's book by Malcolm Bradbury, and starring Geraldine James (Lady Maud), George Cole (Sir Giles) and David Suchet (Blott), and Directed by Roger Bamford, it was shot like a film, one shot at a time, but on several occasions, we used the second camera with Dave Hunter operating, as a second unit. Dave shot the sequences of the earth-moving equipment, the blowing up of the gorge, and Sir Giles's Rover hurtling onto the motorway, and Phil Jones was with me in London, where we shot scenes at the flat of Sir Giles's mistress. Phil also shot Blott's flashback scenes of leaving Germany and being taken back to Handyman Hall by Lord Handyman.

The large Grade II listed Welsh country house, built 1803 to 07 in a picturesque castle style, called Stanage Park, and owned by Mr & Mrs Jonathon Coltman-Rogers, was set in a three-hundred acre park located in the Welsh Marches, and was the location for Handyman Hall, where many of the scenes were shot. We also recorded scenes in the lovely Shropshire town of Ludlow, and in the Avon Gorge in Bristol, where Production Designer John Bone had Blott's gatehouse home built. Later scenes needed to show the destruction caused by drunken motorway construction operatives, so John Bone's team built a pair of semi-detached houses in Deddington village square in Oxfordshire. Despite only having a front, two sides and a roof, they were realistic enough for a local milkman to leave two pints of milk on the doorstep with a 'Welcome to your new home' message. Blott's local pub was also shot in Deddington.

I haven't listed all the different locations, but for economic reasons, time and money, all the scenes for the six episodes are shot at one location before moving on to the next, and scenes were rarely recorded in story order. As an example, there were several scenes, spread throughout the piece, to be recorded in the dining room at the Hall. The room would be dressed, the lighting rig put in and we shot all the scenes, taking two-or-three days. Then we would move on to shoot all the scenes in, say, Sir Giles's office and repeat the process.

Working alongside David Suchet was fascinating. Over the period of the six episodes, his character Blott, developed from an apparently simple gardener into a confident member of the landed gentry, and David had a graph of this progress so that when it came to any scene, he knew where on the character's trajectory he was supposed to be and tuned his performance accordingly. I also realised quite early on that David liked to know the shot size when I was focussed on him, so I got into the habit of gesturing to him with my hand, where the bottom of frame was, be it waist, elbow or neck, as he adjusted his performance to the size of shot. The closer the shot the less you need to do with your face.

We had to shoot a scene where Blott discovers a stash of World War II armaments in the cellars under Handyman Hall. Of course, Stanage Park had cellars, five or six cavernous rooms, three of which had locked iron gates through which David and I spotted large numbers of wooden boxes containing classed growth Bordeaux wine.

Another performance that I admired was that of Simon Cadell's portrayal of Dundridge, the hapless civil servant with O.C.D., who is sent to sort out the planning mess in Cleene Gorge. His slow decline into madness was masterful. I saw him a few times after Blott, when I called backstage after the theatre show he was in, and at a West End Theatre Awards ceremony I was involved in televising, he introduced me to Stephen Fry. Memorable because it was the limpest, dampest hand shake I've ever experienced. After every evening theatre performance, Simon would calm down with a large cigar and a bottle of Champagne before getting a taxi home. It probably killed him. He died of cancer, aged forty-five.

We had a two-day visit to Handyman Hall by Tom Sharpe and Malcolm Bradbury around the time Lady Maud was turning the estate into a Safari Park. A monitor and a speaker were set up in a room in the Hall where they could watch the recordings. Both pipe smokers, they would sit in their comfy chairs, puffing away and chuckling together. At one point somebody overheard Tom Sharpe exclaim "That's a good line...I wish I'd thought of it."

At the end of the shoot, David, Geraldine, Roger (the director), the future Mrs Winser number two and I were invited to dinner with the Coltman-Rogers. David and I were thrilled as we hoped we might get to be served one or two bottles of claret from the cellar. Unfortunately, the grand dining room was unavailable as design were still 'undressing' it, so we ate in the kitchen, and when Jonathan came in with the wine he said,

"I can't find the cellar keys, but I think this Cote du Rhone will be alright".

Happily, it didn't affect a very enjoyable and memorable evening.

Ironically, one evening Geraldine and David came to dinner at a cottage I was renting near Chew Magna for the Avon Gorge sequences, and we sat long into the night watching the opening ceremony of the Los Angeles Olympics.

The show transmitted in the Spring of 1985 and, almost a year later, I was called in to Head of Cameras Office to be told I'd made the final four nominations for a BAFTA Craft Award. Again, Kodak wined and dined the camera and editing nominees in March, this time at the Royal Garden Hotel. The awards presentation evening was again at BAFTA headquarters in Piccadilly. And I didn't make the top spot for the second year running.

A single play I was quite proud to have been involved with was "The Best Years of Your Life". The story involved a promising seventeen-year-old apprentice footballer who is diagnosed with cancer. Initially he lies to his friends, teammates and himself about his illness and pretends that his condition is not serious. After an operation fails to remove the tumour, and he is told that his disease is terminal, he is forced to come to terms with his condition, as are his father and older brother.

It was written by a young man, Clive Jermain, who was suffering terminal cancer himself. The director, Adrian Shergold, needed to shoot several scenes on location, (with the family home and the local pub being recorded in the studio), most memorably at Stamford Bridge, Chelsea Football Club's ground. Using the single camera unit, SCU4, I shot scenes in the team changing room, where the youth team were in the communal bath, a long conversation as the elder brother and a friend walked the length of the pitch, and a much more difficult shot, a complete 360° track around three young players, including the lead character in his wheelchair, on the centre spot of the pitch, at dusk, with all the floodlights on. The difficulty with a circular track, a narrow-gauge railway that the camera dolly runs on, is that it is always likely to be in the back of shot, and you must get the camera very low to avoid seeing it. It took me a few goes to get it right. I also recorded many scenes in hospital, including the heart-breaking last scene. Clive, the writer, spent a lot of time on location in his wheelchair, very much enjoying watching the process of getting his work on screen.

Just before transmission in May 1986, the BBC arranged for a press preview showing at BAFTA headquarters, and asked Clive who he'd like to invite as guests. He asked for, amongst others, Joanna Lumley, David Putnam and me. After the showing, I was talking with Clive when both Joanna and David came up to talk to him. Known for her generosity, I noticed Joanna take a ring off her finger and give it to Clive.

Adrian Shergold, the play's director, interviewed Clive three times in 1986; first during the making of the play, then just after the play was shown, and finally in the December - the end of an extraordinary year for a young man living with a threatening and incurable illness. With remarkable frankness, Clive talked of the play and its impact – it was well-reviewed by many publications using words like 'outstanding', 'heart-breaking', 'overwhelming triumph' - but also about himself, his life and cancer.

"If by anything I say or convey I can help somebody understand that people with terminal illnesses aren't contagious … if it makes cancer easier to accept, then it will have been worthwhile".

It was such a privilege to have known that young man, even for just a few weeks.

Before I recall that which I can remember of the last drama I worked on with the LPU, I have a recollection of recording the final of 'The Prince of Wales Award for Industrial Innovation and Production' at Highgrove, for 'Tomorrow's World". I can't remember who or what won, because they pale into insignificance compared to the memory of being offered a drink by Prince Charles, while Princess Diana and the two princes, aged five and three played around nearby. The crew of about eight of us were all invited to the courtyard between the estate's garages, where the butler had a drinks trolley.

"Would you like a beer?" said Prince Charles.

"Thank-you, Sir, but I don't drink beer," I replied.

"What would you like?" he said, gesticulating towards the trolley.

"A gin and tonic, if I may."

The butler poured what I can best describe as a large double.

***

It was becoming quite clear that dramas recorded on location were from now on going to be shot on one camera, even though the two-camera unit, the LPU, had been allocated to the programme. It had its advantages. There were more seats able to view the incoming pictures, and the sound was relayed on a quality speaker.

It was Fay Weldon's novel "The Life and Loves of a She-Devil", adapted by Ted Whitehead and produced by Sally Head that was to be the series I was to work on. I'd worked for Sally Head before on 'The Detective'. Briefly, the drama tells the story of Ruth who lives in a standard modern house on an estate. She is overweight, not attractive and looks after two children, a dog, a cat and a guinea pig. Her husband, Bobo, is an accountant and a philanderer and manages the accounts of a rich and attractive authoress of romantic novels. He can't stand his wife and moves in with the writer, Ruth sets out to seek revenge.

It starred Denis Waterman as Bobo, Patricia Hodge as Mary Fisher, the writer, and Julie T. Wallace as Ruth.

The director Philip Saville would be a first for me. He came with a reputation as a pioneering and innovative director with many plays and films to his credit including Alan Bleasdale's 1982 drama 'Boys from the Blackstuff'. He was the first and only director I have worked with who seemed to know exactly how the whole series of four, fifty-five minutes episodes would look like when finished. One example that I remember is a scene that ends with the shot moving up Mary's bed, as she lay in tears, continuing up her bedhead, that mixed through to the camera moving, at the same speed, up Ruth's bed to see her smiling. The two shots were recorded three weeks apart.

The casting of Ruth was interesting. Julie T. Wallace, a virtually unknown actress with a few fringe theatre credits to her name, beat off a dozen or more experienced rivals to the role. Saville was looking for an actress over six feet tall, capable of looking hideous but still sexy, and publicised his search in the press. Julie replied with a five-page letter which showed, Philip said, an extraordinary understanding of the book. Having won the part, Julie had to gain a stone and a half, wear false teeth and have full "ugly" make-up, and she was unforgettable as Ruth, the spurned wife.

Shot in two, six-week blocks, with a week off in the middle, we recorded at multiple locations. The lighthouse at Beachy Head near Eastbourne in East Sussex, called Belle Tout, probably the most memorable, but there was a modern house on an estate near Swindon for Ruth's house, an Elizabethan mansion near Windsor, (the judges house), the literary awards ceremonies were in a hotel in Bristol, as was Bobo's office, and an ultra-modern house, which I think was in Derbyshire, for the Californian clinic where Ruth is transformed into Mary Fisher.

I was joined on the LPU by John Hawes as my number two. Unlike previous number twos, John totally accepted that the director wanted to work with the same person behind the camera, and was a tremendous support to me, and dealt with all the background stuff, like getting a different lens or camera mount onto location. He also took the second camera off and recorded some shots of the sea in various lighting conditions which Philip used as bridging shots, some wide shots of the lighthouse from distance and one or two helicopter shots.

We started the shoot at Ruth's modern house on the Swindon estate, and the first shot was a test of my hand-held camera capabilities. Philip was seeing if I was up to the task. I suspect failure would probably have been the subject of a difficult conversation. The scene was Bobo's departure from the marital home, where I had to follow him, at pace, as he went from the front door, through the dining room to the lounge, picking up a few personal effects as he went, and then back through the kitchen to the front door, and end on a close-up of a distraught Ruth. I passed.

We shot all the scenes at Ruth and Bobo's home, finishing with the burning down of the house, before moving to Belle Tout where Patricia Hodge joined the shoot. The first thing Philip did when we got to Patricia's first scene was to look intently at her face, and then turn to me and say,

"Don't ever let me favour the right side of her face".

In almost every one of Patricia's scenes she was on the right side of frame, favouring the left side of her face. I have never encountered that before, or since. Towards the end of the shoot, Patricia said,

"I've heard it said, and I agree, everyone should work with Philip Saville. Once!"

We recorded several helicopter shots, coming in off the sea to rise up to the lamp house at the top of the lighthouse, all a bit risky, as Philip insisted on coming up in the helicopter with me, and putting the aircraft on the upper limit of its payload. On one run in over the sea and up over the cliff edge, there was a drastic loss of lift and we nearly pitched into the ground.

Afterwards, over a couple of large brandies at the production hotel, the pilot told me he didn't think he was going to be able to collect the aircraft and had picked the spot where we were going in.

Philip wanted a shot looking down from the cliff top out to sea which then spun round and elevated up the cliff face to reveal Bobo and Mary on the balcony of her lighthouse home. The only way to achieve this was a very long crane arm with a remote pan and tilt head. This would be a first for me. The camera is mounted on a panning head at the front of the long end of the arm. Commonly called a 'Hot Head', the pan, tilt, zoom and focus controls are wired back to a pan and tilt head at the shorter back end of the counter balanced arm. There was a TV monitor showing the camera's output in front of me and I swung the arm and operated the remote head to achieve the shot.

On what was the best take for the performance of the actors, there was a twitch as I moved the arm a little to the right to include Mary's man servant. I asked Philip if I could do it again, but he said the performance was great and he would cover it in editing with a clink of glasses. It worked, the sound distracts the viewer, and you don't notice the error.

I'm also pleased with contributions I made to some of the iconic images in the series. Towards the end of part one, there is a scene where Ruth has decided to become the 'She-Devil' and disrobes. To convey this, the shot was of a corner of the bed with items of clothing, and finally her wedding ring, dropping into shot. The next shot was to be of Ruth looking into the mirror on her wardrobe door. I noticed that the doors were bi-fold and that if you opened them five or six inches, you couldn't see Ruth's reflection. So, I suggested to Philip that the shot started with the opened doors, and Ruth's hand coming into shot first and closing the doors to reveal the red-eyed She-Devil. Philip liked it, and we shot it that way. Also, there is a recurring image of the She-Devil, a head and shoulders shot backed by flames. John King, the Engineering Manager tasked with lighting the show, was having trouble making her look demonic. I had memories of a book I had read on still photography lighting techniques. So, I said to John,

"I've a vague memory that lighting from underneath makes people look evil - might be worth a try".

It worked. Technically he was my boss, so I had to be a little diplomatic.

Towards the end of the shoot at Belle Tout I overheard the Production Designer Humphrey Jaeger talking about the scene where Ruth goes to Zurich to deposit all the money out of Bobo's clients' accounts, and how they were going to have to make Heathrow look like Zurich. So, I floated the idea that we take a camera, a video recorder, and a sound recordist to Zurich. We could do the return trip in a day, and it probably wouldn't cost any more. They did the sums, and we went to Zurich, taking the kit as hand luggage. It paid off. You cannot shoot snow-capped mountains with a zoom out to an airport, however good you are at set-dressing Heathrow. Swiss Air were very helpful, and Philip managed a "Hitchcock", and put himself in one of the shots.

The show transmitted in the autumn of 1986 on BBC 2. February 1987 and I was in Head of Cameras' office to be told that not only had I been nominated for a BAFTA again, this time with John Hawes, but also John King was nominated for the lighting. As nominees we had to submit an episode for the judges to view, and the Producer, Sally Head, had been on the phone asking me to submit episode two. The series itself was up for best drama series and Julie T. Wallace for Best Actress, so Sally wanted different episodes to be submitted in each case, so that the judges would see the entire piece.

Kodak wined and dined us again, this time back at the Howard Hotel. It wasn't for me to tell them that I had absolutely no influence over what video tape the BBC bought. Way above my pay grade.

Sunday March 15th, and John and I, with our partners, were on a morning train to Manchester where we had been booked into the Britannia Hotel. At about four o'clock, dressed in evening wear, we were collected and taken to Granada Studios by coach, visiting the Coronation Street set on the way. The studio had a two-tier stage at one end, the lower level of which had two, ten-seater dining tables at each side, and the rest of the studio floor was set out with more dining tables. We were wined and dined, which lasted until about eight o'clock. The live television show, with entertainment – Shirley Bassey for one – was due on air at nine. There were too many awards to include them all in the live show, so some awards were presented before-hand, including John King getting the nod for best lighting.

I'd become aware that the awards were being announced by an actor or actress from the show for which people were winning. So, when Julie T. Wallace stepped up to make the announcements, I had the feeling, that this time I'd got it. And so, it proved to be. As she handed me the bronze mask, Princess Anne said,

"Congratulations, that looked as if it was fun to do".

Then when I got to the bottom of the stairs at the back of the stage, the first person I met was Sir Richard Attenborough, who shook my hand and said,

"Well done, lovie".

A week later, at the BAFTA Production Awards at the Grosvenor House hotel in London, 'The Life and Loves of a She-Devil' won best drama series, beating the favourite, Dennis Potter's 'The Singing Detective".

Chapter Eight
Astronomy & Gastronomy Part I
or Moore of a Good Thing

Still dining out on the stories from the trip to the Soviet Union, the same team - Pieter the Producer, Angela the P.A., Doug the Sound Recordist, Patrick Moore and I - reassembled at Gatwick one sunny Sunday in August 1991, for the ten-past-one p.m. TWA flight to Baltimore, Maryland, USA.

There was a programme to be made about the successful science achieved by the Hubble Space Telescope, despite the mirror problems. A second programme updating the work of the 200inch telescope at Mount Palomar near San Diego in southern California, and two further programmes in Hawaii, one about the American 'Keck' 396inch segmented mirror telescope, which was in the final stages of construction, and the second about the two telescopes in Hawaii that Britain has a majority interest in, the United Kingdom Infrared Telescope and the James Clerk Maxwell Telescope. Additionally, further material for the thirty fifth anniversary programme, "Space for Astronomy" could be recorded at many of the locations we were to visit. In three and a half weeks we were hoping to come back with four and a bit programmes. If that wasn't enough excitement, this was my first trip to America.

We landed at Baltimore Washington International over an hour and a half late. Immigration and customs were, compared to reports from colleagues who had been to the States before, unusually swift. We bundled all the gear into the Hertz courtesy coach, leaving hardly any room for other passengers, and were bussed to the lot to collect our hire cars. With the back seat of the Ford "Aerostar" folded down we shoehorned the boxes into the vehicle and led the way out of the airport and onto the freeway. Before I'd worked out the scale of the map, we'd missed the right turn north onto the Washington Baltimore Beltway.

Within a couple of miles there was another right turn and we picked up the agreed route through town and out to the North. Right on Franklin, the one above Pratt, left up Charles and left again at the one after Thirty-third. There were a lot more Japanese cars than I had expected on the roads. The seemingly endless one-way streets made navigation a bit difficult, and all the cars, be they Japanese, American or even the occasional BMW, had five huge rear brake lights, that created a blinding blaze of red at traffic lights.

As we arrived at our hotel, the "Inn on the Colonnade", bellhops scuttled to assist the instant the handbrake was applied. A spacious, air conditioned, marble floored, colonnaded foyer greeted us. This was a relatively new building with three floors of hotel rooms, above which another five or so floors were condominiums;

the most luxurious of which had, amongst other things, a 100ft balcony, five bedrooms, four and a half bathrooms, two libraries [one fiction and one non-fiction], one-hundred-and-seventy-five-thousand dollars' worth of interior design of your choice, four parking spaces and a Rolls Royce Corniche thrown in all for the asking price of $1,300,000. Cheap at the price but I wondered what half a bathroom looked like?

We had arrived at seven-thirty p.m. Baltimore time, got to the hotel by just before nine p.m., but our body clocks told us it was two a.m., so we had a couple of drinks and a starter from the restaurant menu of shrimps on ice. Shrimps!! In my world they were king size tiger prawns.

On Monday and Tuesday, we recorded at the Space Telescope Science Institute (hereafter "STScI"), a department of the Johns Hopkins University, and probably unique in being a university science faculty entirely devoted to one piece of equipment, the Hubble Space Telescope. We interviewed Eric Chaisson about the telescope's science programmes and the results they were getting back from it, and James Westphal about the Wide Field Planetary camera, one of the five instruments aboard the space craft. We recorded a sequence as their Operations Room took command of the space craft to target a star and then hand it back to the Goddard Space Flight Centre, a NASA establishment just over an hour's drive down the road towards Washington DC and Wednesday's location, where we got their Operations Room to recreate the other half of the star targeting sequence. We successfully interviewed Dr Stephen Maran about the Goddard High Resolution Spectrograph, another of the instruments aboard the HST. All in all, a good start to the trip.

We ate at a Thai restaurant near our hotel in Baltimore on both the Tuesday and Wednesday nights. Just the four men on Tuesday as Angela, having managed to purchase a portable electric typewriter, decided to stay in her room and type up the shot list, and, on Wednesday, just Doug, Angela and I, as Pieter and Patrick were having dinner with Dr Stephen Maran. The portions of food even in Thai restaurants were huge, far too much. We were never able to finish it all, and when the food was placed on the table we were encouraged to

"Enjoy".

On Thursday, we were back at STScI for further interviews, firstly with Duccio Macchetto who gave us an overview of the achievements of Hubble and talked about the possibility of a 'Hubble II', and, secondly, with Dana Berry, who worked wonders in the audio-visual workshop massaging images into wonderful computer graphic representations of what the space craft was doing and seeing. Everybody at STScI seemed totally addicted to the Hubble and the "day of aberration", (when it was discovered that the primary mirror had been made incorrectly), was remembered as a cathartic day in all their lives. Fully grown men were known to have cried.

In the evening we went to the harbour in downtown Baltimore, now a pleasure area and tourist attraction with tall ships tied up along the jetty, shopping malls, pedestrian walkways and restaurants. We chose to eat at a Greek restaurant, Patrick's favourite, and sat outside on the veranda overlooking the harbour. All four of us, poor Angela was still typing, decided on the meze for a starter and selected four different main courses. The meze was more than enough to eat, so I was pleased that I had ordered the "baby" rack of lamb. When it arrived, it was nine chops, not to mention the French fries and side salad!

Saturday, we moved south, flying to Orlando in Florida, where we picked up the prebooked hire cars and drove to Titusville, a small town thirty miles to the east of Orlando. Our base for the next three days was to be "The World Famous" Best Western "Space Shuttle Inn", - their modest appellation not mine. Titusville looked to me to be the America of the road movies. A motel at a major road junction, Interstate ninety-five and State fifty. It was only two stories high with a designated car parking space for every bedroom and surrounded by Diners and Gas Stations. The nearest diner, just twenty yards from the motel was "Miss Diane's Space Shuttle Lounge and Restaurant' offering everything you could eat from the hot buffet for $7.95 and live country and western music Thursday, Friday and Saturday nights. In the lounge everyone was wearing Stetsons, tight jeans, checked or tartan cowboy shirts and cowboy boots. The dancing was "ballroom of romance" crossed with a barn dance - very formal and somewhat stagey. The dance floor had mirrors all down one wall and the dancers watched their own reflected moves. The band - "Kenny Mclaughlan and the Hired Guns" - (The hottest Country and Western Band in Brevard County, as the posters modestly proclaimed) -

played gentle country and western including a large selection of Eagles numbers. We had a few drinks and moved through to the restaurant where we decided to go for the house speciality of prime ribs, an all-inclusive meal of soup, 12oz of steak with potatoes and salad, roll and butter all for $9.95. Huge portions again, and it seemed to be the done thing to leave food on the plate. We moved back to the lounge for a couple of nightcaps. Patrick was a bit "tired and emotional" and put his head down on his folded arms on the polished wooden bar. Further down the bar a stetsoned local asked,

"Is your friend a mahogany inspector?"

Sunday was a day off. Doug, Angela and I went to EPCOT, part of Disney World, where we had morning coffee in France, lunch in Japan, and dinner in the "Coral Reef", the restaurant attached to the Living Seas pavilion. Having chosen from a full and varied fish menu, we ate staring into the aquarium. The evening ended with a magnificent firework, laser and light show that would put the combined efforts of Jean Michelle Jarre and Genesis to shame, and they did that every night throughout the season.

Monday, and we were back to work. We spent the day at the John F. Kennedy Space Center, another NASA establishment built on the swamp lands down the Atlantic coast of Florida just to the north of the Cape Canaveral Air Force Station. We recorded pieces to camera in front of the Shuttle "Discovery", strapped to its rockets on pad 39a, primed and ready to go; more links for the thirty fifth beside a Saturn 5 rocket laid out horizontally; and then recorded inside the Vertical Assembly Building, probably the tallest single-story building in the world and so huge it has its own internal weather system. (The Americans assemble the rocket and space shuttle vertically and wheel it to the pad in that state whereas the Russians build Buran horizontally and stand it upright when it gets to the pad). The Americans used six-hundred gallons of paint just putting the stars and stripes on the side of the building. Way up above, eagles or hawks of some kind circled over the top.

At another part of the Cape, further south in the Air force part, we recorded a piece from Patrick on the launch pad that Alan Shepherd took off from and another piece in front of a Mercury rocket. While we lunched in the NASA canteen, Pieter checked through his shooting list and declared that we were doing very well with much more than half of the day's work done. Unfortunately. he hadn't taken into consideration the unpredictability of the Southern Atlantic States' summer weather and we lost over two hours' shooting time because of a tremendous electrical storm. The Space Center was put on what they called a "phase two" alert, which meant that nobody was allowed out of doors until the Space Center's met office declared the "all clear". We were told that they were on the verge of bringing "Discovery" back from the launch pad to the Vertical Assembly Building, but as quickly as it came, the storm disappeared, the skies cleared, and the damp heat returned.

The following morning, Tuesday, and we were on the move again. The Florida countryside that we drove through on our way to Orlando International Airport was flat and covered in low scrub and I spotted Louisiana Herons, Egrets and a baby Alligator along the way. Motoring in America produced linguistic surprises every time a navigational decision had to be made. We had to select from beltways, turnpikes, interstates, freeways, medians (central reservations) and ramps (exit slipways), reinforcing the adage that Britain and America are separated by a common language.

We changed planes at Dallas Fort Worth, the largest airport in the world in size terms, with four parallel runways. As the passengers "deboarded" the plane, a member of the Delta Airways staff was there to explain where they needed to go to get their connection, in our case, Houston. As we took off from Fort Worth, we saw the classic "Dallas" skyline, the skyscrapers with the reflective glass walls so familiar to anyone who had caught the opening titles of the TV series.

We repeated our well-drilled routine at the Airport. We all mucked in to get the luggage and the kit very close to an exit door, and while Angela, Patrick and I stood guard, Pieter and Doug went off to get the hire cars. Like most airport terminals, this one was completely air-conditioned and non-smoking. I slipped outside for a cigarette only to find that, within the time it took to smoke it, I was drenched in perspiration. When the cars arrived, we loaded up and drove out of Houston to the southeast, and to the "Ramada South Inn" on NASA Road One. It was another classic roadside motel. The decor in the hotel's communal rooms, which they proudly claimed in their brochure to be Olde English, was an appalling mix of styles - part English Tudor wood, part Greek columns and part pseudo mediaeval stone walls. Unusually for a motel, they had their own restaurant where we ate that night. The food quantities, although slightly smaller than in Florida, were still massive. We left the air-conditioned restaurant at ten to ten p.m. to walk across the open courtyard to our rooms and collided with a wall of heat.

We spent Wednesday working at the Johnson Space Center just a couple of miles down the road from the motel. We recorded several pieces to camera in front of a lunar landing module and Apollo 17, both of which are on display in the permanent museum they have at the Space Center. We also recorded a piece to camera inside Mission Control, not through the observation glass, but on the floor right next to the flight director's console.

It had taken a bit of prising out of him, but we had discovered that it was Doug's birthday on that Wednesday in August. While Angela and I were waiting at Houston airport the day before for Pieter and Doug to pick up the hire cars, we'd found, in a local tourist guidebook, a restaurant just down the road from our motel. We decided to treat Doug to dinner.

The "Crazy Cajun Food Factory" was a large wooden shack with a corrugated iron roof. Neon "Bud Light" adverts hung from the ceiling. The tables, capable of seating eight, were covered in red and white checked plastic tablecloths. There were jam jars for glasses and kitchen roll for napkins. We sat on bench seats. The restaurant was packed, bustling and noisy and we were lucky to get a table. Our waitress was "Berlie the Girlie", or so her lapel badge told us. While we were waiting for the starters, a Steamed Boudan (a spicy sausage) plus a side order of Sauteed 'Gator (alligator), we were each given a couple of spoonfuls of "Aint Maudies Red Beans" and rice, and a Hush Puppy (a croquet of mashed, spiced chicken). When we'd finished the starters, we were given samplers of Chicken and Sausage Gumbo and Shrimp Etoufee; for the main course Patrick and I went for Panee Combo (Shrimp, Scallops, Fish fillet, Crab fingers, Oysters, Smothered Taters and Hush Puppies all lightly battered, and pan fried in butter). As the menu said, *"it'll make you get down on the floor and roll"*. Angela, Doug and Pieter went for the eight-way Cajun Shrimp Combo - fried shrimp, sauteed shrimp, Cajun boiled shrimp, New Orleans B-B-Q shrimp, on special tonight. Cajun, Country and Western, and Blue Grass music tapes played in the background, much to Patrick's discomfort.

It turned out that "Berlie the Girlie" was from New York. She was outrageously upfront; slim, wide mouthed, hair constantly being tossed to one side,

"How you doin?",

"Here you go, you guys",

which seemed to cover all ages and sexes.

"That's neat",

"You're welcome",

"You mean you wanna whole bottle of wine?".

The shotgun patter was relentless, but it made for an unforgettable evening.

Thursday saw us on the move again. We left the "Ramada" after a reasonably early breakfast and drove right through downtown Houston to the International Airport on the north side of town - we had arrived at Hobby Airport in the southeast. The check in, though claimed to be kerbside, wasn't really and we got stung $150 for excess baggage and I had to shuffle the gear around to get each piece under 100lbs.

We flew into Los Angeles over fifty to sixty miles of the giant computer logic board of Californian suburbia that stretches from San Bernardino in the east, over Riverside, Ontario, West Covina, Monterey Park and Culver City to Los Angeles International on the west coast. All the main roads at right angles to each other and the blocks of identical houses with their drives reaching out to the road looked like massive integrated circuit boards.

We went through the usual routine of getting the kit from the carousel onto the trolleys and to the car and drove out to the northeast, past the Los Angeles Dodgers baseball stadium, to Pasadena, where we were to overnight at the Travelodge Pasadena Central on East Colorado Boulevard. As we had arrived at the hotel mid-afternoon, Doug and Angela decided to complete the set by going to Disney Land at Anaheim in Southeastern Los Angeles. I had spotted an Apple Dealer two doors down the road and, as I was having trouble with the Mac Portable's keyboard, I declined Disney Land in favour of trying to get it sorted.

Patrick, Pieter and I ate out that night at the nearby Ocean Coral Mandarin restaurant. It all tasted very good, but we had to leave half of what we ordered as the portions were back to massive again. I somehow thought that the West Coast would have a slightly better attitude to food. We were offered doggy bags but declined, it being sometime before I would be back home with my dogs.

The Pasadena Travelodge is the first motel where we couldn't get breakfast within twenty yards of our rooms. They offered instant coffee and a Danish if you were early enough, and I wasn't. I'd become very used to American breakfasts. Always instant service of a glass of iced water, eggs any way you want 'em, ham, grits, waffles and syrup, and bacon - always streaky, always very crispy – cremated really.

So, Friday morning we arrived at the Jet Propulsion Laboratory (JPL) at eight thirty a.m., sans breakfast for all of us except Doug who had got up early and gone to Denny's, one of a chain of all-day diners. We recorded an interview about the Wide Field Planetary camera mk2 and shot cutaways of the engineers constructing the instrument that was to be taken up by a Shuttle to the Hubble Space Telescope, to replace the one that was there. Patrick did pieces to camera in front of full-size models of the Voyager and Galileo space crafts, all black and gold, and then we interviewed Ellen Stofan, in front of a mock-up of the Magellan probe that was circling Venus. It was the most glamorously decorated Space Craft I'd ever seen, decked out in white and gold. It only needed a candelabra to look like Liberace's piano. We also recorded a piece to camera in the Deep Space Network control room which, at the time we were there, has been constantly sending and receiving signals from the two Voyager space probes for ten years or more.

We finished recording around five p.m.. Before leaving for the three-hour drive to Escondido, we decided to grab a bite and a drink. The first place we came to, was a "Drive In" McDonalds, where we pulled up in front of a menu board. After about twenty seconds a disembodied voice, emanating from the centre of the menu asked what we wanted to order. Doug spluttered out "two orange juices and a portion of MacNuggets". We then eased the car forward five yards to a booth where a 'human' took our money, and then forward another five yards where an arm poked out of a window with our goodies in a bag. We then drove round into a car parking space and drank our drink and ate our chicken nuggets.

The journey south, out of the flat Los Angeles sprawl that is surrounded by hazy, barren, red and orange mountains, took us down one-hundred-and-twenty miles of interstate freeway - six lanes, sometimes eight, of solid fifty mile-an-hour traffic in each direction - where were all these people going?

Saturday, and we were away by eight a.m. for the hour-long drive up Mount Palomar where we had to shoot the interior of the two-hundred-inch reflector telescope, the dome of which is some one-hundred-and-thirty feet high. With three six-hundred-watt lamps? I managed to borrow four working lights from the observatory staff which, with 9 dB's of gain in the camera, produced acceptable picture quality. The observatory staff were all very welcoming and helpful, and we were treated to lunch and dinner at "the monastery", the residence available to visiting astronomers. When we got back to Escondido, at about nine p.m., I gave the bar a miss, tidied up the gear and attempted an early night.

I slept solidly until seven a.m., woke slowly, had a gentle breakfast at TGI's next door to our motel, and 'veged out' in front of the Disney channel for an hour and then packed the gear. We set off up the San Diego freeway to Los Angeles at about one p.m.. We had a wonderfully hassle-free check in and, as Pieter had managed to negotiate the upgrade from steerage to Ambassador class, we were invited into the Ambassador Club lounge, a haven away from the crowds. The flight was very comfortable, with only six seats across the width of the wide-bodied Lockeed TriStar.

We landed at Honolulu, on the island of Oahu, at nine-forty p.m. Hawaiian time, (twelve-forty p.m. Los Angeles time). We shoe-horned the equipment and our personal luggage into the courtesy coach and were bussed the five-minute ride to our accommodation, the Plaza Hotel, Honolulu International Airport, 3253 n. Nimitz highway. All our rooms were in a block which had been built right underneath the highway. I guess we all thought that at night it would be reasonably quiet, nobody in their right mind would build a bedroom block that close to a major road. It proved to be as peaceful and comfortable as spending the night under Hammersmith flyover in a tent.

It was the noisiest, hottest and most expensive place we stayed throughout the entire trip. None of us got more than a couple of hours' sleep.

Not surprising then, that we awoke very tired and more than a bit ratty. We got away by seven-thirty a.m. to catch the nine a.m. Aloha flight to Hilo on big island, Hawaii. We managed to get the gear booked on without incurring excess baggage charges, a constant source of worry to Pieter as it could add considerably to the programme budget. We were met at Hilo airport by Malcolm Smith from the British joint Astronomy Council, the administrative body that organises the running of the United Kingdom Infrared Telescope (UKIRT) and James Clerk Maxwell Telescope (JCMT) up the mountain. The "serious" truck we had ordered was not big enough, we'd been given an Isuzu Trooper, so we loaded in as much as we could and then Pieter took Doug off to get a second vehicle while Angela, Patrick and I took a taxi to the Joint Astronomy Council offices to register and to meet up with them. Once signed on, we drove out of Hilo, west along the saddle road which runs in the valley between the two mountains of Mauna Kea and Mauna Loa, and climbed the nine-thousand feet to Hale Pahaku, the accommodation and canteen block for all the resident astronomers working up the mountain. It was quite refreshing to think that we would be here for a week and could unpack properly.

Pieter's original intention was that we should then have the afternoon off to acclimatise but it had become apparent that the only time we could interview Jerry Nelson, the man who first came up with the idea of putting thirty-six hexagonal mirrors together to form the ten-metre Keck Telescope, was that afternoon. So, we lunched rapidly on sausage and chips, loaded up the trucks and went on up to 13,650 feet to the Keck telescope to do the interview. I felt a little lightheaded - Doug and Angela felt a little worse. Pieter seemed OK but Patrick was quite wobbly, although he was very reluctant to admit it. We shot the single, the two over shoulder two shots with Jerry Nelson, and left Patrick's close-up until another day and came down to Hale Pahaku for supper - Hawaiian short ribs and rice and peas. The standard of cooking was good transport cafe. I retired to my room, was asleep by eight-thirty p.m. and slept solidly for nine hours.

The following morning, I awoke before the six a.m. alarm I had set and looked out of my bedroom window and saw just the top of Mauna Loa peeping out from a sea of cloud. We breakfasted at seven a.m.. I had the scrambled eggs, the same frazzled streaky bacon that we have become accustomed to across the whole of America and do-it-yourself toast and honey. We set up in the library at Hale Pahaku to interview Ed Stone about the Keck. Angela and Patrick were not feeling too good, so after the interview Doug, Pieter and I went to the summit to shoot wide angles of the exteriors of all the telescopes and Malcolm Smith, whom we were to interview in the afternoon about JCMT and UKIRT, said he would bring the others up after lunch.

In a small hut outside UKIRT, the catering people from Hale Pahaku provided lunch at the summit. We sat outside looking down on the clouds and the island of Maui away to the west, eating veal cutlets with rice and green beans. Douglas Adams got it wrong. This, was the "Restaurant at the end of the Universe"!

Hale Pahaku phoned the summit to say that Angela was feeling worse and that they had advised her that she should return to sea level for medical attention. Pieter decided that no further risks should be taken, and she should return home. We interviewed Malcolm, out on the cinder and ash from the volcano, with the two telescopes for which he was responsible in the background. Moving about at this altitude was exhausting, - there is only thirty-nine percent of the oxygen you get at sea level - so Doug and I took everything quite slowly, deliberately considering every move to ensure that we had everything we needed to do the job, and no more. About four p.m. Pieter called it a day, feeling that we had been at the summit long enough for one day, and we returned to Hale Pahaku.

The rooms were spartan, not unlike a university hall of residence, but at least there was a desk large enough to put the "Mac" on so I could keep the diary up to date. Supper that evening was fish, chips, peas and carrots. The fish was Marlin, a sort of cross between shark and tuna, the carrot old and woody and virtually inedible. The four of us played doubles at snooker - if nothing else it produced a few laughs - and I retired to bed at nine-thirty p.m..

I arose very early Wednesday morning having hardly slept at all. I had woken up many times during the night worrying about the shape of the baggage reclaim carousels at Gatwick and having had a row with the airport manager because our equipment boxes were bashed about. I think I might have had a slight "altitude problem"!

We went up the mountain that morning at eight a.m., to record some general views as the weather was producing better pictures in the mornings than the afternoons. We shot wide angles of the telescopes set against the backgrounds of the island of Maui and the still active volcano of Mauna Loa. We were on Mauna Kea and I was at a loss as to how they could say that of two volcanoes thirty miles apart one was extinct and the other not.

After lunch at the "Restaurant at the end of the Universe" we shot inside the Keck. When completed, (it now is of course, as is Keck 2), this telescope will be the world's largest and most powerful for optical and infrared astronomy. In addition to its size, it is unique in design. It will hold thirty-six hexagonal mirrored segments, each about six feet across, in a honeycomb array that functions as if it were a single mirror. The unorthodox, segmented mirror, equivalent in area to a single mirror thirty-three feet across, avoids the difficulties of shaping and mounting a large piece of glass. With increasing size, a large glass mirror eventually deforms and loses the precise curvature needed to focus starlight. Actuators - precision, motor driven screws that drive a hydraulic lever - create the microscopic motions that keep each segment aligned with its neighbour. Capable of repositioning segments by less than a millionth of an inch, one-hundred-and-eight actuators operate under computer control to maintain the mirror arrays light-focussing shape. Current astronomical thinking puts the farthest object so far recorded at between thirteen and sixteen thousand million light years away, which means that the image as recorded is an ancient snapshot of what happened that many thousands of million years ago. The greater the light collecting power of the telescope, the fainter the image it can record and so, by reaching deeper into the universe, the Keck will reach further back in time and observers hope that they will discover the very beginnings of the universe.

Mauna Kea, besides being the name of the highest part of the volcano, is also the collective name of a whole series of cinder cones, each of which has been named. From what appeared to be the third highest cone, Pu'u Poli'ahu, there was a wonderful panoramic view of all the telescopes, and a wonderful location to do an opening piece to camera. Two things had so far conspired to prevent us recording this piece. One the shot is back lit, very, until well after two p.m., and two, the weather clamped down about lunchtime and we could hardly see the telescopes for cloud. So, we took the decision to come off the summit for an early supper with the intention to return afterwards to get the evening light. We left Hale Pahaku at five-forty-five p.m. and drove up towards the summit. As we came up out of the clouds it snowed. I made a note in my diary,

"August 29th, 1991, Hawaii - snow - must have a word with my travel agent".

We returned to base camp for coffee and two games of snooker, which Doug and I won, to lead three to one in the series.

Friday morning, we left at seven a.m. in the hope of better weather. We drove up through the clouds to the top of the cinder cone, Pu'u Poli'ahu, that overlooked the ridge with most of the telescopes on and stepped out of the trucks and into a howling gale. Even with anoraks and hats we found it extremely cold, but by leaving Patrick in the truck until the last possible moment and by using the vehicles as windbreaks, we managed to do all the pieces to camera that Pieter had planned from that location. Everything was usable if the weather did not improve, but good they were not. We got down to JCMT as quickly as possible and went inside and made coffee. We used the rest of the morning to record some detail of the instrumentation on the bottom of the telescope and, after lunch, as the weather had lifted slightly, we returned to our vantage point on Pu'u Poli'ahu and repeated the pieces shot earlier. Then we went back to the telescope and interviewed Richard Wade about JCMT and its achievements. Pieter was spending part of the evenings reviewing the tapes and logging the shots and he said that if everything looked and sounded OK, we could be finished a day ahead of schedule.

We breakfasted at Hale Pahaku for the last time at around seven-thirty a.m. and then gently packed the trucks with our personal luggage and the equipment. Even at nine-thousand feet we quickly ran out of puff carrying 100lb cases of kit. We drove off the mountain, winding our way down to the saddle road where we turned left and back into Hilo, a day earlier than scheduled. Pieter had managed to get us booked into the Hawaii Naniloa hotel for an extra night. The hotel was a wonderful breath of comfort and my room on the eighth floor looked out over Kuhio Bay and on up the centre of the island to the top of Mauna Kea, where, when the cloud cleared and the sun shone, I could see the telescope domes glistening white on the skyline.

We decided to spend the rest of the afternoon in the Hawaii Volcanoes National Park where we drove round the summit caldera of Kilauea, which is two and a half miles long, two miles wide and four-hundred feet deep. Everywhere we went steam seemed to be venting from cracks in the earth. Even I, with my almost extinct sense of smell, was able to detect the odour of sulphur. Collapses that are smaller than the summit Caldera, are known as pit craters. The upper reaches of Kilauea's rift zone are dotted with these depressions, giving the name "Chain of Craters Road" to the road that leads to the sea. The road was blocked by lava flows in 1986, reopened and blocked in 1987, reopened and blocked again in January 1990. We decided to drive down "Chain of Craters Road" to the blockage. The twenty-three-mile journey winds off the mountain down to the sea, where sixty to seventy cars were already parked. At the end of the queue the road disappears under a swathe of shiny black lava, looking as if someone had poured an immense bowl of crunchy, brittle, black meringue from the top of the mountain away to our left. More than a mile away, across this moonscape, dotted with scrambling humans picking their way over the lava between orange and white marker cones, great clouds of steam billowed up from the water's edge. For forty-five minutes we picked our way towards the steam clouds, between piles of 'a'a lava that looks and feels like clinker, and across pahoehoe lava, the smooth billowy rope swirls that occasionally crack under foot, leaving paths of broken black ceramic tiles. The marked route took us forty yards past the steam, so that when we reached the edge of the cliff and looked back, we could see red hot molten lava pouring into the sea from under the path we had walked over. It was awesome to realise just how fragile and volatile this Earth still is.

Monday morning was spent idling in the sun, out on the hotel lawns overlooking the bay, and in the afternoon, we went shopping for souvenirs, but after three weeks everyone now just wanted to get back home.

The flight into Honolulu with Aloha Airlines was fine and on time, and we learned that, from here on, we were upgraded to Ambassador Class all the way back to Gatwick, and, even better, we could clear American customs with the equipment at Honolulu and check it right through. That was the good news. The bad news was that the incoming flight was an hour and a half late. The next stage of the journey, via Los Angeles, was to St. Louis, where we were scheduled to have a two and a half hour wait for the connecting flight for the final leg back to Gatwick. This meant that, if they didn't turn the plane round in less than an hour, we would have zero time to change planes in St. Louis. We started researching when the next flight out of St. Louis was and hoping they ran at least a daily service. We finally took off at one-fifteen a.m., two hours and twenty minutes late still not knowing if we would make the connection. When we landed at Los

Angeles, we were all told to get off the plane and announcements would be made as to further routings. Fortunately, TWA decided to originate the Gatwick flight from LA and, within twenty minutes we were back on a different plane that would touch down in St. Louis but was going right through. For a few seconds Doug and I worried about whether the equipment had transferred, but very quickly decided that somebody else could sort that out if it all went wrong, we were on our way home.

We touched down in the UK at seven-twenty a.m. Thursday morning, thirty-seven hours after I last saw a bed. We waited at the carousels for the kit and, much to our surprise, everything appeared and none of it was damaged. The runabout from Television OB's base at Kendal Avenue turned up on time and we were back there by nine-thirty a.m.

First thing Sunday morning I went to Bolton to start work on a Children's drama.

Chapter 9
Camping, Canal Boats, Caravans and Cottages

Many times, an Outside Broadcast would require the crew to stay away from home overnight, or more often, many nights. The responsibility to find suitable, and affordable, accommodation was ours. We were paid a twenty-four-hour allowance to cover accommodation and a supplement to cover the extra cost of a breakfast, a lunch & dinner bought in restaurants and cafés. For most great sporting events, choice was often limited as the fans who attended had, often, booked their accommodation at least a year in advance. We would be told for certain about three weeks in advance, when the crew rotas were published. Mostly, we tried to find accommodation within a fifteen-mile radius of the event, which for cricket at say, Edgbaston, Trent Bridge or Old Trafford wasn't too difficult.

The Open Golf Tournaments were much harder. The event had to take place on a links course, which meant it was on the coast, and the search area inevitably halved, except for Royal St. Georges at Sandwich that offered only a forty-five-degree wedge of East Kent in which to find somewhere to lay one's head. For the Open in 1981, the first to be held in Sandwich since 1949, we had to get inventive. Driving in was a non-starter as the queue of cars would tail back for miles. It didn't matter that much to most of the spectators if they were half an hour later than they had hoped, but for the entire television production team and crew, they had to be in well before the first tee-off time. We had to be close enough to walk in or, as some of the crew did, cycle in. They secured accommodation in Canterbury and brought bicycles in or on their cars. Early in the morning, their cars left in their hotel car park, they rode the fifteen miles into the golf course. In my case, a colleague had a small campervan and had secured a pitch at a camp site just a few hundred yards west of Sandwich village, which he invited me to share. When asked where we were staying, we just replied,

"The Transit Motel".

Because of the nature of the hours we had to do, Bed and Breakfast establishments were too restrictive. Breakfast at nine a.m., in by ten thirty p.m., and queuing for the bathroom, just doesn't work. Hotels that could provide *en suite* rooms, early breakfasts and a night porter were often more expensive than our allowance could stretch to. But I can never forget the strangest B&B set up I ever experienced. We were at the Silverstone Motor Racing Circuit in Northamptonshire for the 1965 British Grand Prix. Accommodation was extremely difficult to find, but Steve Chilver managed to find four rooms for Frank Hudson, Stan Bale, himself and I. It was in a vicarage. Only there weren't enough rooms, so Stan Bale and I were sent to the private homes of two of the parishioners who had a 'made up' spare room.

Presumably, there was some financial remuneration for them, but we never found out. However, there was room for everybody at dinner, around a long refectory table seating twenty people, with the Vicar at the head of the table in an armchair with a high back more akin to an Archbishop's throne. While young ladies, presumably from the village, served the guests, which consisted mostly of the Ferrari F1 team, including the driver Lorenzo Bandini, the Vicar gently succumbed to the pleasures of alcohol. (A few weeks later, there was an article about the place in one of the 'red tops'). Also memorable was the informality of an F1 Grand Prix at that time. I wandered around the paddock taking photos of the cars and drivers. Amongst many, I have pictures of Jim Clark and Lorenzo Bandini, including one where he is sitting in the cockpit of his Ferrari, casually reading a magazine while a Dunlop engineer checks tyre pressures. (For motor racing fans, Clark won, Graham Hill came second, John Surtees third and Lorenzo Bandini retired on lap two).

Occasionally, if the weather was set to be fair, we camped.

August 1977, and the crew I was on, were to record a 'Songs of Praise' in Margate. We had a Camera Supervisor, Ian Gibb, on attachment from Television Studios, who, when it was suggested we camped for the one night we had to be away, leapt at the chance, saying that he had a very large frame tent, with a sewn in plastic ground sheet that would sleep all four of us. He could also supply four airbeds, all we had to do was bring a sleeping bag. We arrived at the church in Margate after lunch to install the cameras and sound equipment, followed by the usual production facilities check. We then headed off to the camp site, helped Ian with putting up the tent, inflated our airbeds and laid out our sleeping bags. After a trip to the communal toilet block for a freshen up, we went off to a local hostelry for dinner and a few drinks. During the evening, there was an unexpected thunderstorm, which hung around in the area almost until closing time. It had blown over by the time we walked back to the camp site. My colleague Graham Goldston unzipped the doorway of the tent and launched himself on to his airbed, causing a tidal wave that washed over everybody else's bedding. The tent had leaked extensively, and the plastic groundsheet, with its three-inch-high walls, had formed a shallow swimming pool. A very damp and uncomfortable night was had by all.

When not gainfully employed by the BBC, the hobbies and interests of O.B. staff were many and varied, so when the opportunity to combine work and an extra curricula passion is offered, it is snapped up. Dave Bevan, the Sound Supervisor allocated to the third test between England and the West Indies that was held at Old Trafford, Manchester in July 1976, was looking for colleagues to join him in hiring a canal boat for the seven-night stay. Canal boats were his passion. Having gained a reputation as someone who was happy to cook, Dave put the idea to me and the rest of the camera crew. I can't remember who the fourth shipmate was, but Graham Goldston was certainly part of the company. We boarded the canal boat at Preston Brook on the Bridgewater Canal, which is a sixty-five km canal stretching from Runcorn to Leigh, passing through Manchester. Constructed over two-hundred and fifty years ago by the Duke of Bridgewater, it is the first true canal in England. Built at one level, its route follows the contours of the land to avoid the use of locks and includes the well-known "Barton Swing Aqueduct" which passes over the Manchester Ship Canal. Being the Summer, we were told that we couldn't moor in the same place for more than two nights, so, to have cars for the morning drive into Old Trafford, two cars would go ahead to our next planned stop with one car returning to the boat. Then we would cruise north towards Manchester while I prepared food. First thing the next morning, someone would take the driver of the car left behind, back to where it had been parked, to bring up the transport for the day's drive to work.

Currently in the seventies, five-day cricket test matches did not play on Sundays. So, we were joined by four or five other members of the crew for a day's canal boating. We went into Manchester, passed a tall, grey and dirty industrial block situated on a long bend of the canal. Rounding the corner, we noticed the name on the side and up near the top of the building. "Kelloggs". We took the boat over the Barton Swing Aqueduct, and, down and back up, the Anderton lift. A relaxing journey through some of Britain's industrial heritage. One evening, after eating, and with the sun having just set, Graham was trying to take some photos of his shipmates, sitting at the stern. Bemoaning the lack of adequate light, Graham said,

"I could really do with a flash".

Almost instantly, out of a cloudless sky came one single bolt of lightning.

No one spoke for quite a while.

The following year we were back in the same area for the 1977 Grand National at Aintree Racecourse and, having enjoyed the canal boating experience the previous year, we again booked a canal boat out of Preston Brook. Being March, it was a lot colder, but on the upside, we could stay in one place for the duration. Once we'd settled on a suitable mooring, we were soon entertained for twenty minutes by a hyper-active Kingfisher that was flying up and down the opposite bank. You don't see that in many B&Bs.

On the Thursday evening, the four shipmates, engineer Pete Lester, who'd brought his banjo with him, and cameramen Keith Gibson, Robin Sutherland, who had just returned from a three week holiday in Nepal and was sporting a fez, and I invited producer Ricky Tilling, and two production secretaries to join us for dinner on the canal boat. An opportunity they jumped at. I can't remember exactly what we had as a main course, but I remember the starter, and that we finished with cheese. It's hard to believe that a boiled egg covered in mayonnaise, served on a lettuce leaf, used to be offered as a starter in restaurants in the Seventies, but then so did a glass of tomato juice So, I made egg mayonnaise – how could I forget – it took me almost an hour to get the mayo to emulsify.

Thinking back, the main course was probably a dish I did quite a few times when we self-catered, because a lot of the preparation could be done ahead. Roast a chicken the day before, allow it to cool and refrigerate. The following day get someone to strip all the meat off the chicken carcass into bite-sized pieces. Meanwhile make a large saucepan of *"Ratatouille"*, add a slug of sherry, add the chicken and allow to warm through, take off the heat and add cream, salt and a fair amount of black pepper. Serve with rice, eat with a fork. I didn't invent it, nor did I name it, because today it would be very non-PC. It was called *"Poulet Spastique"*.

It was about four a.m. when the second bottle of port ran out. We were exhausted from laughing, particularly at Robin, who had tried to play George Formby songs on Pete's banjo while wearing his fez.

Later that morning, I was on my rostrum, pleased to have the camera as support when Cliff Morgan, the Welsh Rugby International, and then, Head of BBC Outside Broadcasts, brought Des Lynam up the ladder and onto the rostrum. Cliff, always friendly and approachable, slapped me on the back, and asked how I was.

"Fine," I lied.

Des was there to do his television screen test, having so far worked as a radio journalist and presenter since 1968. He got the job.

The golf courses at Gleneagles Hotel in the Perthshire countryside are beautiful, peaceful and uplifting places to spend time. Around 1975/76; it could quite easily have been both and I've merged the memories into one trip. We were there for a couple of weeks to cover a Professional Golf Tournament and the following week, a USA v GB Pro-Am tournament. We chose to self-cater in caravans on a site just outside of Crief. As usual we brought with us non-perishable supplies and a couple of days' worth of edible provisions, to tide us over until we'd found the local suppliers. High up on the list of consumable non-perishables was two cases of Calvet "Vieux Bordeaux", bought from the much-missed Augustus Barnett's for 49p a bottle. Even back then, an extremely pleasant wine at an amazingly reasonable price.

As to the golf, (having interrogated Google and the BBC Genome project), I believe in the first week, it was the Double Diamond Golf Classic which involved a tournament between eight teams, the four home nations, Continental Europe, the United States, Australasia and the Rest of the World. Some of the top golfers of that era took part, including Tony Jacklin, Brian Barnes, Dai Rees, Christy O'Connor Snr, Seve Ballesteros, Johnny Miller, Bob Charles, Gary Player. Nowhere near as much pressure as a Major, the players enjoyed themselves and it was a pleasure to watch.

The second week was even more fun, an International Pro Celebrity tournament entitled "The Bing Crosby Cup", GB v USA, played between well-known names from the world of show business led by a couple of professional golfers, Johnny Miller for the USA and Tony Jacklin for the Great Britain team. We recorded eight matches. I suspect they were played over nine holes, one in the morning, and one in the afternoon, where the pro golfer paired with a different celebrity for each match. Peter Alliss walked the course with the players having a chat between strokes. The programmes went out in January 1977. The stars included amongst others, Bing Crosby, Burt Lancaster, Dick Martin, Admiral Alan Shepard on the USA team and Sean Connery, Jimmy Tarbuck, Jackie Stewart, Henry Cooper, James Hunt, Bruce Forsyth for the Brits. We were extremely fortunate to see that many celebrities all together in the same place.

But it wasn't all work and no play for the happy campers. We booked tickets one evening at a theatre with a pre-show dinner at the attached restaurant, near Strathallan. I cannot recall much about the food, other than the starter, which was half a stuffed green pepper that repeated on us all for most of the next day. (I've learnt since that a green pepper is an unripe red pepper, which probably explains the gastric problem). The entertainment in the theatre was the Scottish folk / comedy duo, Robin Hall and Jimmie MacGregor. I know we all had a great evening even if I can't remember any of the music or most of the jokes. But the one funny story they told that I do remember, was when they were touring with Jimmy Shand and his Band. Apparently, Jimmy liked a "bevvie" or two after a concert but was always up bright and early the next day for a full breakfast. On this particular morning he ordered his usual fruit juice, porridge, with salt not sugar, a full Scottish cooked breakfast, sausage, bacon, eggs, mushrooms, black pudding and grilled tomatoes followed by white toast, butter and honey. As he was finishing his cooked breakfast, the toast arrived but without butter or honey. He caught the waitress's eye and asked for the butter and honey. Minutes later she returned with a dish of butter,

"And the honey?" he said.

The waitress came back with one of the little catering jars of honey, about an inch and a half tall and even smaller in diameter.

"Thank you," he said, "I see the hotel has a bee".

Another unpressurised and enjoyable golf show that we recorded was "A Round with Alliss". A series of programmes in which Peter Alliss played nine holes of golf with a range of guests from the world of sport and showbusiness, at different courses around the country. I remember the series we recorded at the Trevose Golf & Country Club, Constantine Bay, near Padstow, Cornwall. I cannot recall all the guests that Peter interviewed out on the course, but Jimmy Hill the former Fulham player, Coventry City manager and Match of the Day presenter was one, and Alec Bedser, the England cricketer who took one-hundred-and-four wickets against Australia was another.

It was the accommodation and catering arrangements that were different and probably unique. The golf club had a terraced row of lodges out on the course where we slept, and we ate in the clubhouse restaurant. Very good meals and a great wine cellar. So much so that one evening I couldn't resist a bottle of Chateau Margaux 1970 at a steal of a price of £25, about £100 in today's money. You probably won't find a bottle retail today for less than £300 and about a grand in a smart restaurant.

***

If we were required to stay in one place for more than a week, it was cottages that we preferred to rent. We could have a bedroom each, come and go as we pleased, make tea or coffee whenever, have friends, colleagues and loved ones down for weekends and invite cast and other crew to dinner.

We had a cottage near Glamis Castle for the recording of Shakespeare's "As You Like It" and, amongst others, we had James Bolam, who played Touchstone, for dinner one evening. I did ask Helen Mirren, but she declined.

Having actors for dinner didn't happen too often, it was mostly fellow crew members who were only too glad to get out of their hotels. But I do remember the cottage we rented near Burwash, East Sussex, while recording "Gentle Folk". In the lounge there was a very comfortable, bottle green velvet covered, wing-back armchair, so comfortable that Trevor and I used to take it in turns to sit in it. One evening we invited some of the cast in for a drink and a chat and the actor Christopher Strauli turned up in a bottle green velvet suit, sat in that chair and virtually disappeared.

For the two-week recording of "Heart Attack Hotel", Johnny Johnson and I rented a cottage in Llanthony, in the

Vale of Ewyas, a deep and long valley with glacial origins within the Black Mountains in Wales, seven miles north of Abergavenny and within the eastern section of the Brecon Beacons National Park. The village is on an unclassified road leading northward to Hay-on-Wye, where our location was. The cottage was beautifully situated just across the road from Llanthony Priory and the Llanthony Priory Hotel, which, I checked recently, has no televisions in the rooms, no mobile phone signal, and for stargazers, no light pollution. On the drive up the unclassified road, over the mountains to Hay, we often disturbed a Buzzard feeding on roadkill.

We had the middle weekend off during the shoot, so we invited two of the cast, Hugh Fraser and Amanda Hillwood, to Sunday Lunch. Very pleasant.

Over the years recording dramas around the country, we've stayed in classic black and white timbered houses in Herefordshire, Georgian townhouses in lovely villages like Cranbrook in Kent and stone cottages in the Test Valley, but my favourite was probably the one I rented for "Blott on the Landscape", on a hill over-looking Chew Valley Lake.

Chapter 10
One Shot at a Time

It was becoming clear that, with directors wanting to shoot dramas with one camera, the LPU was too big and had too many staff with it, to continue. For drama, one cameraman, one sound supervisor, one sound assistant, an engineer to control camera technical quality and run the tape recorder, and a lighting engineer would be the basic requirement. Add a rigger driver/film grip to assist with camera dollies and drive a small truck with seating for four and off you go. Fortunately, we already had SCU4.

With camera technology improving to the point where broadcast quality cameras had interchangeable backs, offering cable output to a portable recorder or cable connection to a control box in a mobile control room as one option, or a dockable tape recorder as another, and the fact that cameramen were now allowed to do simple lighting, meant documentary style programmes and interviews could be done with a crew of two. So, a small number of Portable Single Camera units were put together with a camera, lightweight tripod, a small three lamp lighting kit, and an assortment of microphones, all packed into a Renault 'Espace'.

We used a PSC for several "Sky at Night" location shoots in the UK, including Jodrell Bank and twice to Patrick's house in Selsey, but I also did a little 'goose chasing' for Sports Department.

"Hurry up and get to Newcastle Football ground".

"OK we're here. What next?"

"We wait and see if the manager turns up."

Apart from one or two memorable occasions, I hated it.

After Bob Champion and his horse Aldaniti won the 1981 Grand National, "racing's greatest fairy-tale", the jockey founded The Bob Champion Cancer Trust in 1983. His triumph, while recovering from cancer, was made into the film "Champions", with the actor John Hurt portraying Bob Champion. To publicise the Cancer Trust, John Hurt rode Aldaniti, in short stages, from its stables to Aintree. I was sent to cover an interview somewhere in the Midlands. At that time, I was a smoker, (I've given up now - three-fifteen p.m. on 17th October 1993 – not that it bothers me) and I lit up a Gauloises. Within seconds, John Hurt came up to me and said,

"Would you mind if I had one of those".

Obviously, I didn't say no.

In 1986, Sports Department were to cover the European Athletics Championships to be held in Stuttgart, West Germany, and they wanted some slow-motion close-up shots of athletes in action for the opening title sequence. Material shot at the usual 25 frames per second when slowed down to, say 5fps, were very jerky and the viewer notices every step. A super "slo-mo" camera and recorder, which recorded material at 125fps, and could be slowed to 25fps allowing very smooth slow-motion pictures, had just been built, and was to be at an athletics event at the Olympic Stadium in West Berlin, then in East Germany. I, along with Assistant Sports Producer Chris Lewis, (aka The Ginger Tom – he had ginger hair and you can imagine the rest) were to fly to Berlin and meet up with the equipment at the infamous Stadium, built for the 1936 Olympics, which the Nazis used for their "Aryan" propaganda, which was upset by the four gold medals won by Jesse Owens, the black athlete from the USA.

I met with Chris at his local "watering hole" in Twickenham for lunch on a Thursday, before the late afternoon flight to Berlin. On our arrival, we presumably got a taxi to our hotel, I have absolutely no memory of the journey, or of which hotel or where it was. We then went out for a few (more) drinks and some food. The following morning, we went to the "Olympiastadion" to get a feel for the place and meet with the crew of "super slo-mo". Having excerpts from the films made by Leni Riefenstahl during the 1936 Games running through my mind - they made movie history for being highly sophisticated and technologically pioneering works, as well as for their highly dubious ideological slant - along with the foreboding effect of the Germanic-style monumental architecture, the experience was bone-chilling.

We met up with the crew, a couple of technical guys, a recording engineer and a camera assistant to help me. Despite using my minimal schoolboy German language skills to break the ice, it was clear that the female camera assistant resented my being there, believing she was quite capable of getting the shots and saw no reason to fly in a cameraman from the UK.

Anyway, we were not due to record any shots until Saturday, so we left hoping feelings would have softened by then. Chris suggested we go to Checkpoint Charlie and have a look round the Museum named after the famous crossing point on the Berlin Wall and created to document the so-called "best border security system in the world" (in the words of East German General Heinz Hoffmann). On display were the photos and related documents of successful escape attempts from East Germany, together with some of the escape apparatus. All quite moving. Chris then suggested we pop over into East Berlin, just to see the difference.

So, we joined the line, found out that we had to exchange at least 10DM into East German Marks, getting ten for one in return. It was quite scary being eyed up and down by the East German soldiers in a cubicle with a mirror behind me, but they let us both through. Stepping out into the light, the first impression was of dark grey, almost black tenement blocks and there being nobody about. We wandered aimlessly for a bit, being a spur of the moment decision we didn't have a map, until we stumbled onto a distinctly commercial street where the hospitality industry was alive and kicking. We both felt it was time for a drink and went into a bar that was offering Champagne by the bottle at 20D, i.e., one tenth of the East German money that we couldn't exchange back into West

German currency on our return. When we had finished our fizz, we left a healthy 5D tip and went in search of the most expensive lunch we could find. The details escape me, but we had three courses with wine, and we were there for quite a long time. We then went to see the Brandenburg Gate from the East German side, and finally, with great relief, crossed back through Checkpoint Charlie into West Berlin.

It was back to work on Saturday evening, recording close-ups of the athletes over a period of about four hours. Every time I had help from the camera assistant I said thank you in German, be it *"Vielen Dank"*, *"Danke schön" or just "Danke"* and by the end of the evening I was getting a reluctant smile, and we parted on friendly terms.

***

But enough of sport – there were, for me, more interesting and enjoyable assignments.

I was booked to operate a hand-held camera at a 'Genesis' concert from the Lyceum Ballroom in London's Strand on 7th May 1980. It was part of their "Duke" smaller venues tour. The TV Director, Tom Corcoran, arranged for our lighting engineer and I to go to the Hammersmith Odeon concert at the end of March to see what we were in for. I very much enjoyed the music and the 'light show' and said so at the interval. I asked our lighting engineer,

"Are the cameras going to be able to cope with that?".

And then in the second half they turned on the rest of their lights! An awesome display.

On the day of recording, our lighting engineer spent the afternoon with Genesis's light show director working through the lighting sequences and getting him to raise the levels in the dark bits and reduce the levels in the brightest parts to bring the range to within the handling capabilities of the cameras. During the afternoon we had a visit from Head of OB's who was concerned about sound levels damaging the BBC staff's ears. When I was asked whether I was happy to be on stage with such high sound levels, I said,

"It's OK, but then I like the music. It would be different if I didn't."

About an hour before the show, Tom Corcoran the TV Director took me into the band's dressing room, mainly for the band to know who was going to be loitering on the edge of the stage.

A most enjoyable night offering shots of Tony Banks and his keyboards, and profile shots of Phil Collins when he was doing lead vocals and replaced on drums by Chester Thomson.

In the run up to the annual Chelsea Flower Show, comprehensively covered by the BBC, some pre-shooting is required, mainly interviews with the exhibitors at their nurseries and in the case of vegetables, their farms. A crew from BBC Midlands got to go to St. Lucia to interview a group of ladies who were going to showcase the flowers of the Caribbean in the Great Pavilion.

I went to a mushroom farm in, of all places, the Midlands. We shot pictures of the sheds where the fungi were grown in the dark, occasionally having manure thrown all over them, (reminded me of lower middle management), and then the packing line in a huge building with articulated lorries from all the major supermarkets, lined up outside. The line we 'filmed' of plain white mushrooms being packed and labelled ran for ten minutes for Tesco, then ten for Sainsbury, ten for Asda and finally, ten for Marks and Spencer. Same mushrooms, the only difference, the price, and the best before date. M&S had the shortest best before and the highest price.

A more enjoyable time was had doing pre-shoots for "One Man and His Dog", which meant a trip to the Lake District to shoot pretty pictures of the landscape around the area where the competition was to take place. I also shot portraits of different breeds of sheep, which in one case involved getting in a pen with a 'tup', the northern term for a ram, who didn't much like my company.

Other animals I encountered on the children's natural history programme "Caterpillar Trail" were far less threatening. Approximately ten minutes long, and broadcast around four p.m. on BBC1, it ran from 1985 to 1990 and was presented by Stuart Bradley and Nicola Davies. It was a gentle introduction to nature and wildlife for, mainly, primary aged children, but anybody could learn something from the programmes.

Using our single camera unit, SCU4, we went to East Anglia to make two programmes, first about Otters and the second about Heavy Horses. The Otter Trust was begun in 1971 by Philip and Jeanne Wayre. They purchased farmland on the banks of the River Waveney, on the border between Suffolk and Norfolk, and established a charitable trust with the avowed aim of providing habitat and caring for Otters. The Otters were in pools behind sturdy, three-foot-high, chicken wire fencing, to stop them getting out and to stop children slipping into the pools. We recorded an interview with one of the keepers, a piece to camera by the presenter Nicola Davies and I spent some time recording pictures of the Otters. The fencing meant that all the images of the animals were looking down on them so I asked if I could go inside the fence, to get the camera much nearer the ground, to be at the Otters level. Permission was granted, so after putting on my Wellington boots, I went into the enclosure. I thought that to begin with I'd just stand still and allow the Otters to get used to me, guessing that they might be frightened. I needn't have worried. Within seconds they were investigating the camera tripod and seeing if I had any food down the legs of my Wellington boots – very inquisitive little beggars.

We moved on to The Norfolk Shire Horse Centre in West Runton. The centre brings together a collection of different heavy horses, Shire, Suffolk Punch, Clydesdale, and two I had never heard of, Percheron and Ardenne. The horses are paraded in front of their stables during each open day for the visitors to watch. We recorded an interview and portraits of the different breeds of heavy horse, many of which are rapidly declining in numbers, as the work they used to do has been replaced by mechanised farming equipment.

The next little programme was the River Exe from Source to Sea. The Exe rises at Exe Head, near the village of Simonsbath, on Exmoor in Somerset, about eight and a half kilometres from the Bristol Channel coast, but it flows more or less due south, so that most of its length lies in Devon. It flows for ninety six km and reaches the sea at the Exe Estuary, on the south coast of Devon. Historically, its lowest bridging point was at Exeter, which is the largest settlement on the river, but there is now a viaduct for the M5 motorway about three kilometres south of the city centre. We started just outside Simonsbath where the Exe was a fast-flowing, one-foot deep, clear stream. I had with me a waterproof, periscope lens. Standing in the middle of the stream, I was able to record a shot looking down stream and then lower the lens until it was beneath the surface to see what was going on in the water. We recorded our presenter "pond dipping" to show the larvae of many insects, like dragonflies, damselflies, and mayflies. We then went into the middle of Exmoor to record a piece about the Exmoor ponies and, finally, to Exmouth itself. The Estuary is famous for its wildlife – in particular, the huge number of birds which over-winter in the area, including Avocets, Black-tailed Godwits, Bar-tailed Godwits and Brent Geese. But birds were hard to spot as most had moved to their breeding grounds.

Other gentle, interesting trips were to the New Forest to see the range of deer that call the Forest home – Fallow, Roe, Red, Sika and Muntjac. Then to a private house on the outskirts of Southampton, that belonged to a lady who had ten or more bird feeding stations in her back garden. From her kitchen window we were able to record various Finches, Sparrows, Nuthatch, Robin, Song Thrush, Blackbird and three varieties of Tit all in the space of an hour.

In Axminister we recorded a piece about bats – the mammals, not the ones made from willow. We were at the local bat hospital, run privately by a very enthusiastic lady, who was keen to show our presenter, Nicola, the structure of a Pipistrel. It was in her hand, the warmth of which was waking the Bat from its torpor. She asked if we could stop "filming" for a few minutes, so she could put the Bat in the freezer for a couple of minutes to "shut it down". Sure enough, ten minutes later we were able to continue recording with the bat back in hibernating mode.

In early Spring 1985, the BBC's Religious Department, for whom I had worked many times, were to record two "Songs of Praise" programmes in Europe, for which one of our two camera CMCRs was booked, plus our single camera unit, SCU4, to record interviews and location shots, and then join up with the other unit for the church services. The first location was to be the World Council of Churches in Geneva, the second, the ecumenical Monastery in Taizé, thirty-three km northwest of Mâcon, and nine km north of the town of Cluny in the region of Bourgogne-Franche-Comté in eastern France.

So, engineer George Wagland, Sound Supervisor Chris Holcombe, Engineering Manager John Scarr and I, flew to Geneva, picked up a hire car which had been prebooked for us, a comfortable Mercedes as it turned out, and found our hotel. Terry, our Rigger Driver, had driven SCU4 to Geneva and joined us at the hotel.

The next morning, we set off to the location. Once the centre of the Reformation, Geneva is now the place where the superpowers meet to talk about peace and where the churches meet to talk about unity. To celebrate its birthday, "Songs of Praise" was to visit the headquarters of the World Council of Churches, which brings together over three hundred Protestant, Anglican, and Orthodox churches from over one-hundred countries. We recorded interviews with representatives of the many different churches in their own chapels, dotted round the city, with Cliff Michelmore asking the questions. Most memorable being the Russian and Greek Orthodox chapels, which were heavily decorated in black, gold and red. We then recorded the members of the Council's staff, and their families, singing their "Songs of Praise" for Whit Sunday in the Council's chapel.

The following two days were given over to driving to Cluny where our accommodation was booked for the second location. We stopped overnight '*en route*' in Bresse, where at dinner I suggested that we ought to eat *'Poulet de Bresse'*, the famous French chicken with its white feathers, red combe and blue legs, only bred in the region and the only French chicken with an *'Appellation Controlee'*. We finished the meal with a cheese course so that we could have the local speciality, *'Bleu de Bresse'*.

Lunch the next day was taken in a restaurant in the Beaujolais Grand Cru village of *'Moulin-a-Vent'*, the highest rated of all the Beaujolais Crus, basically because I wanted to visit the eponymous windmill. On top a small hill, surrounded by vines, as far as the eye could see, it was everything I expected.

We checked into our accommodation, a small commercial hotel, and went out to explore Cluny. It owed its early importance to its celebrated Benedictine abbey, founded in 910 by Duke William the Pious of Aquitaine, and once the largest in the western world. Both town and abbey suffered during the religious wars of the sixteenth century, and the abbey was suppressed during the French Revolution and closed in 1790. The centre of the town is strewn with parts of the destroyed abbey, with more, relatively, modern buildings built onto, or even on top of the ruins, of which the Hôtel de Bourgogne is one. I made a note of the hotel's details for future reference and have stayed there a dozen times since, *en route* to and from holiday destinations in Provence and Tuscany.

The Taizé Community is an ecumenical Christian monastic fraternity in the very small hilltop village of Taizé, at the Southern end of the Cote Chalonnaise wine region. It is composed of more than one hundred brothers, from Catholic and Protestant Christian traditions, who originate from about thirty countries across the world. It was founded in 1940 by Brother Roger Schütz, a Reformed Protestant, (whom we privately referred to as *"Le Grande Fromage"*). Taizé has become one of the world's most important sites of Christian pilgrimage, with a focus on engaging with younger people. Over one hundred thousand young people from around the world make pilgrimages to Taizé each year to pray, study the bible, share experiences and work in the community. The Church of Reconciliation, at the centre of the village, was inaugurated on 6 August 1962. It was designed by a Taizé member and architect, Brother Denis. Young Germans from the Action Reconciliation Service for Peace, created for reconciliation after World War II, assumed the work of building it. Dotted around the small hilltop are the stone or wooden accommodation for the monks. There are two large carparks for the many day visitors, and a shop selling CDs of the chants and hymns used in the services, books of the writings of Brother Roger, and ceramics made in their own, on-site pottery. Most of the young people who visit, and numbers are massive at Easter, camp in the surrounding fields.

With Geoffrey Wheeler asking the questions, we spent two or three days, (mists of time and all that), interviewing several monks from different Christian denominations about their life and work, including Brother Roger, and some of the young visitors, as to what draws them to the place.

The two camera CMCR then joined us for the recording of the Easter "Songs of Praise" in the Church of Reconciliation. Viewed from above, the floor plan is reminiscent of the shape of an aircraft carrier. Benches and chairs were largely dispensed with in the church. The brothers sit on meditation stools or directly on the floor, as far as their health allows. There are tiered concrete seating for visitors around the perimeter walls, apart from the south wall which consists of eight stained glass windows and the only source of daylight. Services are conducted by candlelight.

When the monks realised that a lighting rig was going into the church, they were very concerned that the unique atmosphere of their candle-lit service would be lost. Very much aware of this, John, our lighting engineer, kept the light level as low as could be tolerated by the cameras. After the recording, the monks were invited into the CMCR to watch a replay, and I have this lovely memory of concerned monks queuing up at the back entrance to the truck, stepping inside to watch for a minute or two, and appearing out of the front door, smiling.

***

Later in 1985, but before I worked on "She Devil", I worked for the director Jack Gold on the location shoot for the play "Me and the Girls". It was one of a series of stories by Noel Coward, and starred Tom Courtenay with Nichola McAuliffe, Philip Voss and Robert Glenister. Jack had directed numerous 'Wednesday Plays', the children's drama "Little Lord Fauntleroy", and "The Naked Civil Servant" with John Hurt playing the part of Quentin Crisp. "Me and the Girls" centred around the character of George Banks, (Tom Courtenay), who'd had an extremely busy life full of young women; his dance troupes that had toured the world. But, nearing the end of his days, it's not just the girls that he recalls.

I remember one shot I had to do, which was a track-in, corner to corner, across the floor of a very large, carpeted room to the desk where Tom Courtenay was sitting. Just as I was thinking, "how the heck am I going to do that without revealing the camera track", the designer, Oliver Bayldon, said,

"I'll get the boys to roll the carpet back to the desk, and then you can lay the track. We'll cover it over, and then as you track in, they will roll it up in front of the dolly".

Every day's a school day!

The final adult drama I worked on, and in my humble opinion the best work I did, not to mention the most satisfying, was the serial, "King of the Ghetto", set in and around Brick Lane, in the borough of Tower Hamlets. Brick Lane is in the heart of the East End and is one of London's most iconic streets. Historically it's been home to French Huguenot, then Jewish immigrants, and now it's a centre for the Bangladeshi community. Along with its heritage, Brick Lane is known for its food. The famous selection of curry restaurants and twenty-four-hour beigel shops are London landmarks. In line with the vibrancy of the area, you can find cuisine from all over the world; Turkish, Japanese, and Argentinian to list a few.

The Director was Roy Battersby, who had made documentary features for the BBC programmes "Tomorrow's World" and "Towards Tomorrow", and, in the 1970s & 80s, many dramas mostly for ITV companies. He had been a Trotskyist for some years, becoming a full-time organiser for the now defunct Workers' Revolutionary Party, alongside Vanessa Redgrave. The association had ended by 1981, but the connection led to his being blacklisted by the BBC. This was his first programme back. Married to actress Judy Loe, widow of Richard Beckinsale (Lennie Godber in "Porridge"), and consequentially, the stepfather of the actress Kate Beckinsale. He went on to direct drama productions such as "Between the Lines", "Inspector Morse", "Cracker" and "A Touch of Frost." In 2005, his film Red Mercury was shown at the Montreal World Film Festival.

The drama, a serial in four fifty-five-minute parts by Farrukh Dhondy, is set in and around Brick Lane. Tim Roth plays a white man living in a Bengali neighbourhood. He organises a squatting campaign, much to the annoyance of the local labour-controlled council. Bengali youths roam the streets scaring away National Front skinheads, and Gwyneth Strong plays white liberal Sadie Deedes who argues for an Islamic school. Zia Mohyeddin plays Timur Hussein, a Bangladeshi businessman who accrues wealth and power by doing shady deals with criminals, the police and local politicians.

Tim Roth was a totally different actor to David Suchet, with whom I worked on "Blott". Tim was a totally instinctive actor who quite often couldn't say what he was going to do physically, saying 'you'll just have to follow me". He had made a huge splash in the British TV movie "Made in Britain" (1982), playing a young skinhead named Trevor. He worked with director Mike Leigh on "Meantime" (1983) and debuted on the big screen when he filled in for Joe Strummer in the Stephen Frears film "The Hit" (1984). After "King", he gained more attention for his turn as Vincent Van Gogh in "Vincent & Theo" (1990). While on "King," I was very much aware that his ambition was Hollywood. He had acquired an American girlfriend, and he moved to Los Angeles, caught the eye of the young director Quentin Tarantino, got the part of Mr. Orange in his heist movie "Reservoir Dogs" (1992), and then in the film "Pulp Fiction" (1994). In 1995 Roth picked up an Academy Award nomination for his campy turn as a villain in the period piece Rob Roy.

Tim Roth's style of acting reminds me of a well-known and often retold story about Laurence Olivier and Dustin Hoffman when they were making the John Schlesinger movie "Marathon Man". Before the famous scene where Hoffman is in the dentist's chair and about to have Olivier torture him with the drill, Hoffman went for a very long run so that he appeared on set sweating and hyperventilating. Olivier is reported to have said,

"What on Earth have you been doing?", to which Hoffman replied,

"Getting into the right state for the scene". To which Olivier retorted,

"Have you tried acting, dear boy".

The love interest, Sadie Deedes, played by Gwyneth Strong, who is probably best known now for playing Cassandra in "Only Fools and Horses", and the 'heavy' Sammy was played by Ian Dury, who was adding acting to his CV after a successful career as the vocalist in the bands 'Kilburn and the Highroads' and then 'The Blockheads'. I remember one day when Ian was on location, I was opening a packet of *Gauloises*, or it may have been *Gitane*s, (I've given up now - three-fifteen p.m. on 17th October 1993 – not that it bothers me), when he came over to me and said, in his gravelly voice,

"'Ere, can I have one of your serious cigarettes?"

I first met Roy, (Battersby), on the banks of the upper Thames. I was engaged in recording some location shots for a Children's period drama. When he and the producer Stephen Gilbert arrived, I was in a small boat in the middle of the river recording a scene for the series, the name of which has completely escaped my mind. Once ashore, we started talking about the look he was after for "King". He wasn't a fan of the zoom lens, it being too easy to change the lens angle, rather than move the camera, with the perspective changing when cutting from one side of a conversation to the other. Also, he liked 'dirty frames', which means having something out of focus at the edges of the shot which adds a slight feeling of claustrophobia. There being no way of using fixed lenses on the camera, we agreed that I would find four different focal lengths on the zoom and only use those angles. I asked what lens angles he was used to working with when using 16mm film. He said he wouldn't know because he relied on the film cameraman with whom he was working. He could, however, give me the telephone number of a camera man who could tell me. So, I got to phone Chris Menges, the Oscar winning Director of Photography on the film, "The Killing Fields", and camera operator on one of my favourite films, "Local Hero". He gave me the focal lengths of a standard kit of four lenses used on 16mm film cameras, and I then converted them to focal lengths on the zoom I was to use, to achieve the same lens angle. Then, throughout the shoot, for all dialogue scenes I set the lens angle from one of the four lenses in my 'theoretical kit' and moved the camera to achieve the matching shots.

Roy and I got on very well, to the point where, on occasions, just he and I would watch the actors run a scene, and then he would turn to me and say, "OK, how do you want to shoot it?". I'd suggest a way the scene could be shot, and, if Roy was happy, we'd call John, the Lighting Engineer onto the set and explain what we wanted to do and leave him to light it.

We used a couple of camera mounts that I'd not come across before. An electrically powered vehicle not unlike a 'mini moke', which we used for part of the car chase in the opening sequence, and for a travelling shot down Brick Lane as a group of Bangladeshi youths were delivering 'flyers' to every shop or house in the road. With all the shops displaying saris, bails of material or even food, it was a vividly colourful scene. The other mount was basically a wooden platform with very softly inflated rubber wheels at each corner, which a film grip / rigger driver would push. We used it for a very long walking and talking scene between Sadie and Saliq, a young Bangladeshi. We were able to start the shot with the camera ahead of the couple, let them close up and pass us on the left-hand side, cross the road in front of us, and then we pulled up along-side for the end of the dialogue.

Recording of the sound was achieved by having the actors rigged with radio-mics.

Apart from bringing in Dave Hunter and a second camera to cover the burning of the local school, we could only do it once, and Robin Sutherland, who had specialised in operating a camera while riding pillion on a motorbike, for one travelling night shot of an attack on a shop window, every other shot in the two hundred and twenty minutes was mine. And the collaboration I had with Roy, was the most satisfying of my career.

At the end of the shoot, Roy gave me a book by William Goldman, a famous Hollywood script writer, (Butch Cassidy and the Sundance Kid; All the President's Men), called "Adventures in the Screen Trade," a title I had thought of using for myself.

***

I'm not totally sure why, but, apart from the odd location inserts, adult dramas stopped for Tel. O.Bs. But I'm going to hazard a guess. The television system was invented, developed, and controlled by engineers, who have traditionally been responsible for applying light to a set or room to ensure that the camera produces the right amount of electronic signal. On a film set, the Director of Photography was often second only to God. Before 'video assist', a system where a little bit of light from the back of the film camera's lens went to produce a video signal, the only people who looked through the film camera's viewfinder were the DOP and the director. So, the set designer, costume designer and make-up artist had to rely on the DOP to say if everything in shot was correct. (I used to surprise a lot of set designers by offering them a look through my viewfinder – I didn't see the point in being precious about it, and shooting drama is a collaborative process).

Apart from a rare few, (on OBs, Hu Cartwright, John Mason, Clive Potter and John King spring to mind), Lighting Engineers tended to light the set, whereas the DOPs lit the shot. So, once small electronic cameras became available to hire from the independent facilities companies, and editing video became a lot easier, Directors realised that they could shoot video and work with their favourite DOP.

Fortunately, Children's Drama Department continued to use OBs for a few more years. In early Autumn 1986, using the small single camera unit SCU4, I spent six weeks in East Anglia for the Christmas ghost story, "The Children of Green Knowe", based on the first book in a series by Lucy M. Boston. The story is about,

"Tolly, a schoolboy, whose parents live abroad, is about to spend Christmas at his boarding school, is summoned to Green Knowe, a very old house in the Norfolk Fens to spend Christmas with his Great Grandmother Oldknowe. Tolly soon becomes aware of other presences in the house and the story follows his exploration over the days before Christmas as he discovers things about Green Knowe's previous occupants who lived in the time of Charles II".

The production called for the old house to be surrounded by flood water, (Tolly finishes his journey by rowing boat), coated in snow, and the site of a battle between ancient good and evil. The location we used was Crow's Hall, a grade II listed, sixteenth century, moated manor in Debenham in Suffolk, and Special Effects Department provided the snow.

Great Grandmother Oldknowe was played with charm and warmth by Daphne Oxenford. People of a certain age will remember her voice, as she had been the narrator of "Listen with Mother" from the 1950s to the 1970s and had also been one of the original "Coronation Street" cast. A year after "Green Knowe", she would materialise as a hologram archivist in *"Dragonfire"* the last story of "Doctor Who's" twenty-fourth season. I became good friends with Daphne and stayed with her and her husband, a theatre obsessive, at their house in Altrincham and when she was working at the ITV Studios in Teddington, she stayed at my home in Surbiton. After her husband died, she moved into Denville Hall, a residential Care Home for all theatrical professionals in Northwood, Northwest London. I enjoyed several lunches with her and other 'luvvies' from the theatrical world. Conversations were at the same time both humorous and sad, as their collective memories faded.

"Surely you remember – oh what's his name - you know the one - he came down the stairs in that play by – whoever it was?"

It was a very enjoyable shoot, even though they say never work with children, animals, and boats, (they rarely go where you want them to), and I got on well with Colin Cant, the director. Apart from covering the house, trees and lawns in fake snow, Special Effects were kept busy on several night shoots, providing heavy downpours of rain and massive wind machines to create the howling gales the scenes required. (While doing some research to check some facts. I discovered that all four episodes are currently available on youtube.com).

It was in 1988 when I worked for the first of three occasions with the director Christine Secombe. As the niece of Harry Secombe, she had the same bouncy enthusiasm for everything and was a joy to work with. Christine directed many "Jackanory" and "Playaway" episodes before moving to directing Children's Drama, which previously had included "Jonny Briggs" and "Aliens in the Family". Our collaboration started with the location shoot for a six-episode adaption of Philippa Pearce's novel, "Tom's Midnight Garden". Paul Harding also recorded material for the programme at a different time and place. The story is about the eponymous Tom, who is staying with his uncle and aunt because his brother has a contagious disease. When he hears their grandfather clock strike thirteen, he makes a strange discovery - a doorway back in time where only a friendly girl called Hatty can see him.

The only sequence I can remember is when Tom opens the door to discover the secret garden. I tried a version of the famous shot in "Jaws", where the camera tracked in and the operator zoomed out to keep the person in the frame the same size, but the World around him got wider. Not sure I pulled it off.

Christine, however, was happy to have me back in 1990 to record all six episodes of "Dodgem", entirely on location. The series follows the adventures of the main character, Simon Leighton (Sean Maguire) as he enters a children's home because his father is reeling over the death of Simon's mother and is unable to look after Simon. In the children's home, Simon's only friend is a wild girl, Rose Penfold (Lucy Speed). They hatch a plan to escape the clutches of Social Services and join a travelling funfair.

We used locations in Hampton for the school and care home, Teddington for Simon's home, a court room in Richmond, (could be wrong there) and Devizes, where there was an erected travelling fairground. Both Sean Maguire and Lucy Speed went on to have successful adult acting careers.

The series was put up for a Royal Television Society Award in the Best Children's Drama and Light Entertainment category, as was "Maid Marian and Her Merry Men", the next series of which was being shot in Somerset by Dave Gautier. I was asked if I would go down to the location and take over from Dave so that he could go to the RTS awards show. So, I did a day recording in woods near Minehead at a place called Porlock, with director David Bell, and "Dodgem" won the award. Duh! The producer of both series, Richard Callanan, wrote to me on the success of "Dodgem" ending with,

"Dave gets to go to the ball, and your show wins the prize. Life's a bitch."

I was reunited with director Colin Cant on "Dark Season" a science-fiction television serial for adolescents, screened on BBC1 in late 1991. Comprising six twenty-five-minute episodes, the two linked, three-part stories tell of the adventures of three teenagers, Marcie, Reet and Thomas and their battle to save their school and their classmates from the actions of the sinister Mr Eldritch, who gives, free of charge, each kid at their school a powerful computer. The class swot is turned into a mutant by her computer and its controller. Investigating, the three discover that the computers are a part of a plan to rule the world. They need to find Professor Polzinski. With the aid of the Professor, Eldritch is stopped. In the second three episodes, a team made up of blonde women dig up the school field to find a wartime computer Behemoth with the power to destroy the world. Marcie employs her super intelligence to lock horns with Eldritch for control of the world. Another round in the age-old war of good v evil.

It was the first television drama to be written by Russell T. Davies and is also noteworthy for co-starring a young Kate Winslet in her first major television role, aged sixteen, and only two weeks after finishing her GCSEs.

Russell T. Davies was a BBC staff producer working for the children's department at BBC Manchester, running the summertime activity show "Why Don't You?". He had gained some television writing experience scripting the comedy dubbed version of "The Flashing Blade" for the Saturday morning children's programme "On the Waterfront" in 1989, and the children's sketch show "Breakfast Serials" the following year, but his real ambition was to write television drama. To this end, he wrote an on-spec script for the first episode of "Dark Season" – originally titled "The Adventuresome Three" – and sent it directly to the Head of Children's Programmes, Anna Home. Impressed, she asked Davies to write a second episode. As luck would have it, Tony Robinson decided to take a break from co-producing "Maid Marian and Her Merry Men", so a slot opened up in the Children's BBC schedules for late 1991 and Home decided to use "Dark Season" to fill it. She then commissioned Davies to write the remaining episodes of the serial. The series was recorded in Mytchett, Surrey, Farnborough, Hampshire, (Woburn Avenue), the long-closed Robert Haining Secondary School, and at the BBC's Ealing Studios, in the summer of 1991. Like Kate Winslet, Russel T. Davies went on to greater things with the very successful revamp of the "Dr Who" series.

Colin Cant came to Tel. OBs base in West Acton to meet with Lighting Engineer, Geoff Rathbone, and myself to discuss how to convey evil on the screen without the use of visual effects. I have had my leg pulled about it ever since, but I came up with the idea of putting one camera panning head on top of another, but at ninety degrees, so that I could pan left and right and up and down as normal but tilt the camera sideways as well. In a situation where 'good' and 'evil' confronted each other, when looking at 'evil' I could tilt the camera to the left, and conversely to the right when looking at 'good'. There was quite a bit of scepticism about, especially from Producer Richard Callanan, but it worked, and he wrote to me afterwards, saying he shouldn't have doubted me, which was gracious of him. The adult members of the cast included Bridget Forsyth, memorable as Thelma in "Whatever happened to the Likely Lads", and the outrageously camp Jacqueline Pearce, probably best known for her role as Servalan in "Blake's Seven". Also, I thought that Grant Parsons, who played Mr. Eldritch, was extremely brave to play the entire show from behind dark glasses.

My most memorable scenes were in Ealing Film studios, not because of what I did, but because of where I was. Such a privilege to get to work in the oldest, continuously working studio facility for film production in the world. They were started in 1902 but came to prominence in the 1930s and '40s, when Ealing Studios made their name with comedies, featuring musical stars like Gracie Fields, Stanley Holloway, and George Formby. The post-war era saw an explosion of Ealing's hallmark black comedies, satirising British life and society at the time. These classics include "Whisky Galore!", "Kind Hearts and Coronets", "The Ladykillers", "The Titfield Thunderbolt", "The Lavender Hill Mob" and "The Man in the White Suit".

Michael Balcon ran the Studios until 1955, when the BBC bought Ealing and based its Film Department there. At its peak, fifty-six film crews used the studios as a base for location filming of dramas, documentaries, and other programmes. Countless iconic BBC TV shows of the sixties, seventies and eighties were produced in this period at Ealing. To name just a few, they include "Cathy Come

Home", "Z-Cars", "Colditz", "Porridge", "Monty Python", "The Singing Detective" and "Dr Who".

Ealing Studios, now under private ownership, continues to host the best of British drama, from TV hits such as "Downton Abbey", "The Durrells" and "The Crown", to acclaimed films like "The Theory of Everything", "The Darkest Hour" and "Bridget Jones".

My last shot for the "Dark Season" series, was in the Studio with the water tank, the same tank that was used in the movie "The Cruel Sea", and for the drowning scenes at the end of episode two of "Tenko". Standing, with cold water up to the top of, and often over, my chest waders, I recorded the final moments of the drowning of The Behemoth.

I was back at Ealing Film Studios in the autumn of 1991, for the last of my three Children's Dramas directed by Christine Secombe, and the last drama I ever did. With a screen play in six parts by Julia Jones, it was based on the award-winning children's novel by Gillian Avery, called "A Likely Lad". Set in Lancashire in 1900, it follows the story of Willy Overs (played by Lee Brennan), who at fourteen was old enough to leave school and whose father appeared to have a very firm idea on what his son should do. Willy, on the other hand, had his own ideas on where life should take him.

The first location, the Overs's family home, was a Victorian, two-up-two-down with a scullery and small yard out the back, in Bolton. We recorded several exterior scenes around the house and local streets, but almost all the interior scenes were to be shot last in constructed sets at Ealing Studios. Also, I've forgotten why such a place was required, but we went to Blackburn to record scenes at an imposing house built for a leading Blackburn solicitor at the end of the Nineteenth Century. Called 'Lancrigg', on Gorse Road, it had not changed internally since the early 1900's and was like walking into a museum. Robert Foster, the Production Designer, had absolutely nothing to alter or add, as it was perfect for the period of our story. Outside was another matter. Robert changed the name of the house to 'Laurel Villa'. During the war, as with many other houses, all the gates of the properties in Gorse Road had been collected for scrap metal for the war effort, so new gates had to be made, and part of the Tarmac-surfaced road outside the house was covered in setts to make it look more appropriate for the period, and the modern garage attached to the house was 'disguised'.

We also recorded scenes in the village of Downham in the Forest of Bowland Area of Outstanding Natural Beauty, which lies at the foot of Pendle Hill, close to the thriving market town of Clitheroe. It is often hailed as the most beautiful village in Lancashire, with unrivalled views, unspoilt by overhead wires, satellite dishes, roadside signage, and TV aerials. Perfect for a period drama. Even better, on the recce, John Mason our Lighting Engineer, found an advert in a telephone box, (no, not that sort), for a holiday home to rent in the village, and he booked our accommodation for the duration of the shoot. Probably the nicest daily commute ever, unlike the drive into Ealing every morning for an eight-thirty start. The decision to record the interior scenes in a studio was for visual reasons. If we had recorded in the Victorian house in Bolton, in the very small rooms, the camera, sound assistant and I would have taken up a good part of the room and everything would have had to be shot on a very wide-angle lens. This would have had the effect of making the room look larger than it was, and people further apart. By building a 'set' where each wall could be removed, one at a time depending on which way the camera needed to point, it was possible to have the front of the lens just outside the room, along with the camera mount. Tighter lens angles were used, which helped to convey the cramped conditions in which the Overs family lived. A ceiling was rigged over the set which helped to achieve more realistic sound, and there was an openable hatch in the middle of the ceiling for top lighting, to replicate the illumination from a central ceiling light.

Still leaning on my final drama.

Chapter Eleven
The Beginning of the End

I sat in for David Jones, Head of Cameras, Television OBs, while he went off to Tuscany for two weeks' holiday at the beginning of July 1992. Earlier in the year, March or early April, David had asked me if I would like to do the second series of "Five Children and It", or "The Return of the Psammead", as it was to be known later. Not one to turn down a drama of any sort, I had of course said "yes". If only I had thought it through properly before replying.

Children's Drama Department had requested that Tel OB's service three complete serials, inserts for a fourth, and another twenty weeks work on "Grange Hill" during that year, and David had to allocate the cameramen for the year's work at the beginning of Spring.

"Grange Hill" was easy, as there was an established pattern of rolling the three-man crews through this production, that had worked for some time. David Gautier was the only cameraman that the Director of "Maid Marion", David Bell, had worked with before, and he wanted him again, so that was easily resolved. Colin Cant, with whom both Dave Hunter and I had worked before, was to do another "Sci-Fi" series by the same writer as "Dark Season", called "Century Falls". Marilyn Fox was to direct the second series of "Five Children and It". Both Paul Harding on the first series of the "Narnia Chronicles", and Trevor Wimlett on "Archer's Goon", had unhappy experiences of working with her and were insisting that it was my turn to suffer this year. The location inserts for "Kevin & Co." were to be shot in two weeks in June or July. Paul was the preferred man for that.

Looked at it in isolation, the allocation of cameramen that the various productions were happy with, was relatively simple and straight forward. Dave Gautier would do "Maid Marion"; Paul Harding, "Kevin & Co."; Dave Hunter, "Century Falls" with Colin Cant. Trevor Wimlett was to have a year off from Drama, leaving me with the "Psammead". Fortunately, Marilyn, with whom I had not worked before, was aware of my previous work for Children's Drama and, it was said, was looking forward to working with me.

What David Jones had failed to appreciate, was the effect that the introduction of the Television Resources Review, and then "Producer Choice", was to have on Tel. OB's as it lurched into becoming a semi-autonomous "Business Unit", and the need to think through who was to sit in as Head of Cameras after he was to retire in the August.

Down in the lower echelons of the corporate pyramid, there were whispers that John Birt, DG in waiting, had been chairing a committee to review the size of the BBC's resources in the light of the Governments requirement that twenty-five percent of BBC transmitted programmes were to be provided by Independent programme makers, and the assumption that once "Producer Choice" was in operation, the Producers of in-house productions would *choose* to *purchase* a proportion of outside facilities. Maybe one day the next generation of broadcasting historians will reveal the truth, but Local Managers and staff heard only rumour and speculation of what took place at those meetings. The word 'on the street' was that if any member of the committee disagreed with Birt's "vision" then they could leave.

What, presumably, was a brilliant plan to the Board of Governors and the Board of Management, was to the staff at the bottom of the heap, a tragedy. The BBC Television Film Studios at Ealing, that historic site, which prior to the BBC's custody, had been responsible for the Ealing Comedies and "The Cruel Sea," was to be sold off to an outside company, and some studios and office space rented back. Apart from the Natural History Unit, all network Studio and Outside Broadcast Operations were to cease in Bristol. Likewise, Birmingham, Scotland and Wales were to lose their Network OB capability, and there was to be a reduced fleet in both Manchester and at Kendal Avenue.

Locally, the direct impact was that an originally planned fleet of six large, ten camera capable, colour mobile control rooms [CMCRs] was being cut to four, the three, medium sized CMCRs cut to two, and all the single channel units [SCU's] were to be done away with. In real terms, this meant that thousands of BBC staff, ninety people at Kendal Avenue alone, who had given the best part of their lives to Public Service Broadcasting were to be made redundant. Talent and expertise, for so long the backbone of the Corporation's reputation, were to be discarded, dumped, disposed of.

Furthermore, as the details of "Producer Choice" emerged, it was rapidly perceived by those operational staff that remained on the "shop floor" of broadcasting, as an appallingly misnamed plan to radically alter the financial structure of the Corporation in such a way as to price out all those unique practices, which had given it a world-wide reputation for standards and quality.

To hear the DG elect and members of the Board of Management, claiming that they would uphold the Corporation's aim of providing high quality, distinctive programming, while at the same time driving through a policy which was turning the Programme Makers, the Studio, Outside Broadcast, and Film facilities Units, the Designers, Make-up and Special effects groups into little businesses, which were required, not only to trade with each other, but compete favourably with the "free market' outside and to operate in such a way that they broke even, was, to say the least, downright insulting to the many thousands of staff who had spent their entire careers striving to put the highest quality programmes on air. Worst of all, it convinced them that they had totally failed to understand what made the Corporation what it was. How dare they lay claim to ownership of the quality and the professional standards. What right had they, the Board of Governors and the Board of Management on their highly paid, politically appointed, short term contracts, to take any credit for the internationally renowned reputation of the Corporation.

They were caretaker managers. It was the Producers, the Directors, the Actors, (who preferred to work for "Auntie" because of the creative atmosphere, even though it was for less money), the Designers, the Make-up Artists, the Cameramen, the Sound Operators, the Engineers, who made the programmes on which the Corporation's reputation was founded. Heads of Finance, Directors of Personnel, Chiefs in charge of Policy Unit, even Director Generals don't win BAFTA's year after year. Time and again, over the decades, while so-called leaders and managers came and went, most of the Production and Craft Award ceremonies were dominated by the Corporation's programmes and staff. Furthermore, those winners that no longer worked for the Corporation, had more than likely been trained there. Away from those somewhat self-congratulatory evenings, where Drama and Documentary take most of the honours, the world at large also appreciated the Corporation's coverage of Sport and Events. Soccer, Cricket, Wimbledon and Grand Prix Motor Racing, Operas, Concerts and State Occasions, all heralded as second-to-none by other Broadcasting organisations still striving to emulate the way we did it.

It was clear to me and to most of my colleagues, that those now in charge had either, arrogantly failed to identify why the BBC had retained its reputation for so long or had a politically motivated agenda to destroy the Corporation's unique position in British Broadcasting.

Most of the staff in my department tended to believe it was the latter. They couldn't believe that these people could not see the consequences of their actions. To turn the

Television Service into something over two-hundred separate business units, each one with a business plan loaded with corporate overheads, valuations for rent plucked out of the air, with their own accountants, controlling offices full of assistants dealing with estimates, invoices, cash flow, phased income, spending limits, capital depreciation, utilisation statistics, all loaded onto the rate per hour for staff and equipment that had to be charged to the programme making departments, which then had to bear comparison with free market rates, was bound to cause a complete about-turn in attitude.

Instead of local managers working to provide the best available staff and facilities to each programme, while at the same time thinking to the future, by bringing on young talent, experimenting with new techniques, and encouraging producers to take risks with new equipment or people, they were now required to become salesmen.

Producers, Directors and Production Managers, who for so long we had related to as colleagues and part of the same creative team, were now to be dealt with as "customers" to whom our services had to be sold, not only in competition with other resource areas within the BBC, but also in direct comparison with the external facilities providers. Rumours circulated about wave after wave of highly paid Management Consultants, who were brought in from the likes of KPMG, Coopers & Lybrand, Deloittes et al, to set up accounting practices, new costing systems, productivity audits, and market comparisons.

Staff weren't, in principle, against business efficiency, they felt they knew where the waste was. But what they saw happening was more expenditure in precisely those areas that are not reflected on screen, while cuts were being made at the sharp end. Moreover, the perpetrators of this plan, had, at a stroke, totally changed the atmosphere in which programmes were made. The artisans of the industry no longer talked in happy excited huddles about this or that programme that they had, or were about to, work on. The conversations were now about rates per hour, discounts, winning or losing contracts, staffing levels, pension provisions, and redundancies. Creativity and fun had been replaced by cynicism and fear. Trying to get the feelings and fears of the staff fed up the chain to the top was virtually impossible. Any manager who tried to pass upwards the concerns of his staff would be deemed as having failed in his duty to indoctrinate them with the "message" and would fear for his own job.

A non-believer himself, which was more than likely the reason why he was replaced before his due retirement date, Ted Bragg, Head of Television Outside Broadcast Resources, and his management team had to produce the Tel. OB. business plan. Income and Expenditure accounts had to be worked out. Income was to be derived from the sale of staff, equipment and services to programme makers, the rates for which could only be intelligent guesses, based on a combination of outside rates, what it was felt the internal market could stand and an estimate of how much work the Department could hope to retain with the reduced fleet. Expenditure was, for the most part, dictated from "the Centre".

A charge for rent was imposed by a new department set up to control the Corporation's property interests. This was rumoured to have been set at a figure close to £25 per square foot, when all around the West Acton area Industrial sites were on offer at £8 -£10 per square foot. Any sane business operation with an overhead like that would seriously consider relocating, but that was not allowed. Current Asset Values for all the equipment that we operated had to be negotiated, so that interest charges could be levelled on assumed borrowings from the corporate centre. Salaries, and Travel and Duty Allowances were set centrally. A charge for Corporate Overheads was apportioned, to cover central Finance, Personnel, Policy and Planning, Equal Opportunity, Health and Safety, and Occupational Health. All these figures seemed to have been plucked from the air with a damp finger and without fairness or logic.

Two examples which pointed up the absurdity, and finally convinced me that accountancy was not an exact science, was Occupational Health and the Catering Subsidy. Studio Production Resources, the programme making operation at the Television Centre, had a staff level of over a thousand. Kendal Avenue had four hundred and fifty staff, yet the Occupational Health levy for Tel. O.B.s was rumoured to be £22k, just £2k less than Studio Production Resources. Where was the fiscal logic in that? The Catering Subsidy was even more ludicrous. If the Corporate charge was divided by the number of meals taken during the year in the Kendal Avenue canteen, it worked out at nearly £10 per meal. It would quite clearly be cheaper to shut the canteen, stand outside the door and give everyone £5 to go and eat somewhere else. The fact that probably ninety-five percent of the staff based at Television centre ate in the canteen, and only about twenty-five percent of Kendal Avenue staff ate in their canteen, (the other seventy-five percent were dotted around the country making programmes), hadn't seemed to occur to the bean counters.

It was not surprising then, when rumours emanated to the effect that the first attempt at a business plan, which was supposed to "break even", showed a £9 million loss. This, together with the fact that Ted Bragg was alleged to have dismissed the 'centrally' installed Consultant, who was assigned to assist with the preparation of the business plan, with the words, "…go home, sonny, we have been doing simple maths for years.", must have been enough to convince Television Service management that a change at the top of Tel. OB's must come sooner rather than later.

In January 1992 I think, after Ted Bragg had revised the business plan, presumably under pressure from his masters, he called a general staff meeting in the canteen.

He was an Outside Broadcast man right through to his very soul, even to the sole of his golf shoes. He'd come up through the ranks, becoming first an Engineering Manager, where for years he was responsible for organising the technical arrangements for all the Golf Tournaments that BBC Sport covered. Then he became Head of Tel OB. Operations, basically the second-in-command, where he was responsible for the management of all the Engineering Managers and had Head of Cameras,

Head of Sound and Head of Lighting under him. Finally, when Roger Jeffcott moved on, Ted Bragg got the job he had always wanted, Head of Television Outside Broadcast Resources. He really loved big live OB's and considered that they were the only real reason for the existence of the department. He was an aggressive, ebullient, some would say irascible, defender of traditional multicamera OB's. This at times had its disadvantages when others in the department were trying to expand the range and scope of the programme types we serviced. Ted Bragg felt that we shouldn't be doing drama and documentaries, pussyfooting around with one camera for weeks on end, and, at times, would give these production departments the impression that OBs were less than committed to what they wanted to achieve.

Some three hundred or so members of staff, everyone who was not out working on a programme, were packed into the canteen that day, as Ted Bragg stood up, not much more than a year after being appointed to the job he had always wanted, to announce that he had to shed ninety jobs if OBs were to survive. It was quite clear to those of us sitting nearby that he was holding back the tears. Here he was, aged fifty-nine, at the apogee of his career, having spent all his working life as the staunchest defender of Tel OBs, having to prepare twenty percent of its staff for the sack. Every section was to be affected. Rigger Drivers, Communications engineers, Mechanical Workshops, Sound Operators, Cameramen, Video Tape Editors, Secretaries, Planning Office staff, even Management. Voluntary redundancies were to be sought first.

Applications were to be submitted by the end of June, with termination at the end of October. Any shortfall in the required numbers were to be made compulsorily redundant by the end of March 1993, in time for the start of the first year as a Business Unit.

At the end of the meeting, staff from each section went off into huddles, remembering only the total numbers to go and the number to be lost from its own section. There were to be eight losses in the Camera Section, and opinions and guesses as to who, and how many, might volunteer for "the early bath" were soon to be whispered in corridors and corners around the building. Which management posts were to go was also the subject of much speculation. Clive Potter, as Head of Lighting, had retired in the previous October and his post had never been filled. Jeff Baker, who was Assistant Head of Tel. OB. Ops, had very recently, and very quickly, applied for and got the job of Head of Open University Production Resources. Rumours were rife that he had been told to apply, and again, that post had not been filled. John Hughes, Head of Tel. OB. Ops, was still there. Dave Jones was to go in August, and Ted himself was to go in October. Would he be allowed to put in place a new management structure before the new man in charge was appointed? If not, would there be a Head of Cameras? Would there be a combined Head of Cameras and Lighting? If that was to be the case, then there was no chance that a cameraman would get the job, as the Engineering Managers would never tolerate a cameraman as being responsible for their lighting standards.

So, a couple of days before David Jones left for his Tuscan holiday, I asked him who he'd decided was going to sit in and run the Camera Section after he retired, until such time as a decision was reached as to when and if the post was to be filled. Dave's reply was that only Paul Harding or I could do it and that as I was due to start "The Return of the Psammead" at the beginning of August, that it would have to be Paul. My heart sank, and I realised, perhaps for the first time that I thought I should do the job. And this was not going to help. I will never really know, but perhaps at that moment I indicated this in some way, through bodily posture or an attitude that I struck, because Dave then said that he thought that perhaps Paul didn't have the "political" astuteness to deal with the months to come and that he wouldn't have crewed up the Dramas this way had he known, but there it was. I have to say that I seized on that as an opportunity to open the discussion. I said that, in a talk recently with Paul, I had got the impression that he was not looking forward to sitting in the office and that maybe Dave should talk to him about it. Not that I in any way wanted to denigrate my friend Paul's abilities, but, if it was possible, even at this late stage to reorganise the cameramen for the dramas, with production's blessing, would he, David, prefer it. I was to do a recce with Marilyn Fox, for the "Psammead" shoot the following day and it was decided that I should go through with that and keep quiet for the time-being. While I was away, David telephoned Paul with his change of mind. There was, apparently, a vehement exchange which resulted in both men being left hurt and confused. David left for his holiday saying that it was all a mess, which was the last thing he wanted prior to retiring, and that if I could sort it out then I should do so. I immediately wrote the following letter to Paul, but despite this, my relationship with him has never quite been the same. Perhaps Paul thinks that I manipulated the whole situation, and perhaps, without really knowing it, I did.

Dear Paul,

We must talk. It appears that Dave has gone off at half-cock over who should act after his departure without a full discussion with the parties concerned. I am also aware that I may have contributed to the problem by misinterpreting the short conversation we had on the subject. I gather that the possibility that you and I might be swapped has caused you some upset. That is the last thing I wanted to happen, and if I have in some way been responsible, I apologise.

I inferred from our brief exchange on the subject, that you were not really looking forward to sitting in the office. That was clearly a mistake. When David suggested that, with a bit of shuffling of staff, it may have been possible that I could sit in, I told him my interpretation of your feelings. I did state that he had to talk to you first and find out your reactions for himself and sound out Children's Dept. to any camera staff changes on their upcoming dramas. It would appear that it hasn't happened the way that it should have.

What I feel to be important, is, firstly, that there should be no bad feeling between us, this is not a competition, secondly, especially in this time of change, that there should not be any departmental splits and fragmentation because we all have too much to lose, and, thirdly, that if you want to sit in the office then you should do so. You will have my total and whole-hearted support.

I am at home on Sunday if you would like to talk on the phone, or we can leave it until we are both in Base on Monday.

Paul was firmly of the opinion that he was never going to sit in the office after that, and that he did not wish to take over the Drama that I was scheduled to do, and that David had created this mess and he could sort it out. The only way the situation was going to be resolved was if Dave Gautier would be prepared to take over "The Return of the Psammead" just one week after finishing "Maid Marion" and, not only would production find that acceptable, but would they accept a replacement for a week while he was on holiday. Fortunately. they did, and everything had calmed down by the time David returned from his holiday, although, apart from the formal goodbye buffet lunch in Base, Paul refused all invitations to any of David's farewell parties.

Chapter 12
Astronomy and Gastronomy Part 2 or finally once Moore

It was on the flight to Sidney in the January of 1994 that I ventured the opinion that,

"All these white domes on the top of inhospitable mountains look a bit samey to me and I'd like to find a way to put the air fare on the screen - make it more obvious to the casual viewer where in the world the programme is coming from".

Pieter retorted

"You'll just have to get me a close-up of kangaroo - pan to telescope then".

We were going for two weeks to collect material for the "Story of the Telescope" and to make two separate programmes on Australian Optical Astronomy and Australian Radio Astronomy. This was the time when New South Wales had tremendous fires, and the press in Britain gave it considerable coverage, some going as far as to imply that the whole state was ablaze. In the time we were driving through the state, some thousands of kilometres over the two weeks, only on one day were we aware of smoke haze in a distant valley.

On the second day of the trip, we went to Coonabarabran, some seven hours driving to the north-west of Sidney. Memorable for the lack of traffic, the gum trees, the sulphur crested cockatoos and the 'Neighbourhood Watch' signs; (given the lack of houses for miles I guessed they were looking for neighbours). We soon realised just how vast Australia is. The Anglo Australian Telescope is situated at Siding Spring in the Warumbungle Mountains, a few miles west of Coonabarabran, and on the edge of a national park. During the next day, I inquired as to whether there were kangaroos in the park and was it possible to see a telescope dome. The reply to both questions was affirmative. Early that evening we put the kit in the hired Toyota Torego, (Previa in the UK), and drove into the park looking for 'roos. It didn't take long. We were soon gently out of the van and recording pretty, but irrelevant, shots of families of marsupials when the park ranger turned up. Unbeknown to us, a permit is required for professional "filming" in the park. Somehow Pieter managed to sweet talk him into allowing us a bit of time to try and get a shot of the telescope. We must have looked funny to the others in the truck, as Pieter and I crept around the back of a herd of 'roos, me with the camera, Pieter with the tripod, trying to look inconspicuous and harmless. Eventually we got ourselves into a position where I could get a close-up of a single kangaroo and then tilt up to the ridge of the mountain and the gleaming white dome of the telescope.

A Kangaroo featured prominently at the next observatory, seventy miles further north at Narrabri. This is where six of the eight radio antenna that make up the

Australia Telescope are situated. We were to be accommodated at the observatory, unlike at Coonabarabran where we stayed in a local motel. This gave the staff and resident astronomers just the excuse they needed to put on a barbie, thankfully well into the evening, as daytime temperatures had reached the mid-forties centigrade. It was during the meal that Pieter found he had an unusual dinner guest to feed. Kangaroos had wandered around the observatory site all day, but this one had plucked up the courage to invite himself to supper.

The drive south to the Parkes Radio Telescope took us past the vineyards of the upper Hunter Valley and Mudgee – excellent but as far as I have been able to ascertain, unavailable in the UK – and across innumerable named creeks, but not one called Jacobs. The Parkes Telescope, though it usually works alone, is the seventh dish in the Australia Telescope array. We recorded the observatories director, Dr Alan Wright, inspecting the equipment at the focus of this huge dish in sweltering temperatures. Doug said that he now knew what it felt like to be a prawn in a wok!

There wasn't to be a Southern Hemisphere trip in 1995, but in May of that year we went to California for a seven-hour, overnight flight at forty-two-thousand feet in a military C130 Starlifter with a sunroof! Operating out of NASA's Ames research establishment, Moffett Field, the C130 Starlifter, had been specially designed to carry a telescope behind pressurised bulkheads and, once it had attained operational height, (between forty-two and forty-five thousand feet), which is above ninety-five percent of the Earth's atmosphere, a hatch slides open to allow the telescope to observe. This was, (it is now decommissioned), the Kuiper Airborne Observatory, and the subject of a complete programme in itself, and a part of the "Story of the Telescope".

Our motel, (large rooms, huge double beds, the usual great shower that blasts you to the back of the cubicle; apology for breakfast; reception has a coffee percolator and a selection of 'Danish' pastries), was in Mountain View, to the south of San Francisco in 'Silicon Valley'. Other townships familiar to computer buffs are Cupertino – Apple Headquarters; Palo Alto – where Xerox had their Research Centre, (hence "Parc") and where the Graphical User Interface, basis of the Macintosh OS, was developed. The road south-southeast through 'Silicon Valley' is also the road to San José. Doug and I managed, with great difficulty, to resist the temptation to stop the car, gain the attention of a passing pedestrian and sing the old Dionne Warwick song "Do you know the way to San José?"

Most mornings, Doug and I would take breakfast at "Ken's" twenty-four – Hour Restaurant next door to our Motel. I was getting addicted to sour dough toast and whipped butter, but I managed to resist a "weasel" – a dish of ground beef with cheese melt.

Pieter's organisational skills were virtually flawless. Where he did seem to slip up was in organising the schedule in such a way that we just missed the first available flight home and had to spend a further day away, kicking our heels trying to think of something to do to kill the time. So, on this spare Friday in May we just got into the Ford Windstar and drove north through the Napa Valley, tasted a few wines, bought some Cabernet Sauvignon from a small vineyard to ship back, had a little lunch, headed south through Sonoma County, stopped to take photographs of San Francisco through the arches of the Golden Gate Bridge, parked the car at Fisherman's Wharf, took a Tram Car up those switch back streets of "Bullet" fame to the centre of town, got a cab back and drove into Chinatown for dinner. Well, what would you have done?

In 1830, William Herschel's son, John, took a twenty-foot telescope to the Cape of Good Hope to observe the far southern sky, and, although the telescope is no longer there, it's location is marked by a monument in Cape Town. That, and the Innes Refractor in Johannesburg, were of sufficient historical significance to the "Story of the Telescope" to warrant a trip to South Africa in January 1996.

Johannesburg, was the most threatening city I've ever been in. Our hotel, the Karos Johannesburger, was on the corner of Joubert Park, then a cardboard city, although everyone seemed to have a VW Caravanette. We were continually warned not to go outside the hotel unless we stepped into a pre-ordered taxi from the hotel's list. Four people were shot in the area the day before we arrived, and muggings are commonplace, everyday occurrences. At night, the recommendation is to drive through red stop lights, it being considered safer than stopping, as you are more likely to be relieved of your car at gun point than be hit by another car. The view from my room at the back of the hotel was of tower blocks of very run-down flats that was immediately reminiscent of the worst parts of Tower Hamlets.

Professor David Block, whom we were to interview the next day, had arranged to take us out that first evening to a typical South African restaurant, the "Carnivore", but he phoned to say he had stomach-ache and left us to our own devices. Pieter tried to book several places from information provided by the hotel, but nobody seemed to answer the phone. We took the decision to eat in. Fortuitously, as it turned out, as Tuesday night was "Stir-Fry" night in the restaurant, the only night the fare changed all week, and a Zulu-speaking Chef, he also spoke English and Afrikaans, was on hand to prepare beef or chicken with the spices of our choice.

We spent the whole of Wednesday working in Johannesburg. The hotel's car park was in the basement and accessible directly from our ninth floor rooms by lift, so we were able to load our VW Caravanette with kit and passengers and drive out to the locations. In the morning, we went to the Johannesburg Observatory, hidden away behind a barbed wire-topped fence, containing a historically important telescope, the Innes Refractor, where we did a Patrick piece to camera for the fortieth Anniversary Programme. The Observatory is sighted on a ridge in what is now a suburb. Before the town was developed, it was quite a good observing site as Johannesburg is at six-thousand feet. above sea-level. While shooting the exteriors, we became aware of a white butterfly migration to the NE. We were told it happens every year, they move from the Eastern Transvaal to the Orange Free State, and that as yet, nobody knows why they do it or sees their return!

We took up the Observatory's kind offer of coffee, so rare on "Sky at Night shoots, before driving to Witwatersrand University to spend the afternoon making a programme with Professor David Block entitled "What's the Matter between the Stars?". This professor's office not only had a solid wooden lockable door but also an iron bar gate, like a prison, to prevent intruders, presumably students, from entering uninvited. Despite it being the summer vacation, parts of the university were open. Students were booking courses, paying fees, etc. and the Campus Coffee Shop was doing brisk business - the closest we got to lunch that day! The stainless-steel machine that dispensed coffee and hot water had a notice 'scotch' taped to it,

"Due to the number of tea bags being stolen, they will now be issued by the cashier, but only after payment."

Thursday morning, we flew to Cape Town, and arrived at our hotel, the Capetonian Protea at Roggebaai, near the waterfront, around lunchtime. Having been fed on the plane, we immediately took ourselves off for the afternoon to Cape Point Nature reserve. Standing at Cape Point, where you can see both the Atlantic and Indian Oceans at the same time, I recalled that, at some moment during the Second World War, my father would have sailed past here on his way to Madagascar. That evening, we went to the newly renovated dock area for dinner. Like

Sidney, San Francisco and Baltimore, the area seems to have been designed and built in that 'Disney not quite permanent film set style', with the same mix of retail outlets and ethnic restaurants. Patrick was still partial to Greek food and Retsina - well no one's perfect - so we decided to eat at the "Greek" fish restaurant. Fortunately, wines other than Retsina were on the list, as the meal bore so little resemblance to anything Greek I had eaten before, that I have no doubt that the cook probably didn't even know where Greece was!

Friday, first thing in the morning, we went to the Grove Primary School in Claremont, a Cape Town suburb. In a small courtyard at the school, was an obelisk marking the sight of the first Southern Hemisphere Telescope set up by John Herschel to observe the Southern Sky. We had a nice surprise, as neither Pieter nor Patrick were aware of its existence, as the school's janitor brought out a model of Herschel's first telescope made by one of the school's former pupils which we used as part of Patrick's piece to camera.

We moved on to the Cape Observatory in Cape Town, now the administrative headquarters of the South African Astronomy Observatory's operation, to meet with and interview the director, Dr Bob Stobie. He suggested that, if we completed our schedule in Cape Town in time, we should lunch at the Rhebokskloof Winery in the Paarl wine region, which is *en route* to Sutherland, the South African Astronomical Observatory's current operational site three-hundred-and-ninety kilometres away to the northeast of Cape Town in the Karoo Mountains. The entire team thought that was as good a reason as any to get on with the interview and Patrick's piece to camera. We managed to find an interview position with Table Mountain in the background and, as the site was well planted with exotic trees and plants, I was trying hard to get as much as possible into the shots that said, "South Africa", "air fares", "heat", "exotic location", etc. Dr Stobie pointed out that most of the trees here were not, in fact, indigenous. The Eucalypts, and even the Oaks had been imported, and there was a growing body of opinion that considered that anything not indigenous should be eradicated. After all, in the Cape Park Nature Reserve alone there were more species of flora than in the whole of the UK.

We interrupted the five-and-a-half-hour drive to Sutherland, which took us through some stunning scenery enlivened by troops of baboons on the move, with lunch at the suggested winery, Rhebokskloof, on the northern slopes of Paarl Mountain. As he was the local, and quite obviously a regular at the establishment, we got Dr Stobie to choose the wines. An interesting Chardonnay / Riesling blend to go with the starters, and a wonderfully fruity Pinotage - a grape variety unique to South Africa - to wash down the roast leg of Springbok. Up at the Observatory site on the mountain there were Springboks aplenty. The site was fenced off from the rest of the land around and now held nearly three-hundred animals from a small herd of thirty introduced when the observatory was first established. Now all we had to do was get them to walk between the camera and the telescopes. On the second day on the mountain, after we had finished recording the scripted material, we decided to spend an hour or so seeing if we could get ourselves into a position where we had a shot of telescope domes and these shy gazelles. The hired truck we were using had a tailgate that split horizontally so we could set up the camera at the back and record without getting out of the vehicle. There were a couple of small herds, only eight to ten animals in each, within four or five hundred yards of the domes, but finding a position for the truck where there was a chance that the Springbok would walk between us and the domes took some time. Eventually we positioned ourselves with the domes ahead of us and the animals two hundred yards away to the right, gently grazing and drifting right to left. Then they stopped moving and started to turn around and drift right. I said that someone had better sneak out of the van, walk directly away from the animals and then go round in a big circle at three hundred to four hundred yards away and try to ease them across the shot. Pieter volunteered. Back at the truck it was like being in the commentary hut at "One Man and His Dog".

"I think he went a bit wide on the out, don't you.?"

"Yes, only nine out of ten for that, but let's see how he does with the lift".

"Oh no, much too quick, only seven points for that".

Fortunately. the tape was running as the Springbok had got wind of Pieter and turned and ran, right to left, across the domes.

The previous evening, we had a rare treat, a look through a telescope. Unusually, one of the smaller scopes at the observatory had an optical eyepiece attached rather than the normal array of electronic detectors. We were each able to drive the telescope across the surface of the moon, virtually full that night. As I panned across the edge of the disc, I could quite clearly distinguish mountains and valleys. Outside the dome, while the others investigated further stars and galaxies, I preferred to watch the dim silhouettes of the Jackals and Crowned Plovers on the skyline. The following morning, Doug, who often got up early and went out for a walk on these deserted mountain tops, reported that he had been sitting out on a rock when these little furry things, not unlike large hamsters, kept popping up around him. Apparently, he'd been sitting next to the Rock Hyrax's communal lavatory, much to their disgust.

As we got closer to the April 1997 transmission date for the fortieth Anniversary programme, the trips got more frequent, and shorter. We popped over to Florence for four meals, three days, two pieces to camera and a cut-away of Galileo's first telescope. A trip to the USA that included Mount Graham out of Tucson, Arizona, to see the Vatican Advanced Technology Telescope (VATT) run by Jesuits, Mt Wilson out of Pasadena, to see the one hundred-inch Hooker Telescope and a return trip to the top of Mauna Kea, the nearly fourteen thousand feet high extinct volcano in Hawaii, to see the second Keck Segmented Mirror Telescope, (we'd seen Keck I on the 1991 trip). Our return from Hawaii included a twenty-hour hiatus in Dallas between flights, so we went to see the exhibition in the book depository, from which JFK was shot. I left with the distinct feeling that there must have been more than one gunman.

We spent three days getting to Cerro Parañal, altitude eight and a half thousand feet, in Chile's Atacama Desert to see the European Southern Observatories' newest telescope, four identical eight metre instruments working in conjunction and, closer to home, we recorded material at the Royal Society, just off the Mall, at Herschel's House in Bath and the Museum at Greenwich. Completing the programme took us to Birr in Ireland to see the virtually restored Rosse reflector, Baltimore for the latest on the Hubble Space Telescope, and, finally, to Selsey, to Patrick's house for the opening and closing of the programme and the final meal; Patrick's seafood salad and a bottle of '89 Burgundy. I know, I know, but somebody had to do it!

The fortieth Anniversary programme aired on 27th April 1997 and, just when I thought it was all over, the phone rang.

"Hi Mike, it's Pieter. Have you got one of your holidays booked for the end of February?"

"No, there's nothing planned till the week before Easter".

"Do you fancy doing a total eclipse of the Sun?"

"Yeah – could do. Whereabouts?"

"From a cruise ship in the Caribbean"

I turned away from the phone and shouted,

"Love, could you pass me next year's diary?"

If my love for the juice of fermented red grapes allows me to retain them, I've enough memories from these 'Sky at Night' trips to last out my days. Some awesome mountain-top scenery, Earth's fragility in Hawaii, the barrenness of the Atacama Desert, the view from Doyle's fish restaurant at Sidney's Watson's Bay, shooting the launch of a Soyuz Rocket in Kazakhstan, roast Springbok and Pinotage, my first sight of a Goldcrest in the grounds of Birr Castle, dinner with the Jesuits who ran the VATT in Tucson, where, when asked if I'd like another glass of wine, I just stopped myself from saying, "Is the Pope Catholic?", and the camaraderie and humour of the team, especially the off-the-wall humour of sound recordist and fellow traveller, Doug Whittaker. Not many people know this, but just about every mountain top in the world that contains an astronomical observatory has now got a piece of rock from a Buckinghamshire garden. Can you imagine the consternation among the next generations of geologists?

Chapter 13
Extra-curricular Activities

Sometime around the end of the nineteen-sixties, or early seventies, my first wife Charmian and I went to dinner with a work colleague, Bob, and his wife, Jane, at their home, just a short walk away from where we lived, in West London. About ten thirty p.m., maybe a quarter to eleven, Bob and I were slowly sinking below the dining table when Jane emerged from the kitchen with coffee, saying,

"Thank God that's over".

Freed of inhibition or tact by the evening's alcohol intake, I mumbled,

"I don't know what the problem is, if you can read, you can cook", to which Jane retorted,

"Well, you cook the next dinner party then!"

On the walk home I thought, "Right, I bloody well will!"

I bought a few cookbooks and started to cook from them whenever I had a day off. Modern British Cookery didn't really start until the eighties, with chefs like Gary Rhodes and Alastair Little, who, with his eponymous Soho restaurant with its short-form menus, changed daily and featuring seasonal produce, became the template for modern British restaurants. Back at the beginning of the seventies, British 'cuisine' included full breakfast, fish and chips, the Christmas dinner, the Sunday roast, steak and kidney pie, shepherd's pie, and bangers and mash, not the sort of fare for a dinner party, so most of the early recipe books I bought were about French and Mediterranean food.

To begin with, I bought two of Elizabeth David's books, "French Provincial Cooking" and "French Country Cooking", both in Penguin paperback editions. Elizabeth David was way ahead of her time, writing in the nineteen fifties and sixties to an audience, whose idea of a change from standard British fare was tinned Spaghetti Bolognese and Vesta packet curry kits. (Not long ago I saw the Hairy Bikers demonstrate a new way of poaching eggs, by putting the egg in its shell into the pan of simmering water for thirty seconds and then cracking it open, (the pre-cooking in the shell starts to set the albumen and restricts the spread of the egg). In my 1966 revised edition of "French Country Cooking", E. D. describes that exact method which she got from a cookery book published by the Buckinghamshire Women's Institute, and she has used the method ever since). As have I.

Another paperback I devoured was "Mastering the Art of French Cooking" by Simone Beck and Julia Child, in two volumes, both of which are more than seven hundred and fifty pages, without a single photograph. Julia Childs was married to an American diplomat who was posted to Paris, where, with not a lot to occupy her time, she signed up to attend Le Cordon Bleu to learn French cooking and was initially met with scepticism as she was the only woman in the class. She and Simone Beck set out to write a cookbook for the American housewife with the time, money and a lack of concern for calories.

It was made into a biographical comedy drama in 2009, starring Meryl Streep and Amy Adams and written and directed by Nora Ephron. Meryl Streep played Childs, and Amy Adams played the young New Yorker, Julie Powell, who aspired to cook all five hundred and twenty-four recipes in Child's cookbook in three hundred and sixty-five days.

I can get obsessive about stuff, but not as badly as that. I did though, cook a fair number of the recipes in the book. The instructions are extremely detailed and leave nothing to chance, perfect for a novice. I made, amongst many others, *Coq au Vin,* and *Boeuf Bourguignon*, both recipes I still use today, *Jambon Braisé Morvandelle*, (ham braised in wine with a cream and mushroom sauce) and an ice cream bombé constructed of four layers of different flavoured ice cream, each layer having to go in the freezer for four hours before I could add the next. It took two days. But I loved it, and ever since when guests came to eat, I did the cooking. And still do.

But, in my world, you can't have a good meal without wine, (a meal without wine is called breakfast after all) and I realised I knew very little about it. I was just beginning to understand that there was a vinous world out there beyond Black Tower, Blue Nun, Mateus Rosé, Bull's Blood and Piat d'Or. I was totally confused by the, sometimes, massive price difference between two bottles of wine with labels both containing the word *Chateau*. Fortunately, I found a couple of saviours in the wine writer, Hugh Johnson, and the wine shops of Augustus Barnett. I bought Johnson's book "Wine" (1966), and subsequently, "The World Atlas of Wine" (1971), of which there have been eight editions and, since 2004, co-authored with Jancis Robinson. I found the atlas extremely helpful in establishing where a wine comes from and why it might be superior, and, consequentially, more expensive, to its neighbour.

The theory was fine, but did it work in practice? Whenever guests came for dinner, I would purchase two, or sometimes three, bottles of wine from the same region, say a *Hautes-Côtes-de-Nuits*, a *Côte-de-Nuits-Village* and a *Chambolle-Musigny*, each name describing an area of land that is progressively smaller than the previous one, and choose to cook a meal that would show off the wines to their best advantage, in this instance, *Boeuf Bourguignon*. By the way, being French wine, one is supposed to know that all three wines are made from just *Pinot Noir* grapes. I wouldn't tell my guests where the wines had come from or how much they cost, and, on more occasions than not, we all agreed that the wine from the smallest area was the best.

At that time in the seventies, to get access to single commune Burgundy wines, or Grand Cru wines from Bordeaux, you needed an account with a central London wine merchant, and I was not able to buy twelve bottle cases of the stuff, which is where Augustus Barnett's off licences saved the day. He would buy large quantities of world class wines in cases of twelve, and then split them up, and sell them by the bottle, enabling Joe Public to occasionally sample good wine.

Then Simon Fone and I had an idea which would enable us to cut out the middleman and get a bottle of good wine even cheaper. We did a little research and discovered that the most common lot size at Christie's South Kensington wine auctions were three, twelve bottle cases. We formed a wine club of thirty-six work colleagues, no more, no less, who paid £5 per month into a bank account, and, after a year, we went to auction and bought twelve three case lots of fine wine. It was a lot of fun, as there was usually a pre-sale tasting to ensure everything we bought was drinkable, and everybody in the club had a twelve-bottle mixed case, usually in time for Christmas. As I had Hugh Johnson's Wine Atlas, I printed up a sheet explaining where the wines came from and what grape varieties they contained.

Simon and I worked together on another project, a grading claim for Outside Broadcast cameramen.

The BBC's staff remuneration system was heavily based on the Civil Service, with jobs that were considered to have equal responsibilities or skill sets, placed on the same grade across the Corporation. Each grade having a five-year incremental pay increase, subject to a satisfactory annual report. In Technical Operations, the scales for camera operators, across the BBC, were 'B' for Senior Cameramen, a post one would have to apply for –

it was not an automatic progression, and grade 'C minus' for basic cameramen. Simon and I considered that there was, in fact, a marked difference between the requirements of working in a television studio and working on an Outside Broadcast, especially on live sports coverage.

In a studio situation, the director would have been involved with the production designer when deciding on the set. He would know where each camera was on the studio floor and would have worked out a shot list for each camera and, if anything, didn't work as expected, he could leave the gallery, and come down onto the studio floor to work it out. Whereas, on an Outside Broadcast, the director was in the control van outside the ground and could only see what was beamed to the monitors in front of him by the cameras inside the stadium. Our case was based on the fact that the director didn't direct the cameras but chose the appropriate picture provided by the cameramen, albeit to a brief. The quality of the coverage depended a lot on the cameraman's understanding of the sport being covered and the personalities in the teams playing that day.

During this period in the seventies, I was on the local branch committee of the Association of Broadcasting Staff, through which a grading claim could be made. The current job description for cameramen on Grade 'C minus' said that the cameraman works completely under direction and, as such, has no responsibility for programme decisions. Simon and I rewrote the job description of a cameraman working on Outside Broadcasts to include, amongst many other requirements, the obvious contribution made by Outside Broadcast cameramen to the BBC's reputation for Sports coverage.

Needless to say, the BBC was having none of it. I attended meetings at national level which also failed to convince them. My colleagues and I were not in the mood to take no for an answer. Working to rule, or not doing overtime, were options discussed, all of which could rumble on for months. It was decided that a short, sharp, shock would be the quickest and cleanest way to bring the BBC back round the negotiating table. We walked off the live "Song for Europe" show, five minutes before transmission. Within days we were at an Arbitration Tribunal at ACAS, (the Advisory, Conciliation and Arbitration Service) where we won.

At around the same time, my marriage to my first wife, Charmian, was drifting apart. I'd got married at the age of twenty-two, far too young and with very little life experience and, in hindsight, for all the wrong reasons. I was living alone in London and wanted a permanent relationship. I wanted sex. I was still a virgin. Getting married seemed, at that time, to be the answer.

Charmian was training to be a classical singer, which meant she was permanently in part-time schooling and teaching piano to others at the same time. I had, and still have, a problem with the classically trained human singing voice. I liked many of the tunes, the "Liebestod" from the opera *Tristan und Isolde* by Richard Wagner for one and "Nessun dorma" from the final act of Giacomo Puccini's opera *Turandot* can bring me to tears at the drop of a handkerchief. I however preferred to listen to Pink Floyd, Genesis, Fleetwood Mac, and American West Coast country rock like the Eagles.

As to her other interests, they left me bemused and confused. She started with Palmistry, predicting peoples' future by the lines across their palms, moved on to Astrology, studying star signs and conjunctions at the subject's time of birth, then to Reflexology, an alternative medical practice involving the application of pressure to specific points on the foot, said to correspond to internal organs, and, finally, to Reiki, a form of alternative therapy commonly referred to as 'energy healing,' involving the transfer of universal energy from the practitioner's palms to their patient. After we divorced, her book, "Reiki: Healing Energy for Mind, Body and Spirit" was published and she set up The Light Centre in Bournemouth in 2001 to,

"Anchor in Light and raise conscious awareness of our connection to Source".

According to her website, Charmian has been pursuing her spiritual development for over fifty years and teaching since 1987.

And the lovemaking was probably best described as unsatisfactory. Despite rarely saying no, I never felt she wanted me sexually and I was left feeling that I was no good at it, leaving me uncomfortable in the company of women.

As I could not find it in myself to join Charmian on her pursuit of spiritual development, I started going to music gigs with other people. I saw Pink Floyd preview their album "Wish You Were Here", at Wembley Arena with friend, Simon, where they played "Dark Side of the Moon" as an encore. Later, Simon decided he didn't want to go to a concert at the Odeon, Hammersmith, so I picked up the ticket and went with his then girlfriend to be part of the now, legendary, 1975, first UK concert by Bruce Springsteen and the East Street Band. An electrifying two and a half hours which I can recall at will, as I have the two CD recording of the concert.

A colleague booked six tickets, two for me, to see Pink Floyd's "The Wall" gig at Earls Court and one of the secretaries on the top floor of Kendal Avenue accepted my offer to join me. "*J*" was a tall, statuesque lady with tumbling, curly hair whom I was happy to be with, and she seemed comfortable with me. Our seats were three rows back from the front of the stalls, and it was "the most theatrical concert" I have ever been to. I asked "*J*" if she would like to join me at other concerts if I was successful at getting tickets, so, subsequently, we went to Wembley Arena.to see 'Fleetwood Mac,' memorable mostly for the many costume changes by Stevie Nicks, and 'Emerson Lake and Palmer'.

Towards the end of the seventies, there was a period of about twelve months that had a dramatic effect on my life. No, it wasn't a diet or a spiritual lightbulb moment. It was several encounters with, - and although I completely support the "me too" movement in its attempts to out male sexual predators, admit it ladies they exist, - female sexual predators. Don't get me wrong, I'm not complaining, I just think the pendulum may have swung just a little bit too far one way.

As part of my responsibilities as a member of our local union Branch Committee, it was down to three of us to attend annual conference, in a hotel on the coast, as most conferences are. Don't ask where it was, I haven't a clue. My memories of that event were of being extremely nervous at having to mount the rostrum at the front of the auditorium, with BBC Management representatives in the balcony away to my left and having to make a short speech to the effect that Outside Broadcast staff would not stand for a reduction in our twenty-four-hour subsistence allowance for the privilege of making programmes for the BBC, and that they needed to think again.

Later in the evening, as delegates were milling around, a comely lady, who appeared to be in her early-forties, and from Scotland, approached me, introduced herself as *"F"* and congratulated me on my speech, and said that she often had to come down to London on Union business and that it would be nice if we could meet one evening to take in a movie or go for a meal. Not wishing to appear rude, I said that would be nice, that she could contact me by phoning the switchboard at Kendal Avenue and that they would 'page' me over the tannoy system. I thought that, in all probability, nothing would come of it, and our meeting at conference would be forgotten.

A couple of weeks later, it might have even been a month, and I am in Kendal Avenue when the 'tannoy' says, "Will Mike Winser please come to the phone". I found the nearest booth —there were many dotted around

331

the ground floor garage of Kendal Avenue – pick up the receiver and say, "Mike Winser". A Scottish voice says, "Hello Mike, it's *"F"*. I'm coming to Union Headquarters next week and I'm at a loose end on Thursday evening. Can we meet up?" I say, "that would be nice, where shall we meet?". She says, "The foyer of my hotel, the "Can't Remember" near the bottom of Tottenham Court Road at five-thirty p.m.". "Great", I say, "See you then".

I got a copy of the 'Evening Standard' to find out what films were playing near there and hit upon an 'art house' cinema at the Hyde Park Corner end of Knightsbridge, that was showing Visconti's 1972 film "Death in Venice", one of my all-time favourite films, because it is not a photographed play, but it's the pictures and the camera movements that tell the story and the music from Mahler's third and fifth symphonies reels you in emotionally. When we met, I suggested that we go to see the film. Its first showing was at six-thirty p.m., and that we could find a bite to eat afterwards. *"F"* concurred, and we got a taxi over to the top of Knightsbridge and settled into our comfy seats in a deserted cinema. The arm rest between us was a little on the hard side and we pushed it into an upright position out of the way, and comfortably snuggled a little closer. The film started with lingering shots of Venice and Mahler's sublime music, and I slipped, totally engrossed into the movie. I don't know how long it was before "*F*'s" left hand gently alighted on my right thigh and started softly stroking it. Distracted from the anguish Dirk Bogard's character was suffering, I had a decision to make. Gently remove the hand, ignore it, or reciprocate. Having never experienced a woman indicating her desires before, I decided to reciprocate, and put my right hand on her left thigh and started stroking. Her hand slipped further left and found my growing manhood and continued caressing it. We just managed to stay till the end of the film, but not the credits. All thoughts of finding somewhere to eat vanished as we flagged a taxi back to her hotel. We walked casually though the foyer to the lift, where being alone, the kissing, the unbuttoning and the probing of tongues started. After about an hour of mutual sexual pleasure, we relaxed on the bed, having both been satisfied, twice, and I glowed with the satisfaction of knowing I had been wanted sexually and had demonstrably satisfied a woman.

We met again a couple of months later. This time she was staying at her sister's flat, somewhere out towards Uxbridge on the Piccadilly line. We spent the best part of an afternoon rolling around naked on the aptly named shag pile carpet. We met once more, she was again staying with her sister, but couldn't meet till five-thirty p.m. So, we went to a restaurant for a meal. On the homeward Piccadilly line journey, we were going to have to separate at Acton Town, she needed the Uxbridge branch, I the Hounslow line. We never sat in the seats on the tube, preferring to stand, face-to-face in the corner by the door and allowing the movement of the train to gently grind our groins, while staring wantonly into each other's eyes, alone in our bubble. Apparently, we did not go unnoticed as, on one occasion, a fellow passenger called out,

"For God's sake get a room".

We decided we couldn't part at Acton Town with just a peck on the cheek before one of us left the train, so we got off at Turnham Green where there was a large unlit area of grass. We walked to the centre, as far away from any source of light as we could and began our passionate goodbyes, kissing and fondling erotic zones. Her left hand found my trouser zip, pulled it down and pulled out my erect and proud manhood, bent over and engulfed it in her warm and moist mouth, and gave me the most exiting goodbye present I'd ever had. My legs almost gave way, and I had to hold on to her to stop myself from collapsing.

We never met again but play Rod Stewart singing "Maggie May" or "You wear it well", and memories of *"F"* come flooding back. Technically I wasn't a virgin, but this brief relationship felt like I'd really, really had SEX for the first time.

I was starting to spot how differently women looked at me when they fancied me, and I wasn't about to turn down an offer, as I felt I had a lot of catching up to do after twelve years of a physically unsatisfactory marriage.

We were in Somerset on a drama location, renting a large, five or six bedroomed cottage. The Lighting Engineer, Hu, invited a couple of secretaries from the third floor at Kendal Avenue for the weekend, even though we were working. They spent time in their offices typing up memos and letters about stuff they hadn't seen, and this would enable them to get an idea of what we were doing. *"J"*, the lady I'd been going to gigs with, was one of them, and we sat next to each other at dinner. There was an exciting crackle of static between us, and we had to keep reminding ourselves there were four others around the table. We'd got to the cheese, biscuits and grapes, the easiest last course when self-catering and an Eagles tape was playing on my Walkman, (with battery powered extension speakers). I picked up a large black grape and asked *"J"* if she would like to share it. Our lips came together, juice ran down our chins as Don Henley sang the track, "One of these Nights", (you'll have to look up the first four lines of the lyric) and a tryst was struck, but we'd have to park it for now. This was not the time or place.

The following week, my camera colleague and I were having dinner with *"A"*, the Assistant Producer and the Production Secretary at their shared cottage. I was getting all the signs, hand on leg, breasts rubbed across my shoulders as she passed behind my chair and that look in her eyes. I ended the evening in her bedroom, making love. She was very wanting, I guess it had been a long time since her last coital orgasm.

On the very next programme, I picked up the signals from a lady in the costume department, who I shall call *"C"*. I have no idea what had changed in me, but I had not been used to this kind of attention, and I was enjoying it. We met up three times to have sex, once in a cottage in Herefordshire, once in a Hotel near Russel Square, and, finally, for an afternoon at her flat in Hammersmith. She had a unique, (in my limited experience), modus operandi when it came to having orgasms. Being a gentleman, I would hold back from going for my own pleasure until I could sense that the woman between whose legs I was pulsating was about to join me in the moment of heightened satisfaction. When I slowed down to wait for *"C"*, she said,

"What's up"? I replied,

"I'm waiting for you to catch up".

"No, no, no, please keep going, I'll tell you what to do".

I thrusted deeper and quicker until I came, at which point she shouted,

"Don't move!"

Then after a few seconds she let out a huge exhalation of air, containing the words,

"Oh God! Yes! Fucking, Yes!"

Probably a month later, I was on a drama shoot in Kent and in a rented cottage for three weeks. The second weekend was to be a two-day break and everybody else in the cottage were going to travel home on the Friday night. At last, an opportunity for *"J"* to come down, and for us to honour our tryst. Arrangements were made, and I would meet her at the nearest railway station around Saturday lunchtime.

The Wednesday of the middle week, halfway through the assignment, we invited some other team members to the cottage for drinks and nibbles, amongst them the vision mixer, *"S"*. Everybody stood around chatting, pouring glasses of wine, and eating crisps, olives and pistachios, anything that could be bought ready to eat. Around nine p.m. I decided I'd had enough standing for one day and went and sat in a Chesterfield style leather armchair with wide arms that curled down to the floor. *"S"* came over and I offered her the seat which she declined and sat on the floor leaning against the left arm of the chair. After ten minutes or so she hooked her right arm over my left leg. I thought nothing of it, thinking it was making her more comfortable. Then, a few minutes later she eased my left leg towards her and started rubbing her right breast against it. She turned and looked up at me with eyes that said,

"Take me to bed now".

Where the hell had that come from? Completely out of the blue, but I was not of a mind to disappoint. I leaned forward and put my hand under her arm, caressed her pert little breast, and in a stage whisper, said casually,

"Okay, I'll show you where the bathroom is,"

and we went upstairs to my room. I undressed a very petite, fit body, she went to ballet classes weekly, and we lay on the bed and explored each other's bodies, sometimes face to face, sometimes soixante-neuf. Finally, I entered her, she'd said it was going to be difficult, her small frame making her a tight fit. She orgasmed quite quickly. I hadn't, but rather than use her, I withdrew. We were quite far down the bed and as I hauled myself up towards the pillows, I felt her take hold of my manhood and bring me to orgasm with her mouth. We slept intwined until four a.m., when she said she ought to go. We arranged to go out together for dinner that evening, just the two of us. After the meal, we came back to the cottage and went to my room and made love again, this time we "arrived" together. One of those location flings, where neither party is looking for a relationship. We've worked together many times since, and we continued as if nothing ever happened.

That was Thursday night, and I had about twenty-six hours to wash and dry the sheets before *"J"* was due to arrive.

I met her off the train and we took a bus to the village where the cottage was. We had a pub lunch, listened to, and talked about music, then I made us dinner. All very cosy. We went to bed and made love in a gentle way and slept soundly. I accompanied her back to the train station after a spot of lunch on the Sunday.

I never did find out what turned on her lights.

I still don't understand why, but I kept picking up the signals that I was wanted. I encountered *"D"*, a design assistant on a drama shoot in Hampshire on the edge of the New Forest. When my camera colleague and I first walked onto the location, the design department was already there, having installed some props, and *"D"* and I immediately clocked each other. Her eyes said, "I fancy you", and mine said, "God you're gorgeous", and the inevitable followed. I'd describe her as voluptuous, about five foot six with blonde hair. It was a two-week shoot, with the weekend off in the middle, and my colleagues in the cottage we had rented, intended to go home on the Friday night. For those who were staying, there was to be a gathering in one of the local pubs, with a local band for entertainment. *"D"* asked me if I was going home for the weekend or staying and going to the party. I replied that, as I didn't have a car, I could stay but only if she could run me back to the cottage in the hire car she had for the shoot. She said that would not be a problem.

Friday evening, and I was dropped off at the pub by a colleague on his way home for the weekend. I mingled and chatted with several of the crew who had stayed, and eventually ended up having a slow dance with *"D"*. With our bodies pressed against each other, it was quite clear that I was aroused.

"Shall we go now?", I said.

Once inside the cottage, we couldn't get our clothes off fast enough as we moved swiftly through to the bedroom. The bed was higher than most, and when she sat on the end of it, she was at the perfect height to receive my manhood. She lay back and I started long slow strokes while caressing her melon-sized breasts and tweaking her nipples. As her breathing got faster, so did my stroke rate, and we both vocalised loudly as we orgasmed in unison. We spent an hour cuddled up, chatting as I stroked her body.

"Have you got any plans for tomorrow?", I said.

"No", she replied, "What would you like to do?".

"What I'd really like to do is buy a copy of the Guardian and a bunch of grapes, then go into the New Forest and make love in the open air".

"Great idea", she said.

As she was leaving, she said,

"What time shall I pick you up?"

"About ten o'clock?".

"Yes, see you at ten".

And she did. And we did.

"R" was the cashier behind an iron grill in the Kendal Avenue cash office. We had always chatted amiably on the rare occasions that I popped in to cash my expenses claims. About four or five weeks before Christmas, she asked if I'd made any plans. I said no, and that my wife and I were separating and that I'd not really got around to contemplating anything festive. She said that she couldn't offer me Christmas lunch, but would I like to go to dinner at her place next week. I said that would be lovely, and we compared diaries, made a date, and she gave me her address and phone number.

On arrival at her first floor flat, I was introduced to her Red Setter. I didn't ask, but I did wonder how it got through the day while she was at work. We were four at the table; she had invited a couple of girlfriends along as well. It was a very pleasant evening and, when we all got up to go, she whispered in my ear,

"You don't have to leave".

I went and sat on the sofa and patted the dog. After saying goodbye to her friends, she came and sat beside me, put her arms round my neck and pulled me towards her. I slipped my hand under her jumper, heading for her breasts. I heard the front door shut and withdrew my hand rapidly as a man, who I assumed must have been the boyfriend, said forcefully,

"I think you'd better leave".

I got up off the sofa, drew myself up to my full height and said,

"You two need to talk",

I grabbed my coat and let myself out. Fortunately, there was a public phone box on the corner outside her flat, and I called a cab.

A couple of weeks later, I had reason to be in Kendal Avenue and I went to the cash office to see how she was.

"I'm fine", she said, "He's gone. Can you come to dinner this Friday?".

This time it was just three of us and the dog. At the end of the meal, the flatmate said she'd do the dishes and then go to her bedroom. The dog, *"R"* and I went to her bedroom.

"It will howl the place down if I leave it in the lounge".

Naked we lay on the bed, kissing, nibbling, sucking and licking until it felt time to spread her legs and enter the tunnel of love. I rolled onto my back and brought her on top and set her hips rocking slowly up and down while fondling both breasts. Sensing that the end would soon be upon us, I rolled back on top and increased the pace and, as we orgasmed together, the Red Setter licked the crack between my buttocks for that special *'Je ne sais quoi'.*

When I next went to the cash office, early in the New Year, there was a new lady behind the grill. On asking around, I found out that *"R"* had left and gone to Dorset to marry a vicar. I realised she must have handed her notice in before she asked me to dinner and that I must have been part of a plan.

Then Wendy found me.

The same Wendy I first met on "Jude the Obscure" Fortunately, I was ready. Sexually, it seemed she had some catching up to do. In her mid-forties, with a husband who was either at work, or in his office generating work, she felt weighed down by the responsibilities of the house and an acre of garden, his parents who were living with them, two teenage sons experimenting with drugs, and the tenanted house her mother had left her. She needed fun, excitement and to be able to forget her responsibilities. It was a risky game because, not only could we not get enough of each other physically, but we fell in love – we'd found our soul mates. We sought every opportunity we could to have sex. Rooftop car parks, the darkest backstreets of Hounslow, in the long grass in Richmond Park, and, best of all, a weekend in a cottage deep in the Kent countryside where we did just three things. Eat, make love and sleep. I lost count of the number of orgasms we had. We just didn't want to stop.

Eventually, her husband David accepted that he had lost her, and had the remarkable grace to let her go without a row, fight, or litigation.

Early in 1982, Wendy's husband David had been asked to produce and direct "Dylan Thomas, A Celebration" at the Duke of York's Theatre, in London's St Martin's Lane. It was a concert to raise funds for the installation of a plaque to Dylan Thomas in Poets' Corner at Westminster Abbey. Every Welsh performer that was available was going to take part, (known in the business as the 'Taffia'). Richard Burton was to read the part of the narrator in "Under Milk

Wood", which Thomas wrote about Laugharne, the village where he lived. He called it 'Llareggub' in the poem, buggerall backwards.

David asked me if I would take some photographs, black and white transparencies, to be projected onto a screen at the back of the stage during the performances of Thomas's poems. He needed sleazy pictures of the Paddington area of London to go with "Adventures in the Skin Trade", and he needed pictures of 5 Cwmdonkin Drive, Swansea, the house where Thomas was born, photos of paintings that Welsh artists had produced inspired by his poetry, that were in an art gallery in Swansea, a photo sequence of two men drinking inside his favourite pub in Laugharne, and, of course, the boathouse where he lived and his writing shed overlooking the Taf estuary.

"The Swansea Gallery will know when to expect you and will take pictures out from behind glass to avoid reflections and The South Wales Tourist board will ensure everything else will be available. They've booked a room for a night in a hotel on the Mumbles, Wendy can drive you".

"Yes, David".

Sunday, February 8th, 1982, and everybody was at the Duke of York's Theatre by nine a.m. David had to rehearse the entire show but had accepted that it was unreasonable to expect everybody to have learnt their words and opted to allow the actors to read their parts. Wendy and I had successfully achieved our photo assignment and had handed the slides over to the show's designer. When the back-projected pictures came up on the screen during rehearsals, they were upside-down and back-to-front. The designer presented me with the cassettes and said rather brusquely,

"Can you sort it, please?"

Stress levels were rising. I spent a couple of hours going through the slides one at a time - I couldn't just assume they were all in the wrong way round. Wendy, who was also reading a part in "Under Milk Wood", went out into St. Martin's Lane to get pizzas for David, their eldest son Gareth, who was to help handing out programmes, for me and herself.

At curtain up, I had a seat in the balcony and was very nervous, having not seen my rearranged slides projected. Huw Wheldon, who was curating the evening, and later conducting the fund-raising auction, stepped out to explain the evening's performances and the reason we were all here. Thankfully, the back projected pictures were coming up correctly and I was able to relax. I think "Under Milk Wood" concluded the first half and everybody could take a deep breath.

As the second half began, Huw Wheldon stepped out from the wings saying,

"Look who I've found back-stage,"

as he brought on a stunningly beautiful, auburn-haired woman. It was Elizabeth Taylor. The audience went mad, clapping and cheering. After she left the stage, the audience calmed down and the rest of the show went off successfully.

After the show, cast and crew were to go to the Garrick Club for a meal. Wendy and I hung back looking for David. When we found him, he was busy talking to people, but when he saw us, he put our hands together and said,

"You two go, I'll be along in a bit with Gareth".

It felt like he'd given our relationship his blessing. On arrival at the Garrick Club, we were shown to a table with four spaces left and, before we could sit down, we were joined by another couple, Elizabeth and Richard. We had a fascinating hour or so in their company. They obviously adored each other but admitted they couldn't live together. And, yes, she did have amazing violet-blue eyes, enhanced by the violet-blue 'Angora' jumper she was wearing. Richard told the story of Elizabeth dropping the diamond ring, which he had bought for $1.1 million, into the shag pile carpet, where they crawled around on their hands and knees until they found it.

"And then you fucked me," she whispered.

When they decided to go, I shook hands with Richard and, when Elizabeth proffered her hand, I raised it towards my lips, leaned forward and kissed it. Well, I had to.

Richard died in 1984.

David died in 1987.

Wendy and I married in 1988.

In 1995 I was diagnosed with Type two diabetes, a side effect of which is erectile disfunction. The closest I get to an orgasm these days is going for a pee. On the upside, I have four or five of those before lunch.

Chapter 14
The Postscript

Luckily for me personally, my request for redundancy was granted and I escaped the listing ship at the end of March 1994. Lucky also that Pieter Morpurgo continued to want my services on the "Sky at Night" and had me hired in for those occasional "filming" trips.

The final twenty-one months in full-time employment were soul-destroying, and I haven't really gotten over it yet. From August 1992, attending weekly management meetings, first, as acting Head of Cameras and, then, as the penultimate incumbent of the post, they blur, one into another. The all too easily spotted stream of 'consultant speak', utilisation statistics, market testing, multi skilling, "run this up the flagpole" – "put that on the back burner" – "has this been checked with the tea ladies focus group" and the descent of colleagues, who, in times past, one had happily shared the pursuit of quality and excellence, and who had campaigned by one's side for the recognition of the technical and operational contribution of OB staff, now through blind ambition or fear, and, in some cases, the obscenely naked need for power, dropped all past principles in an obsequious attempt to ingratiate themselves with their masters. Not only that, the nearer the top, the more they were sucking the system for personal gain. With the permanent threat of redundancy always in the air, underlings were going to do what you asked, just in case. Never mind the effect on the bottom line. Despite telling the troops that, with a bit of belt-tightening, a reduction in overtime rates, a cut in the subsistence allowance and they would be alright, I believe our bosses knew the game was up, so they might as well look after number one.

And what good did it do. Now there is no Tel OB department at all. First Radio OBs merged with Television OBs, followed by Manchester; downsizing continued, the increase in the use of dual role and multi–skilling furthered the dilution of the skill base. Line management was reduced, and scheduling clerks picked crews on economic grounds rather than the best person for the job. One single Resources Department was created, staff merged with Television Centre, more and more staff went freelance or gave up the business altogether.

Producers and Directors, of course are now mostly independent and are courted and treated as "customers". As a business, whether as an organisation hiring out cameras or OB units, or as an individual freelance cameraman selling his skill, to ensure the customer returns to buy again, the attitude must be, that the customer is always right, even when we clearly know they are not. It is not totally necessary to have any training, or formal qualification, before saying that you are a film or television producer. No longer the traditional route of coming through the ranks with an understanding of the grammar and the rules. Start a Production Company and go for it. So now we've got wobbly vision, with cameras hosing in and out without motive, mantel shelves in the back of shot that slope alarmingly down-hill, on which the ornaments defy the laws of gravity and friction, and buildings that out lean the tower of Pisa. People transport themselves from one side of the screen to the other in the nanosecond it takes to change shot. Why?

I can only presume that someone thinks that abandoning the rules of visual presentation is clever or that it makes for good television. Sometimes it's so bad these days that I shout at my TV set.

You've only got to look at the production credits on simple, basic television programmes to see where the money is going. A recent 'Gardeners' World', featuring one presenter and a garden, had nineteen non-technical credits. Back in the day – one Producer, one Producer's Assistant and a stage manager.

Outsourcing doesn't seem to have reduced the numbers of staff at the BBC, twenty-three thousand the last time I checked, about the same as when I left. What outsourcing has done, as it has in the NHS, is launder licence fee payers' (and taxpayers') money into the pockets of the commercial companies and their shareholders. This is, in my honest opinion, political dogma. It seems that nothing in this country can be done unless someone is making a profit. The losers, in this case, are the viewing public.

But maybe that's where I've got it wrong now. Now it would seem to be no longer about making good television but making money. I can't watch drama these days. I can't see who's talking, it's so underlit, even though I have hearing aids, I miss parts of the dialogue and it's invariably shot in close-up with handheld cameras. They say it's the new "film noir", an artistic decision. Oh, really? Under-light it and shoot in close-up and you don't have to dress the set, because it's out of focus, shoot handheld and you don't have to hire camera dollies, fewer lights, no dollies, no props, less expenditure, more profit. Simples!

And without a whimper, complaint, or tear from Government or public, sixty years of broadcasting history has been written off and the quality in depth of British Broadcasting will, in my opinion, never be quite the same again. The real tragedy is there is no way back.

BBC Television Outside Broadcasts, with all its equipment, Mobile Control Rooms, cameras and cables, sound equipment and staff were sold off to an independent television facilities company for a rumoured £18,000,000, just three times the annual remuneration package allegedly paid to Jonathan Ross.

Says it all really.

With thanks for the good times
Roy Battersby, Christine Secombe
And the cameramen and -women of BBC London Television Outside Broadcasts

| Maurice Abel | Graham Goldston | Phil Nixon |

Steve Adnams
Les Ager
Duncan Anderson
Andrei Austin
Stan Bale
Steve Blatchford
Gordon Blockley
Martine Brigstocke
Chris Buchanan
Stuart Bush

Bob Buttermere
Neil Cameron
Barry Chaston
Steve Chilvers
Ted Cocks
Peter Cook
Stuart Cook
Harry Coventry
Selwyn Cox

Keith Dawson

James Day
Ian Dicker
Chris Eames

Alan Gomery
Mike Graham
Paul Graham

Steve Hall
Paul Harding
Alison Harper (Jones)

John Hawes

Alan Hayward

Jack Hayward
Colin Hazelwood

Pete Hill
Paul Holman
Frank Hudson
Dave Hunter
Alan Jessop
Jonny Johnson
David Jones
Phil Jones
Nick Jordan

Ken Lane

Terry Learner
Dick Lennox
Robin Lewis

Don Oliver
Rex Palmer
Andy Parr

Chris Penny
Colin Perry
John Pilblad

Martyn Porter

Roger Prior

Giles Pritchard
Nick Rodger

Eric Russell
Carol Sadler
Dan Scala
Andy Smith
John Smithson
Chas Snare
Vince Spooner
Ian Stanyon
Richard Stevenson
Robin Sutherland
Andy Tallack
Alex Thomas
Lex Tudhope

Bill Eldridge	Terry Loader	Clive Walker
Gerry Ellis	Jon Lord	Brian Weeks
Bob Everett	Brian Maddison	Chris Wickham
Mark Faulkner	Martin Mansell	Bryan Wilkes
Jon Fay	Peter March	Keith Williams
Ray Fitzwalter	Tony Maslen	Bob Wilson
Simon Fone	Martin Mathewson	Trevor Wimlett
Paul Francis	Pat McLoughlin	Peter Wrench
Keith Furlonger	Bruce Miller	Alec Wright
Dave Gautier	Alastair Mitchell	Derek Wright
Ian Gibb	Ken Moir	Martin Wyatt
Keith Gibson	Tim Moses	